The Wire

The Wire

Urban Decay and American Television

edited by
Tiffany Potter
and
C. W. Marshall

continuum

NEW YORK • LONDON

2010

The Continuum International Publishing Group Inc
80 Maiden Lane, New York, NY 10038

The Continuum International Publishing Group Ltd
The Tower Building, 11 York Road, London SE1 7NX

www.continuumbooks.com

Library of Congress Cataloging-in-Publication Data
A catalog record for this book is available from the Library of Congress

ISBN: HB: 978-0-8264-2345-0
         PB: 978-0-8264-3804-1

Typeset by Newgen Imaging Systems Pvt. Ltd. Chennai, India
Printed in the United States of America

Contents

Acknowledgements

As with any edited volume, and particularly with a scholarly collection such as this, we have incurred many debts along the way. We are grateful to all our contributors, and to the people at Continuum for their assistance in bringing this project to fruition. We would like to thank for their assistance David Barker, Laura Hamilton, and Sam Tucker. We are also grateful to the University of British Columbia Hampton Fund and the Social Sciences and Humanities Research Council of Canada for funding research time. We are grateful to HBO for permission to use the cover images. Above all, we would like to acknowledge our great debt to Hallie Marshall and Ken Madden, for constant support, encouragement, insights, conversations, and (especially) for their tolerance of our obsession with television. Really, it's incredible what they put up with. You have no idea.

"I am the American Dream": Modern Urban Tragedy and the Borders of Fiction

C. W. Marshall and Tiffany Potter

"It's kinda fun figuring shit out."

—*Prez (1.07)*

Requiem for Snot Boogie

A cop and a drug dealer are sitting on a stoop in front of a boarded-up vacant, talking about the murdered man on the street before them. The opening dialogue of *The Wire* (1.01) encapsulates so many of the series' tensions that it is worth spending a moment contemplating the fate of Snot Boogie. Street names are in some ways a cover, hiding who you are: for a while, Little Kevin's physiologically inapt name keeps him safe from police (4.09). But they are also a badge, of honor or of shame. The cop, Jimmy McNulty, contemplates the body on the ground: ". . . his nose starts runnin', and some asshole, instead of giving him a Kleenex, he calls him Snot. So he's Snot forever. It doesn't seem fair." It isn't fair, and the show implicates its viewers in that unfairness by drawing us into a position where we often think of characters only by their street names. Bodie, Stringer, Wee-Bey, and Snoop don't have recognizable first names for most viewers, and even if the names are known (Preston,

Russell, Roland, and Felicia), they never become the primary associations. In editing this book, one of the tensions we felt was the fact that white characters tend to default to surnames or to recognizable corruptions that do not efface identity (Herc for Hauk, for example, or Prez for Pryzbylewski), while black characters, on the other hand, typically default to street names. Even among the police, "Bunk and Jimmy" or "Bunk and McNulty" seems a more natural collocation than "Moreland and McNulty." There are exceptions, of course, and enough exceptions that we can assure ourselves that we aren't just falling into a linguistic trap that the series has laid for us. D'Angelo is D; Prop Joe, Chris, and Wallace are known by forms of their given names; on the docks, the white Thomas Pakusa is more familiar as Horseface; conversely, Avon Barksdale remains little more than an unfamiliar name to the police, his face known only from a boxing poster from his youth, until Herc realizes that he is likely at the East side/West side basketball game (1.09).[1] So the loss of Snot Boogie's birth name proves to be only the first of many examples of the rifts in the maintenance of identity that are created by the conventions of urban life in the Baltimore of *The Wire*.[2]

But Snot does more than this for us. He has been killed, we are told, because he has robbed a craps game.[3] This is something he does repeatedly, whenever the pot gets big enough. In the past Snot Boogie has been beaten for stealing the pot, but McNulty's source thinks this time things have gone too far. The whole process has become almost routine: a regular game, an increase in the stakes, a tempting pot, and Snot tries to get away with his prize, never to succeed. Incredulous, McNulty asks why, given the predictability of this pattern, Snot Boogie was allowed in the game. They had to let him play, McNulty is told: "This is America, man."[4]

We are told in passing that Snot's given name was Omar Isaiah Betts. The series opens, then, with a guy who habitually, compulsively robs the drug dealers of Baltimore, who in the end gets got. And his name is Omar, but as with so many of the series' African American characters, his name has been effaced. So Snot becomes a prototype for another Omar who habitually, compulsively robs the drug dealers of Baltimore. Omar, unusually, has kept his real name, and never was labeled despite the imposing scar across his face that could prompt any number of nicknames. When Omar is killed (5.08), the scene is harrowing because of its apparent emptiness for the larger meaning of the series (fan response to his death is discussed by Kathleen Lebesco in this volume). This loss is reinforced when the city paper declines to run the story of "a thirty-four-year-old black male, shot dead in West Baltimore grocery."[5] The presumed interest of the broader Baltimore community is reflected in this decision, and so the news media further undermine the identities of residents of the projects, leaving street names, chosen by oneself or bestowed by others, with their power both to efface and to create one's identity.[6]

The contrast between Omar and Snot Boogie is instructive. While the latter is merely pathetic, the former "is loved because he is meaner, funnier, cooler and braver than any other character you've ever seen on TV" (Delaney 6). Actor Michael K. Williams praises his character's integrity: "He makes no excuses for what he is. He is not duplicitous in any way. That's not only rare in the show but in real life, too" (Delaney 6–7). We find a heroism in Omar because he only robs from the drug dealers. There is a purity in this vision, as when he insists on paying for his cigarettes after he has robbed a shopkeeper whose store also serves as a drug front (4.03). Such variant visions of the institutions of the heroic in *The Wire* are discussed by Alasdair McMillan and Ryan Brooks in this volume.

In one episode, Omar wears a shirt that proclaims, "I am the American Dream" (2.10). It's a charming, ghastly thought. Earlier in the season, Omar appears as a witness in court (2.06), where he is described by Maurice Levy (one of the attorneys discussed by Lynne Viti in this volume) as "a parasite who leeches off of the culture of drugs." But in playing such a role, he is, as the scene powerfully declares, no different than the lawyer himself. With the irony possible only on a mass-produced t-shirt, Omar proclaims a profound truth.

The phrase "the American dream" was first used by James Truslow Adams in his 1931 work, *The Epic of America*:

> There has also been the *American Dream*, that dream of a land in which life should be better and richer and fuller for everyone, with opportunity for each according to ability or achievement . . . a dream of social order in which each man and each woman shall be able to attain the fullest stature of which they are innately capable, and be recognized by others for what they are, regardless of the fortuitous circumstances of birth or position. (374)

It is an idea that has been corrupted into a drive for financial profit seen in the corrupt politicians and developers who take advantage of Stringer Bell, as he seeks legitimacy for himself and the Barksdale organization (and who is discussed by Stephen Lucasi and Jason Read in this volume). It is an idea that is shown to be a fiction through every episode of the series, as we see characters continually fail to improve their lives, or to escape the circumstances of their birth. In Season One, Wallace selflessly tries to provide family stability to the kids in the low-rises whose parents are, dead or addicted. He makes them lunches from store-bought snack food (1.06) and he helps them with their homework (1.08), providing them with some nurture and continuity, until, that is, he is shot by Bodie and Poot (1.12). The bullied and socially outcast Dukie sees the promise of a life away from the streets, proving competent with the classroom computer and even being promoted to ninth grade (4.11); but, despite the protection offered by Michael for a time, Dukie ends up as just another drug addict living on the streets (5.10).

The Wire shows us an urban America in which life becomes better and fuller for only a precious few (as is addressed by Ralph Beliveau and Laura Bolf-Beliveau in this volume). Opportunity and innate ability seem not to have a place, since mere survival becomes a legitimate measure of success. In the end, Omar lives with integrity, but he cannot achieve that American Dream. His Wild West mentality, the lone frontiersman taming the wilderness of the drug trade, loses focus when he violates his code by acting on his anger. With the murder of his lover, too much has been taken from him, and in the end, his erasure from the series lacks the resonance we expect from a fictional death, particularly of a major character. It has no apparent purpose, except to ascribe value to social forces that we are challenged to understand. The same is true, of course, of Snot Boogie. *The Wire* isn't interested in a dream. This is America, man.

"a simple man, who was horrifically punished"

A term that has frequently been applied to the narrative of *The Wire* is "tragedy." Simon himself has termed the show "postindustrial American tragedy," arguing that

> whatever institution you as an individual commit to will somehow find a way to betray you on *The Wire*. Unless of course you're

willing to play the game without regard to the effect on others or society as a whole, in which case you might be a judge or the state police superintendent or governor one day. Or, for your loyalty, you still might be cannon fodder—like Bodie. No guarantees. But only one choice, as Camus pointed out, offers any hope of dignity. (quoted in Havrilesky)

Tragedy is a concept that Western literature has found difficult to represent since the late-nineteenth century, in part because its central preoccupation, the cost and consequences of greatness, sits uncomfortably with the democratizing tendencies coincident with the effects of the Industrial Revolution. First Büchner, then Ibsen and Chekov, nevertheless found a way to valorize the ordinary individual in their plays, discovering a tragic dignity in ordinary situations and characters.

In *The Wire*, Senator Clay Davis is located at the top of the show's political and economic hierarchies. He is patently corrupt, but nevertheless is able to see himself as a tragic victim. When he is finally required to explain his financial dealings, he calls an impromptu press conference on the courthouse steps. In his hand he holds a translation of Aeschylus' *Prometheus Bound*; while he mispronounces both the author's name and the play's title, he presents himself to the assembled crowd as a traditionally tragic figure, martyred for being "a simple man, who was horrifically punished by the powers that be for the terrible crime of trying to bring light to the common people" (5.07). The ridiculousness of such self-positioning is evident, as Davis presents a summary that might describe Christ as well as it does Prometheus, before it is reduced to a cliché: "In the words of Uh-silly-us, 'No good deed goes unpunished.' I cannot tell you how much consolation I find in these slim pages." The ploy works—the public accepts the story—but in this scene we are also pressed by the explicit comparison of classical tragedy and *The Wire* to acknowledge the inapplicability of traditional theories of the tragic to these narratives.

According to most definitions, the arcs for most of the show's characters are not tragic, but rather merely sad (and Amanda Ann Klein argues in this volume that they are more easily read as melodrama than as tragedy): we regret the murders of D'Angelo Barksdale and Frank Sobotka; we are disheartened at the hardening of Randy Wagstaff;

we are outraged at the murder of Omar Little. But that doesn't make any of these life stories particularly tragic, any more than that of Clay Davis is. There are simply too many stories, too many characters whose experience is presented in *The Wire*, for the focus on the individual to assert itself, as would be required by conventional representations of tragedy. Whenever something bad happens to someone the audience has been led to care about, we are equally committed emotionally to several other characters as well, and inevitably their stories go on. Events have consequences, but they are denied grandeur.

Yet each of them in his own way seems to demand that "attention must be paid," in the words of Arthur Miller's Willy Loman. Miller's 1949 essay "Tragedy and the Common Man" provides a mid-twentieth-century iteration of the idea of the tragic that offers us a starting point for a sense of tragedy in *The Wire*. David Simon is in some ways both author and agent of this revisionist tragedy for an urban generation that has long been excluded from the cultural valuation and social status traditionally required for tragedy. Miller is describing character, for example, when he articulates his sense of the nature of the tragic flaw (a term widely, if misleadingly, appropriated in such discussions from Aristotle's *hamartia* in *Poetics* 13, 1453a), but he might also be talking about the social function of *The Wire* as a series:

> Only the passive, only those who accept their lot without active retaliation, are "flawless." Most of us are in that category.
>
> But there are among us today, as there always have been, those who act against the scheme of things that degrades them, and in the process of action everything we have accepted out of fear or insensitivity or ignorance is shaken before us and examined, and from this total onslaught by an individual against the seemingly stable cosmos surrounding us—from this total examination of the "unchangeable" environment—comes the terror and the fear that is classically associated with tragedy. (4)

Few of Simon's characters demonstrate the wherewithal to enact this demanding requirement, though Stringer's doomed attempt to reject the presumed naturalism of black criminality or Bodie's refusal to soldier on as a mere pawn might come close (Bodie's character is discussed at length by Elizabeth Bonjean in this volume). The show itself, however—and Simon's vision—clearly functions as tragedy in these terms, shaking out what the generally affluent HBO viewer has long accepted, and giving a human face to what is usually written off as unavoidable urban blight, criminality, and addiction. The faces are (mostly) fictional, of course, but their humanity cannot be identifiably false if we are to experience the intellectual and emotional effects of tragedy.

The Wire gives us the deaths of several salesmen, shifting the perspective from the narrative of the single common man to that of disposable men, killed off amid their pursuit of the twisted version of the American Dream that is all that is available to many young men of the Baltimore projects. The men of *The Wire* share with Wily Loman what Miller argues is the tragic element of character (regardless of traditional nobility):

> the tragic feeling is evoked in us when we are in the presence of a character who is willing to lay down his life, if need be, to secure one thing—his sense of personal dignity. From Orestes to Hamlet, Medea to Macbeth, the underlying struggle is that of the individual attempting to gain his "rightful" position in his society. (4)

When Bodie refuses to submit to Marlo Stanfield's new order and insists on controlling his own corner, and then refuses to run from that corner even as Chris and Snoop approach, he claims his rightful place: "I ain't never fucked up a count, never stole off a package, never did some shit I wasn't told to do. I've been straight up. But what's come back?" (4.13). Similarly tragic, and less dramatically noble, Dukie's battle for personal dignity is finally lost when, in the closing sequence of the series, we watch him tie off and shoot heroin, slipping into exactly the "rightful place" that others have always expected of him. The eventual protracted death implied for Dukie is functionally no different than Willy Loman's suicide. Loman just kills himself faster.

Even outside of the projects, the new common man seeks dignity, at times not just for himself, but for those he represents. Frank Sobotka fights for a future that is the same as the past, and his loss is the more painful because his requests seem so eminently reasonable. As Miller points out, if the story is not to be mere *pathos*, "The possibility of victory must be there in tragedy" (7). Until the day he is murdered,

Sobotka—and the viewers—allow for the possibility that his view of the world will win out, and the blue-collar middle class will continue to sustain itself in a Baltimore that values the appearance of wealth and success over the economic survival of its individual citizens. His view doesn't win out, of course, and the "fear of being displaced, the disaster inherent in being torn away from our chosen image of what or who we are in this world" comes a little closer to the HBO viewer, forcing us to recognize that "it is the common man who knows this fear best" (Miller 5). In the words of Helena Sheehan and Seamus Sweeney, "*The Wire* is a Marxist's idea of what tv drama should be. Its specific plots open into an analysis of the socio-political-economic system shaping it all."

Though they may often seem so, tragedy and bleakness are not necessarily the same thing. There are optimistic moments in *The Wire* that prevent any automatic sense that there can be no hope for redemption, that the social ills depicted are irremediable—a feeling that may accompany viewings of Simon's earlier miniseries *The Corner* (HBO, 2000). Bubbles's readmission to his family, Namond's apparently bright future, the elevation of the good lawyer Rhonda Pearlman to the judge's bench, and Kima Greggs's return to motherhood all remind us that change and hope are not impossible. More subtly, the willingness of *The Wire* to pay attention to those whom society often considers disposable allows a consideration of the tension between the possible and the impossible. In modern tragedy, there remains, as Miller argues, "the belief . . . in the perfectability of man" (7). *The Wire* writes starkly of the human costs of a capitalism of the disenfranchised, but, like Bodie, it also refuses to allow the corners to be taken away from the control of those who inhabit them. As television presents the individuals who have dropped below even the standard of the common man in twenty-first-century popular and political discourse, *The Wire* goes beyond Miller's twentieth-century argument that tragedy "is the consequence of a man's total compulsion to evaluate himself justly" (5), to argue that all of American culture must act with justice in this necessarily brutal self-assessment.

Documentary Fallacy

Perhaps as part of this self-assessment, more than any other series, *The Wire* works to confound the line between truth and fiction. Its stories scream of verisimilitude, and the authentic dialogue draws the viewer into a sympathetic consideration of characters who live the sort of lives many viewers will not ever have examined with careful, concerned, critical awareness. Again, the series forces the HBO audience to confront its own prejudices. HBO is a subscriber-based channel, and the bulk of its audience is composed of (comparatively) affluent, middle class, white Americans. Subscribers choose to invest in programming that is assumed to have a certain quality that distinguishes it from "regular" tv. A second audience is generated through DVD sales, another means for direct marketing of quality television to viewers, without the economic pressures of advertisers. This change in television viewing habits, particularly over the past decade, has altered the economic drives of American television.

For these viewers (who through investment in a specialty channel, or through the purchase of DVDs have committed to HBO and *The Wire*), the initial episodes of the series may possess an almost anthropological fascination. Many would not have previously invested emotional energies in caring about the drug problem in urban America and its ramifications. Intellectual energies, sure, maybe. But the veneer of fiction offered by the series in fact stimulates a desire for identification with the characters, immersing the viewer into the heart of an American city.

What we see is a war zone: a side of America that appears extreme—at times incomprehensible—in a representation that is intellectually and morally challenging. The series appears to eschew any episode-based resolutions (as Ted Nannicelli discusses in this volume), preferring instead to offer larger narratives, juggling a Shakespearian cast of dozens of individuals, some of whom have names for us, some of whom are recognized or perhaps only partly recognized by their faces. Five seasons, each of which coheres as a unit, together form a super-narrative that shows the progress of time in a fictionalized Baltimore, but not any clear moral or narrative advance. Faces change, characters enter our awareness or drop from view, but the drug problem (which may be seen as the series' principal concern) persists. There is change rather than advance: whatever closure offered is, painfully, only temporary. By eschewing strong episodic conclusions, *The Wire* offers its viewers a narrative form unlike that offered typically by television, and with a scale (in terms of pure length, obviously, but also in terms of narrative sophistication) unparalleled by most cinema as well.

David Simon and others have drawn analogies between *The Wire* and the nineteenth-century novel, a genre whose sweeping narrative produces a coherent whole, belying its serial origins. Nevertheless, smaller narrative gestures can be pulled out, isolated strands from the larger skein. These strands might concern individual characters or a single episode or group of episodes, which may contain a discernable unity because of a strong or individual directorial hand (see Kevin McNeilly in this volume).[7] Beyond the novelistic, there is also an epic scope to the series, which—over the broad canvas of more than 60 hours of television—takes the time to focus on small details. Given the generic expectation of substantial length, epic can afford to linger over apparently insignificant objects and people, to find virtues in the ordinary, and can take the time to establish the place of the everyday in the larger world depicted. *The Wire* explicitly adopts epic ambitions at different points over its five seasons, perhaps most notably when it chooses in Season Two to examine the death of the urban middle class. The grand theme is not localized in one individual, but is shown to have an impact on many figures, amidst an expansive narrative of dockyard corruption. Yet at the same time, *The Wire* ascribes value to two teenagers sitting on an abandoned couch in the courtyard of a low-rise housing project. So much gets spoken in their silences, as they contemplate the economic implications of the invention of the Chicken McNugget (1.02). The series can even turn an apparently extraneous fish-out-of-water scene, in which Snoop goes to a big-box home improvement store to purchase a nail gun (4.01), into a crucial plot point for the whole of Season Four.

Despite the literary sophistication of *The Wire*, there is an authenticity that bleeds through the screen. Part of the reason for this is the deliberate blurring of truth and fiction that the creators have inscribed into the casting and the characters of the series. Identity is written, rewritten, and overwritten as actors' biographies and previous roles, characters' names, and real-life citizens of Baltimore dissolve into one another, problematizing aggressively any idea of easy constructions or associations of identity. Melvin Williams, for example, plays the Deacon over 11 episodes (starting 3.02). The character is a peaceful community builder, but the role reveals nothing of the actor's past as a Baltimore drug lord, who was arrested in 1984 by series co-creator Ed Burns when Burns was still a Baltimore police officer. After serving as a homicide detective in Baltimore, Burns turned to teaching, a career trajectory echoed (somewhat more abruptly) by the character of Roland Pryzbylewski in Season Four. Jay Landsman, a retired Baltimore homicide detective who features prominently in David Simon's book, *Homicide: A Year on the Killing Streets*, plays police officer Dennis Mello in 18 episodes; actor Delaney Williams plays a character called Jay Landsman throughout the series. Baltimore's first elected black mayor Kurt L. Schmoke appears as the Baltimore Health Commissioner, who advises the series's Mayor on his drug policy (3.11 and 3.12). Grand Jury Prosecutor Gary DiPasquale is played by Garry D'Addario, a former Baltimore Homicide Shift Lieutenant.[8] Recovering heroin addict and musician Steve Earle (who sings the series's title song in Season Five) plays Whalon, a recovering heroin addict who is Bubbles's sponsor. David Constable plays managing editor Thomas Klebanow in all but one of the episodes of Season Five, a character based on former *Baltimore Sun* managing editor Bill Marimow; the real-life editor's name is echoed in that of Charles Marimow, the ineffectual lieutenant of the major crimes unit (beginning 4.03). And Ed Norris, Baltimore police commissioner from 2000–2002, plays a homicide detective in the show, who is also called Ed Norris.

Precisely this overlap—playing a character with your own name, who both is and is not a fictionalized representation of who you are—also affects Felicia "Snoop" Pearson. As she describes in her 2007 memoir, Pearson was born in Baltimore to two crack addicts; as a child she worked as a drug dealer; and in her teens she was sentenced to eight years in prison for killing someone in self-defense. Her real-life recovery and rehabilitation must be measured against the bizarre reflection created by the character she plays in *The Wire*. Snoop's life (and death) in Seasons Three, Four, and Five, which establish her as a merciless enforcer in Marlo Stanfield's drug organization, form a counterpoint to the life she has instead chosen for herself. Pearson was introduced to the writers and producers after a chance meeting with actor Michael K. Williams (who plays Omar Little). The doubled awareness of actor and character serves to reinforce the emotional impact of the character as she moves through the violence that surrounds her, and it certainly contributes to horror writer Stephen King's estimation of Snoop as "perhaps the most terrifying female villain to ever appear in a television series" ("Alarm").

Less directly, the character of Omar (discussed in detail by James Peterson in this volume) is based on a number of real-life individuals who made careers robbing drug dealers in Baltimore. One of these, Donnie Andrews, provides a particularly powerful resonance with Simon's series. After turning himself in to Detective Ed Burns (co-creator of *The Wire*), Andrews was sentenced to life in prison in 1987 for murdering one of the dealers he robbed (see Urbina). But from this, there nevertheless emerges a story of redemption. Two years after his release in 2005, he married Fran Boyd. Boyd is the real woman at the center of the drug-addicted family documented in *The Corner: A Year in the Life of an Inner City Neighborhood*, written by Simon and Burns in 1997. This book was adapted into the six-episode miniseries *The Corner*, that, with *Homicide*, forms a crucial part of the groundwork Simon had established before he began work on *The Wire*. The unlikely pairing of a (rehabilitated and recovered) stick-up man and a (recovered and rehabilitated) drug addict proves to be a real-life fulfillment of the promise the series at times presents to the viewer.[9] Fiction, fact, documentary—blurring these lines and generic distinctions has never been attempted before on television at this scale, and its persuasive argumentation seduces viewers into a larger, albeit mediated, understanding of the urban life of modern America, and provides some sense of hope for the American Dream.

One final example of the elements of truth hiding among the fictional stories of *The Wire* seems necessary here. At the wake of Detective Ray Cole (3.03), a character who had been played by executive producer Robert F. Colesbury (who died unexpectedly after Season Two), police officers sing a 1986 song by the Pogues, entitled "The Body of an American." The song itself is set at the wake of a boxer, who is described as

> The man of wire
> Who was often heard to say,
> "I'm a free man born of the U.S.A."

Colesbury, of course, was a "man of wire", instrumental in the series' production. So indeed is the fictional character of McNulty, for whom a mock wake is held, where the song is again sung (5.10). Again, this "man of *Wire*" is eulogized by Jay Landsman (except it is not Landsman, but the actor playing a version of him, a counter-self). Throughout *The Wire*, names and identities blur, producing gripping television that challenges notions of how fiction works, and to what it can aspire. But all of these themes, it should be noted, had been shown to the viewer in miniature before the first title sequence was run. That initial conversation on the stoop of the boarded-up vacant repeats at times verbatim a true story that Simon tells near the end of *Homicide: A Year on the Killing Streets* (570). From those opening moments of the narrative of *The Wire*, we are forced constantly to reconsider what terms like verisimilitude and authenticity can mean. Nevertheless, we must always remember that as he lies there, dead before the first episode of the series begins, Snot Boogie too offers us the body of an American.

Notes

1. We discuss Herc's investigative career elsewhere (see Marshall and Potter, "Fuzzy Dunlop").

2. The City of Baltimore is arguably a character of its own in *The Wire*, and the representation of the city is discussed in this volume by David Alff, Peter Clandfield, and Afaa Weaver.

3. Viewers of Season Four remember that Prez teaches his Middle School math class basic probability through the odds of craps, and they all become proficient in the skills that Snot lacks.

4. Margaret Talbot expands on the poignancy of this moment in her profile of series creator David Simon: "It was a perfectly crafted setup for Simon's themes: how inner-city life could be replete with both casual cruelty and unexpected comedy; how the police and the policed could, at moments, share the same jaundiced view of the world; how some dollar-store, off-brand version of American capitalism could trickle down, with melancholy effect, into the most forsaken corners of American society."

5. Omar almost loses his name again in the morgue (5.08), where his name tag is left on a body bag containing an elderly white man. This is corrected, but it is worth noting that the date of birth on the card in the morgue is certainly incorrect, off by roughly 14 years. The card indicates 15 August 1960, but other indications suggest Omar was born closer to 1974: he claims to be "about 29" in Season Two (2.06), is 34 in Season Five (5.08), and is apparently 11 or 12 in 1985 (*The Wire: The Chronicles* <http://www.hbo.com/thewire/chronicles/>). This obvious error is most likely not a mistake within the dramatic world, but rather a meta-televisual nod to the birthdate of someone involved with *The Wire* (perhaps David Simon himself, who was born in 1960).

6. When Omar helps a court bailiff with his crossword puzzle, explaining the distinction between Mars and Ares, he could be speaking about any one of the nicknamed dealers in *The Wire*: "Same dude, different name, is all" (2.06).

7. For example, the direction of Clark Johnson bookends *The Wire*: he directed the first two episodes (1.01 and 1.02; also 1.05) and the final episode (5.10). His vision therefore frames the audience's experience of the overall series, but Johnson also mediates the show from within, as he plays city editor Gus Haynes in Season Five. His connection with Simon is longstanding: Johnson also played Detective Meldrick Lewis in *Homicide: Life on the Street* (NBC, 1993–1999), which Simon created.

8. "D." as he was known, was also the inspiration for "G.", Al Giardello, the shift lieutenant played by Yaphet Kotto in *Homicide: Life on the Street*, and in which Gary D'Addario also had a role as a SWAT team commander.

9. Relationships among the representations of women, crime, and the domestic realm are discussed by Courtney Marshall in this volume.

Baltimore before *The Wire*

A Memoir

Afaa M. Weaver

As *The Wire* closes, Michael takes on the work Omar has done before him, robbing the rich gangstas, redistributing the wealth, and upholding a truncated sense of honor and decency in a world ground down into feeding on its own life. He comes into the rim shop with his partner and delivers a gunshot wound to the knee of another gangsta, and makes off with their income, leaving him and his cohorts looking very frustrated there in the rim shop. The rim shop is actually there in East Baltimore where I grew up. It's at the intersection of Gay Street and North Avenue, where Gay Street rises up from the Johns Hopkins hospital area on a 45-degree angle. The rim shop is also where the drug dealers recently had a strategy of handing out free samples near the end of the month when everyone is low on cash. It was a feeding frenzy, a site that seemed more unreal than anything you might want to imagine as all kinds of people scurried over the area as if they were ants on a sugar cube.

In the late 1950s, my parents were among the young, black, working class couples that bought row homes in East Baltimore, many of them from the same areas in Virginia and North and South Carolina. Some people moved into the area from the public housing projects as time progressed. East Baltimore was all white before we moved into the area as part of the block-busting strategies used by real-estate companies nationwide in the 1950s, strategies that made fortunes for them as they resold houses to black folks at exaggerated prices after spreading fear among whites that black folk were coming. We came, and we painted the porches that had never been painted before. We added aluminum porches in different colors, the porch business that is the subject of Barry Levinson's 1987 film *Tin Men*, and we planted vegetable gardens in our backyards. These were southern families, an agrarian culture. We were their children, the bright ones who would do great things in the white man's world, even as they were launching us into it in the days of southern segregation.

The Baltimore of my childhood was segregated. It was also the childhood of Proposition Joe, the master of double dealing.

Joe and I were attending junior high school at the same time. We might have known each other, each of us dressed as we were in those days for success, although the mandatory shirt and tie did not come until I got to senior high at Baltimore Polytechnic. But when I started Herring Run Junior High in 1963, the month of the bombing of the Sixteenth Street Baptist Church in Birmingham, I was part of the train of children of bright hopes that were sent out on buses into white neighborhoods from the circumscribed black worlds of American apartheid. The schoolyard used to film that prequel of Joe in junior high[1] looks remarkably the way my junior high school looks now, although it has gone through several changes and no longer carries the name of the large public park nearby. Joe went wrong, the way a lot of us did in those days, but it was a genteel wrong before the wholesale violence of Omar's generation became the prevailing mode of criminal life. Those of us who went wrong did so in relatively innocent ways that gave way to larger enterprises, and some of us are still in that life. Some of my schoolmates are senior members of criminal life in Baltimore, and some of my relatives have done time in prison for matters serious or not so serious.

Joe and our crowd got to be 16 or so and started hanging out on the corners of East Baltimore where we wore shirts pressed with starch and shoes polished all the way to the stitched soles. We stood there and drank cheap wine and smoked reefer while we imitated The Temptations, The Four Tops, James Brown, The Supremes, Mary Wells, and all the bright fantasia of African American Urban Theater. Violence crept in as if on the feet of giant cats.

If you walked southward from the rim shop along Milton Avenue to the intersection of Federal Street you were at a locus of East Baltimore street life, just four blocks from my parents' home. Lucky's Bar and Cut Rate was the corner landmark. This is where I learned several lessons in the hard and often insane courage of a black man living for the city. We were a group, about four or five of us, and our leader was a member of a respected family. His brother was the lord of that section of East Baltimore. He stood on the corner of Federal and Milton in a top hat and with a cane, the attire that would emerge almost 20 years later in Run-D.M.C., who are now elders of Hip Hop. In the old days of Milton and Federal, these elders of Hip Hop were 10 years old, the little boys.

One night, just one block away from Lucky's, some friends and I were confronted by a slightly older man who was looking to make a reputation for himself. He was holding a .25 semi-automatic, and we were all unarmed. He caught me in the forefront, just in front of the right fender of the car parked next to us. It was a minute or so of menace. There was only one thing to do, and I was prepared to do it if necessary. He was about 20 feet away, and, as the closest person to him, I could rush him and try to bust his heart, scare him down and take the chance of eating a bullet along the way. I had to make the decision in the space of a few seconds, something one of my uncles taught me.

Uncle Jason was a knife fighter who walked everywhere and always carried at least two switchblades. His way of training us when we were kids was to catch us unaware and slam us up against a wall. The knife came up to the sides of our necks instantly, and in the calmest of voices he said, "Now chump! What you gonna do? Huh? Chump!" I learned to monitor my fear and to pray for intervention.

We were saved that night there up the street from Lucky's. The leader of our little gang came up from Lucky's and ordered our would-be killer to put the gun away. That was the hierarchy of things in street life in those days. Much of it was the respect of younger men for older ones, older ones who earned that respect for things that became the myths of life. There was some semblance of that hierarchy when Omar was a young teenager in the mid-1980s. Omar is part of the age group of the elders of Hip Hop. In the prequel that shows him returning the stolen cash to the West Indian man on the bus stop,[2] it is a time in Baltimore when violence and illegal enterprise were worlds away from that night in 1969 under the barrel of the .25 semi-automatic. Heroin was much scarcer in the late 1960s than in the mid-1980s when it became as plentiful and familiar as Kool Aid.

As black Baltimore was burned away and worn down beginning in the 1960s, the jobs that had sustained my parents' generation left the city and the country. They were replaced first with a stark and stunning absence and then with the paper promise of the service industry. From 1970 to 1985, I was a blue-collar worker in the city before going off to Brown University's creative writing program. Proposition Joe was busy building his empire in East Baltimore, one that he set up under the façade of a TV repair shop. It's in a neighborhood where the old row houses were gradually abandoned, as black folks moved to the suburbs. Their children would not know our memories, but they would have the same racist forces set against them in life. These forces could even take the form of the seemingly kind faces that want to assure them that racism is no longer America's problem.

One day in the early 1980s, two men escaped from the Maryland State Penitentiary, known as Central Booking these days. They made their way to a trendy restaurant on Charles Street, two blocks away from Walters Art Gallery. There they made what I can only think was a planned hit and killed one of the restaurant workers. Then in the dead aplomb of street courage they got onto a city bus that was headed toward North Avenue. The SWAT team was assembled, and the two men swore they would not go back to prison. They kept their word. At North Avenue, they got off the bus and had a shootout with the police department, who fired from every available angle. The men died in the streets, shot to death and through death's door to what lay waiting for them in the great beyond.

Omar was just two years away from making that difficult decision of doing what must be done, turning his .38 on his compadres to force them to give him the small cash that was all the West Indian gentleman on the bus stop had at the time.

Milton Avenue went through tremendous changes from the time Proposition Joe and I were in junior high school and in the 20 years up to Omar's emergence as a self-styled vigilante. As children Joe and I could go to the five-and-dime store there on Milton Avenue and with a dollar buy a whole bag of toys. With another dollar we could have gone to the movies next door for 35 cents and had a hot dog and soda for another 65 cents. The only problem might have been Joe's shenanigans.

Partly for amusement and partly to polish his entrepreneurial skills, young Proposition Joe might have stolen something from the five-and-dime, something he probably did not even want. Ever alert, the store clerk would confront us outside, and Joe would begin apologizing for me immediately because, in his sleight of hand, he had put the stolen goods in my pocket. I would begin to apologize and sweat, and we would both be allowed to go. Around the corner, I would jack Joe up and commence to whoop his ass, whereupon he would make me an offer, an offer beyond my imagination. Such is street genius.

Just a few feet away from the place where we were held at gunpoint, around the corner, there is a set of old garages that have mostly fallen down and rotted away. When they were in operation, they were a center for card playing, working on old cars, and drinking. Uncles and cousins of mine hung out there. It was just three blocks from my family house. One uncle of mine would sit in his car in the afternoon sun, listening to his radio. For awhile, he had a '64 Impala Super Sport that he outfitted with little conveniences of his own, such as the one switch in the console that turned on his stereo system. At the time he was my age now, in his late fifties, and now I know that moment of sitting in the sun and rolling back over one's life.

I do it from inside the white world that was legislated away from us when Joe and I were children, and began to deconstruct when Omar was born. Snoop is younger still. She was a tiny girl when Omar was making his reputation, and she grew up on Patterson Park Avenue, two streets over from Milton Avenue and just across from Collington Square Elementary School, where my son entered the Head Start program in the early 1970s. He and Omar are about the same age, and the two of them are rooted in the Baltimore that is rooted inside me, although now I am miles away in the Boston area, a place where the constructs of race are opposite to what I knew as a youngster coming along in Baltimore.

In my moments of greatest discomfort, it is a Boston where the city magazine can run a cover story referring to one of our most prominent black scholars as the H.N.I.C. or Head Nigger in Charge. This Mississippi Up North is a world where the liberal kindness is too often steeped in denial of the very thing it propels from this academic vortex.

Not only is it a white world that feels alien, it is also a black world that feels alien. These are black people I find it very difficult to know. I long for home, a home that is mostly no longer there. Just as Proposition Joe said at the meeting of the dealers, "I think we all see the writing on the wall in East Baltimore" (5.01): Johns Hopkins is buying East Baltimore in huge chunks and has already bulldozed an entire stretch of property from Monument Street northwards to Biddle Street. It feels like an absence in my heart.

When I am more reconciled to the hopeful world the Christian charity of my upbringing taught me to hope and work for, I realize America is home, as difficult as that may be.

Notes

1. In November 2007, during the hiatus between Seasons Four and Five, HBO.com released three short "prequels," called *The Wire: The Chronicles* <http://www.hbo.com/thewire/chronicles/>. One of these features Proposition Joe in 1962.

2. Another entry in *The Chronicles* shows a very young (12-year-old?) Omar, already with his distinctive scar, in 1985.

I

Baltimore and Its Institutions

1

Yesterday's Tomorrow Today: Baltimore and the Promise of Reform

David M. Alff

On 27 July 1996, over fifteen thousand spectators assembled in West Baltimore to watch the dilapidated and crime-ridden Lexington Terrace housing projects implode. A parade, balloons, and speeches from government officials celebrated the dynamiting of a low-income residential complex long ceded to the governance of warring drug traffickers. "What we have done is torn down what essentially have become warehouses of poverty, and what we're creating is town houses of choice," explained Baltimore Mayor Kurt L. Schmoke, alluding to a 303-unit mixed income development that would eventually replace the maligned high-rises. On a gorgeous summer afternoon before thousands of cheering bystanders a sequence of detonations leveled the Kennedy-era towers in seconds (Belfoure, "Baltimore Housing").

The third season of *The Wire* opens with a similar spectacle. This time fictional mayor Clarence Royce presides over the demolition of the public housing projects that Avon Barksdale's drug syndicate controlled in Seasons One and Two. "A few moments from now, the Franklin Terrace Towers, behind me, which sadly came to represent some of this city's most entrenched problems will be gone," proclaims the mayor, to enthusiastic applause (3.01). As Royce speaks, the scene cuts to Barksdale crew chiefs Preston "Bodie" Broadus and Malik "Poot" Carr

23

chatting about the towers where both dealt heroin and where Poot lived
with his mother:

Poot: I dunno man, I mean I'm kinda sad. Them towers were
        home to me.
Bodie: You gonna cry over a housing project now. Man they
        shoulda blown those motherfuckers up a long time ago if
        you ask me. You're talkin' about steel and concrete man,
        steel and fuckin' concrete.
Poot: No I'm talkin' about people, memories and shit.
Bodie: They're gonna tear this building down and build some new
        shit, but people, they don't give a fuck about people.

The camera cuts back to Royce promising that "low and moderately
priced housing" will replace the failed towers, and then back to Bodie
and Poot, and so forth. As the scene proceeds, alternately focusing on
Royce, Bodie, and Poot, each character registers a different response to
the impending demolition. Poot, sentimentally reflecting that he lost
his virginity in Franklin Terrace, laments his loss of home and the
destruction of a site of pleasurable adolescent memory. Royce claims
that "reform is not just a watchword in my administration. No, it is a
philosophy," and gestures hopefully toward a future where the structural
renovation of West Baltimore can revitalize the neighborhood's impoverished community. Bodie, more worried about the loss of his turf than
anything, criticizes Royce's insincerity and Poot's nostalgia simultaneously when he mocks the latter's recurrent bouts of gonorrhea: "No
matter how many times you get burnt, you just keep on doing the same."
Despite the mayor's grandiloquent proclamations, Bodie believes that,
however the city goes about manipulating its "steel and concrete," the
residents will continue feeding addictions, committing felonies, or in
the case of Poot, engaging in dangerous sexual behavior.

Literally and ideologically oblivious to this critique, Royce continues
his stage performance by asking the onlookers, "Now what do you say?
Are you ready for a new Baltimore?" After more applause, the mayor calls
out a countdown and seconds later the towers implode. Unexpectedly,
smoke and debris from the demolition tumble out onto the surrounding
streets, triggering car alarms and choking bystanders. Royce coughs into

his sleeve as black dust swallows the podium. Like Bodie's dismissal of the mayor's reform vision for privileging "steel and concrete" over people, the backfired publicity stunt casts a dark cloud over Royce's vision of a "new Baltimore."

Mayor Schmoke welcomed "town houses of choice." His fictional counterpart Mayor Royce proclaims a "new Baltimore." Talk of change is anything but new in Baltimore, a city perennially dramatized, historicized, and poeticized as the subject of formation and reformation narratives. From its colonial founding on the shores of a remote Chesapeake tributary to its industrial development into a bustling Atlantic harbor in the nineteenth century, to its depopulation, drug epidemics, and race riots in the twentieth, Baltimore has, in the words of geographer Sherry Olson, grown and contracted in a "boom-and-bust-sequence" of "building up and tearing down, swarming and dispersing, getting and spending, birthing and dying, sharing and competing" (xii). By attending so closely to the realities of twenty-first-century Baltimore, *The Wire* has internalized the metabolism of a city historically characterized by boom-and-bust sequences, a pattern traceable through the actions and words of characters on the show.

When series co-creator David Simon deliberately restages an event from Baltimore's history, the destruction of a housing project, and reproduces its accompanying descriptive language, the mayoral speech, he invites his viewers to notice the ways in which reform language and infrastructural redevelopment shape one another, or in other words, to evaluate the disjunctive relationship between the transformation of landscape and transformative rhetoric. By recalling an episode from local history through the invocation of that slippery commonplace, "new Baltimore," *The Wire* both rehearses and challenges a body of promotional rhetoric that has enshrouded and gilded the city for centuries. By populating its scenes with characters whose disturbing narratives resist compartmentalization within political speech, *The Wire* embarrasses Baltimore's project of rhetorical self-fashioning to suggest the inadequacy of such language to aptly describe the city. What, after all, would a "new Baltimore" mean for Bodie and his crew?

In confronting rhetoric proclaiming everything from Baltimore's reform to its resurrection, *The Wire* portrays a city conversant with certain aspects of its history and in denial of others. Through an ongoing serial sloganning project, Baltimore presents itself as Charm City, Crab City, Monument City, The City that Reads, and in the much satirized words of former mayor Martin O'Malley "The Greatest City in America" (O'Mara). For these bloodless clichés, *The Wire* substitutes its own language of the city in the masturbatory tropes of Jay Landsman, the shrewd barter of Proposition Joe Stewart, and the fatal swagger of Felicia "Snoop" Pearson. The conspicuous presence of this kind of language in David Simon's Baltimore illuminates by contrast the corresponding poverty of rhetoric used to address and sell the real-life city.

This chapter examines how *The Wire* appropriates Baltimore's legacy of political rhetoric to uncover the city's strategic foregrounding and concealment of different historic moments. As a televisual annotation of regional history, *The Wire* revises, refutes, and ventriloquizes rhetoric originating in such documents as Thomas Scharf's historical account of Baltimore's founding, Francis Scott Key's poem "The Defense of Fort McHenry," Mayor Robert McLane's rallying response to the Great Fire of 1904, and the Baltimore Urban Renewal and Housing Agency's Inner Harbor Plan blueprint for the city's waterfront gentrification program in the 1970s and 80s. More than merely satirizing the promotional efforts and selective memory of a rusting port city, *The Wire* demands a reimagination of Baltimore broad enough to encompass the contradictions of logical political rhetoric and a profusely irrational urban landscape, and to recover the orphaned accounts, obscured histories, and undocumented lives of a city in desperate need of a more truthful and complex artistic narrative.

The most explicit embodiment of the ways in which *The Wire* appropriates Baltimore's promotional language comes in the character of Tommy Carcetti, a fictional politician whose campaign speeches and policy proposals ostensibly aim to reform the city's infrastructural face and human heart, but whose actions ultimately perpetuate a historic status quo while serving the ends of professional advancement. The rise of the hotheaded, philandering, and masterful Carcetti from the back-benches of city council to the office of the mayor provides the principal political plot line of the third and fourth seasons of *The Wire*. Locating Carcetti within a nearly 300-year tradition of Baltimore orators, it is possible to read him as a pastiche of promises, talking points, motivations, and gestures. By rehashing the reformist language of tomorrow so often deployed by real-life Baltimore civic leaders, industrialists, journalists, and historians, Carcetti personifies the historic incompatibility between municipal rhetoric and material reality, while participating in a mayoral tradition of semiotic inheritance that suggests his actions will reiterate rather than intervene in the idiosyncratic cycles of Baltimore's history.

The City

Assessing Carcetti requires some historical sense of the city he comes to manage: where and what is the city of Baltimore? With characteristic oracular brevity, Reginald "Bubbles" Cousins offers a provocative if incomplete answer when he asserts that "It's a thin line 'tween heaven and here" (1.04). Substituting "here" for the commonplace "hell" makes for striking prosody, but Bubbles's actual location remains ambiguous. Where on the axes of history and geography can we locate a city supposedly bordering on heaven but possibly identical to hell? Historian Thomas Scharf set out to answer a similar set of questions when writing his 1881 *History of Baltimore City and Baltimore County*:

> Surrounded by rugged hills, hemmed in by boisterous watercourses, and flanked by malarious marshes, there seemed little prospect that the rough hamlet planted on this apparently unpropitious site would rise to the dignity of metropolitan honors. (Scharf 47)

Scharf delivers a colorful and tellingly antiprovidentialist account of Baltimore's foundings. Unlike the Puritan Boston that John Winthrop christened a "city upon a hill," or the Quakerly Philadelphia that William Penn envisioned as a "green countrie towne," those who built Baltimore had to claim their city from forbidding woods and infectious wetlands. In Scharf's triumphal formation narrative, it is not God but men who leveled hills, drained swamps, filled hollows, and carved a gridwork streetscape from the grasses and mud of the Chesapeake basin. For Scharf, Baltimore's eighteenth-century ascension into the ranks of America's most populous and commercially vital cities is a great comeback story, bearing tribute to great Baltimoreans who transformed a "rough hamlet" into an urban center.

In its early years, Baltimore defined itself as a site of resistance, whether against "unpropitious geography" or the hostile interventions of Maryland, whose Annapolis legislature favored rural interests over those of the port town. Historian Hamilton Owens comments that "At the very beginning Baltimore Town seemed an alien thing in the body politic of the palatinate on the Chesapeake Bay" (2). Sherry Olson claims this alienation prompted Baltimoreans "to define themselves as a people struggling against the past, resisting the oppressive institutions of the state, surviving in a political environment hostile to cities" (1). Olson's description of Baltimore's dialectical self-fashioning could certainly apply to the fictionalized Baltimore of *The Wire*, whose mayoral and police administrations over five seasons manage to alienate the Maryland Governor (4.13), the state attorney general (3.12), the U.S. Attorney General (5.04), and the Department of Homeland Security (1.13).

With eighteenth-century Baltimore's role as an industrial port serving piedmont farmers in a state run by southern agrarians, the fortunes of the city of Baltimore often ran against those of the state of Maryland. In its first hundred years, the city thrived during wars, blockades, and other political turmoil. Baltimore capitalized on the French and Indian War (1756–1763), the American Revolution (1775–1781), and the French Revolution (1789–1802) by supplying Atlantic marketplaces with cheap grain, incorporating Arcadian, German, and Scottish refugees into its expanding population, and exploiting the American need for a naval fleet to establish a powerful ship-building industry (Olson 11). During the early years of the American Republic, Baltimore grew rapidly through its capacity to address public health crises, domestic economic rivalries, and foreign invasion with large-scale public works efforts. For instance, outbreaks of yellow fever in the early 1800s drove the city to construct a modern sewer and drainage system (47).

Infectious epidemics demanded a civic response in the form of stones and cement. But the British invasion of Baltimore Harbor during the War of 1812 required nothing less than the spiritual unification of a citizenry to support protracted military resistance. The instrument of civic cooperation came in the "The Defense of Fort McHenry," a broadside poem composed by Francis Scott Key in which the American flag serves as visible proof to an astonished city that U.S. forces had repulsed the British fleet:

> What so proudly we hailed at the twilight's last gleaming,
> Whose broad stripes and bright stars through the perilous fight,
> O'er the rampart we watch'd, were so gallantly streaming?
> And the Rockets' red glare, the Bombs bursting in air,
> Gave proof through the night that our Flag was still there.

During the summer of 1812, Baltimore epitomized America's internally divided attitudes toward "Mr. Madison's War," most visibly in the violence of a pro-war rabble whose brutality and intimidation garnered Baltimore the nickname "Mob City" (O'Mara). However, by 1814, following the decisive American victory at the Battle of Baltimore, the city that the British had scorned as a "nest of pirates" could boast itself the birthplace of the text that would become the American National Anthem (Owens 171).[1]

Baltimore's self-descriptive idiom of comeback, transcendence, and the forging of civic coherence through adversity carried through the nineteenth century as commercial trade expanded and residential quality of life declined. Then on 7 February 1904, fire broke out downtown and incinerated all structures within Baltimore's original colonial boundaries, replacing the city's commercial core with a scorched and ghostly void (Hoffer 162, 186). The "Great Fire of 1904" destroyed 1,526 buildings and caused between $100 and $150 million worth of property damage (Hoffer 186; Jensen). On 8th February, the front page of the *Baltimore Sun* reported that fire has "devastated practically the entire central business district of Baltimore" ("Twenty-Four"). A column adjacent to this sober pronouncement catalogued a long list of the addresses, owners, and property values of buildings lost to the flames.

However, in the days immediately following the devastating fire, the same pages of the *Sun* that proclaimed the city's doom published signs of its resurgent life. While reporters mulled over the charred remnants of Baltimore's business district, and the implications of massive insurance pay-offs, the Geo. A. Fuller Co. firm advertised that, "This Company is prepared to immediately commence the construction of buildings in Baltimore in place of those destroyed by the fire" (Geo A. Fuller Co).

Other firms outside the immediate swath of destruction were quick to announce their survival, such as Alex. Brown & Sons, who printed an advertisement in the 9th February *Sun* to "Announce that their building being so slightly damaged by the recent fire and their vaults not being affected in any way, they are ready to resume business as soon as the streets are cleared" (Alex. Brown & Sons).

Mayor Robert McLane personified in the public sector the spirit of resilience already evident among Baltimore businesses. Just three days after the fire, the front page of *Baltimore Sun* declared the need to "raise up a new and greater Baltimore from the ruins of the old." The article relayed news that Mayor McLane had declined offers of aid from the federal government: "I do not mean that we are too proud to ask for help, and if we find that we need it [we] shall not hesitate three minutes about availing ourselves of the many generous and hearty offers of assistance, both financial and otherwise, that have poured in upon us from all over the country" ("To Build a New"). Following this act of civic bravado, McLane proclaimed in an interview with the *Baltimore News*, "We shall make the fire of 1904 a landmark not of decline but of progress" (McLane 269).

In issuing a series of sweeping predictions, McLane assumes a prophetic stance seamlessly undertaken in *The Wire* by fictional mayors Royce and Carcetti. As Scharf described Baltimore's transcendence of geographical and political conditions, and Francis Scott Key versified Baltimore as the site of resistance to national invasion, McLane locates the city's greatest triumphs in a future shortly following its most traumatic calamities. History, of course, has since proven the former mayor's predictions valid. Peter Charles Hoffer, a historian of the 1904 fire, remarks that the widened streets and modern skyscrapers that replaced the scorched ruins of Baltimore's business district "turned the Inner Harbor into a distinct and coherent place" (195).

At the dawn of the twentieth century Baltimore needed to rebuild itself as a modern city atop the ashes of an antiquated one. Fifty years later, Baltimore again faced the imperative of modernization. Following World War II, the city lost over 213,000 residents, many migrating to the surrounding suburbs (Gibson). Between 1970 and 1995, Baltimore lost over 95,000 manufacturing jobs (Olson 392). It was in these years that the city began to see the superblock housing projects and blighted corners that *The Wire* transforms into contested turf between the Barksdale and Stanfield organizations, the vacant rowhomes where Chris Partlow and Snoop stash corpses, and the shuttered commercial store fronts instrumental to State Senator Clay Davis's corrupt urban renewal efforts.

Commercially marginalized by nationwide corporate consolidations while plagued with appalling crime rates and failing infrastructure in the neighborhoods, the city at mid-century responded with an effort to redevelop its under-used Inner Harbor into an entertainment district that would "reinforce Baltimore's image as an urban center of distinction, charm, and vitality" (*Inner Harbor Project*). Authored by the city Housing and Urban Renewal Agency, the Inner Harbor Plan outlined a massive land acquisition and rezoning project that would culminate in the construction of a downtown festival marketplace, the National Aquarium in Baltimore, Orioles Park at Camden Yards, and the Baltimore Convention Center. In 1981, *Time Magazine* proclaimed Baltimore's "renaissance," asserting that "few cities anywhere can boast so dramatic a turnaround" (Demarest).

The Wire

The Wire begins staging its own history of Baltimore at the turn of the twenty-first century in neighborhoods beset with seemingly ineradicable poverty but often literally in the shadows of downtown skyscrapers and within sight of Inner Harbor amenities, in what Peter Szanton calls the "the rot beneath the glitter." Into this world of tantalizing proximity and gross inequity enters Councilman Thomas Carcetti, a scheming agitator driven by his anger at the city's collapse and navigated by his political savvy. Though representing a predominately white, middle-class district in the city's south side, Carcetti sees both human catastrophe and professional opportunity in the crime-ridden streets of West Baltimore, and so uses his position on the Safety Subcommittee as an excuse to court voters citywide.

Carcetti publicly reveals his aspirations for higher office at the end of Season Three, following the revelation of Major Howard "Bunny" Colvin's experiments with drug legalization in the Hamsterdam freezone. Rather than merely blasting Colvin, Carcetti uses the spectacle of a televised safety subcommittee meeting as a prompt for rhetorical bombast:

> we turned away from those streets in West Baltimore the poor, the sick, the swollen underclass of our city trapped in the wreckage of neighborhoods which were once so prized, communities which we've failed to defend, which we have surrendered to the horrors of the drug trade. (3.12)

In Carcetti's figuration, Baltimore is not battling itself in a struggle to reform, but instead a violent and remorseless external foe. Like Francis Scott Key, whose poetry compelled readers to "see through the dawn's early light" as well as the complicated national politics of the War of 1812 to rally around the common good of defense, Carcetti uses the figure of invasion to elide the complexities of municipal management and to explain the city's shortcomings as a simple failure of will. There is obviously some irony in the fact that Carcetti blames the condition of West Baltimore on "surrender," considering that the aggressively original Hamsterdam project constituted the most radical and successful police intervention depicted in *The Wire*. Carcetti builds his reformist candidacy by savaging the reform efforts of others, much like Mayor Royce (and by extension Mayor Schmoke) who applauded the demolition of high-rise public housing while seeming to forget that such towers of the Great Frontier Program were once a welcome antidote to overcrowded and unsanitary slums.

Where Colvin's Hamsterdam rezoned the physical geography of West Baltimore, Carcetti's critique of the project is a nebulous rhetorical gesture to the limits of toleration. By repeatedly declaring that the city has had "enough," the councilman offers only criticism of the present regime while proposing no alternative ideas of his own. City government is to save West Baltimore, but how it is to do so and with what benchmarks it can document this rescue remain unstated. Unaware of funding shortages, the strained relations between the city and Maryland, and the need to broker compromises across multiple constituencies, Carcetti at this stage calls only for "the courage and the conviction to fight this war the way it should be fought" (3.12).

Only after formally declaring his mayoral candidacy does Carcetti offer his own vision for Baltimore. On the night of the Democratic primary, Carcetti and his wife leave the campaign hotel suite to stroll the Inner Harbor. Carcetti looks out over the illuminated waterfront, and muses to his wife Jen, "It could be a great city again. Pull some jobs in. People move back, fix up the houses" (4.06). Carcetti's private thoughts on the economic renewal, repopulation, and repair of Baltimore hardly comprise a unique or actionable plan for reforming the city. Standing in the Inner Harbor, once the sight of conflagration and later the acclaimed landmark of Baltimore's renaissance, Carcetti merely echoes Royce's commonplace call for a "new Baltimore." Carcetti's assertion that "It could be a great city again" also recalls Mayor McLane's 1904 boast that Baltimoreans would look back on the fire as a milestone of progress. To accomplish this turnaround, all that candidate Carcetti lacks, of course, is a fire, a locatable problem that would inflict a finite amount of damage over a short period of time, and which the city could defeat and rebuild around. Instead of fire, *The Wire* shows how Baltimore's civic institutions have suffered from chronic neglect, suburban flight, racism, a depressed local economy, drug dependency, and failing schools. In short, Carcetti faces systemic problems far more complicated than those that McLane attempted to solve in the winter of 1904. When the fictional politician slides into the rhetorical grooves of his historical predecessors, optimistically reiterating yesterday's vision of Baltimore's tomorrow, it remains only for the show's writers to document the ways in which Carcetti fails to answer the challenges of twenty-first century urban management.

In this scene, it is Jen rather than Tommy Carcetti who is more attuned to the physical city. Smelling the night harbor, she notes that it's "a little ripe" (4.06). Where Thomas Carcetti is absorbed in his hypothetical rebuilding of Baltimore, Jen's words remind viewers that gentrification projects conceal but cannot repair the city's decaying underpinnings, its schools, social services, and law enforcement. When Jen notices that the harbor stinks, she literally smells Szanton's "rot beneath the glitter." Like the ominous smoke cloud that swallows Royce's stage at the Franklin Tower demolition, the sensory residue of an ailing city undermines the words that prophesize its recovery.

Unlike his wife, Carcetti cannot distinguish between the rot and glitter, between material realities, and rhetorical hypotheticals. This becomes clearer in Season Four, when the new mayor must contend with the same budgetary constraints, constituent contingencies, and personal politics that hampered Royce and others. Still animated by an optimism in the vein of Robert McLane or Thomas Scharf but sobered by the advice of his savvy and cynical advisor Norman Wilson, Carcetti sets three goals for his administration: a 10 percent reduction in crime, the construction of a "bricks and mortar" public works project, and a strategic evasion of issues relating to the public school system (4.08).

In his first two proposals, Carcetti follows the thinking of the twentieth-century Baltimore executive leadership that grasped only the external symptoms of the city's underlying illness, and accordingly proposed cosmetic solutions, like arbitrary numerical reductions in certain types of crime and Inner Harbor gentrification, while sidestepping issues like education, whose public perception cannot easily be managed with statistical and linguistic manipulation. Carcetti's proposal to reduce crime by 10 percent is meaningless in a city patrolled by a police force willing to massage, miscontextualize, and falsify crime statistics. Carcetti's initiative to build a downtown project simply to put his name on something is practically self-satirizing. Unlike Baltimore's purposeful public works of the nineteenth century (including sewer engineering and road improvements) this compulsion toward "bricks and mortar" as ends in themselves recalls Bodie's observations on the city's pointless deployment of "steel and concrete" and its concern for infrastructure over people. When the administration considers building a harbor promenade walk along the Patapsco River, it does so by prioritizing the interests of a potential Washington D.C. commuter population over the waterfront's traditional blue-collar residents. In an episode appropriately entitled "Know Your Place," city government's disregard for the ports resurfaces in the words of a Carcetti advisor who laments that the promenade could not extend further east because it would run into "the Locust Point Marine Terminal, which unfortunately is still a working enterprise" (4.09).

While Mayor Carcetti's first two initiatives crumble in the crucible of the Baltimore of *The Wire*, his decision to distance himself from the city's failing public school system to "respect the depths" as Norman puts it, holds more protracted consequences (4.08). After learning that the schools have accumulated a $54 million budget deficit, Carcetti is compelled to seek state aid. When offered a bailout by Maryland's Republican government in return for the installation of state oversight, Carcetti elects to retain both autonomy from the state and the $54 million debt. The mayor defends this decision by blaming the state, engrafting himself in a tradition of defiant Baltimore mayors including Robert McLane, who spiritedly declined relief following the Fire of 1904. However, unlike McLane, who dedicated himself completely to rebuilding the city (and committed suicide in May 1904 under the accompanying pressures), Carcetti taps into historic animosity as a means of retaining his personal reputation: "He was gonna make me beg, then call a press conference so the world could see me on my knees" (4.13). Carcetti interprets the political as exclusively personal, reading the situation not as addressing the future of Baltimore's children, but the future of his own political career. By the end of Season Four, the first-term mayor has so thoroughly considered his prospects as candidate for Maryland governor that he rejects state educational aid because the embarrassment would undermine his 2008 gubernatorial candidacy (4.12). By seeking the governorship, Carcetti follows the well-worn path from Baltimore to Annapolis traversed by five former mayors, including William Donald Schaeffer, an energetic promoter of the Inner Harbor, and Maryland's current governor, Martin O'Malley[2] (Archives of Maryland). While none of Carcetti's policies reforms Baltimore permanently, each contributes to the mayor's statewide self-promotion and eventual election as governor (5.10).

In predictable irony, the first-district councilman who called upon Baltimore's resolve to fight has in some sense surrendered his own mission of reform. In *The Wire*, Carcetti's political rhetoric stands in for actual intervention in the same way that Baltimore's many slogans substitute for the city's less easily marketable substance, and the tourist bustle of the Inner Harbor compensates for the lack of cargo passing through the outer one. By understanding Carcetti as the rhetorical sum of his predecessors and recognizing the power of his words to misrepresent and side-step real problems, *The Wire* personifies the need for self-critique within the text of Baltimore's master narrative, for a streetwise Bodie to puncture Royce's inflated speech (3.01), for an embittered

Nick Sobotka to heckle officials at a condo ribbon cutting (5.06), and for Jen Carcetti to recognize that underneath a surface of flowery words, even the most celebrated sections on Baltimore's map can still reek (4.06). The appropriation of historical rhetoric in *The Wire* reveals a city that has always shaped itself more compellingly through dialectical struggle than seductive marketing, and accordingly calls for a more populous discursive realm, in which a cacophony of local speakers and authors can draft, debate, and determine the evolving character of Baltimore's composition.

Notes

1. In an interview with *The Believer*, David Simon delivers a confessedly "useless history" of the final stages of the Battle of Baltimore that deflates Francis Scott Key's patriotic pathos: "In the morning, the star-spangled banner still flew over McHenry and so we had something to sing at the beginning of sporting events, and the British army, having fought the Battle of North Point against Baltimore irregulars to a draw, reembarked on His Majesty's ships and sailed away" (Hornby).

2. When in 2004 the Baltimore public schools faced a staggering budget deficit, Mayor O'Malley, unlike Thomas Carcetti, accepted a $42 million bailout from Republican Governor Robert Ehrlich in return for ceding some oversight authority to the state of Maryland (Craig). O'Malley defeated Ehrlich in the 2006 Maryland governor's race.

2

"We ain't got no yard": Crime, Development, and Urban Environment

Peter Clandfield

Season Three of *The Wire* begins by depicting the implosion of the tower blocks of Franklin Terrace, the dysfunctional housing project that has been central to the first major storyline of the series, the battle of wits between police and the drug gang led by Avon Barksdale. The disappearance of the towers triggers the Barksdale organization's campaign to retrench and defend its territory against its upstart rival Marlo Stanfield, a major plotline for the third season. Yet, the prominence given to the demolition of the towers (and to the various reactions of area residents) points to further key concerns of the season and of the series: ordinary Baltimoreans' need for decent living places, and the city's prospects for renovation and material revitalization beyond the ostentatious redevelopment of privileged areas. This resourceful engagement with Baltimore's urban environment as a subject in itself, and not just a necessary background for conventional crime narrative, is among the distinguishing and sustaining qualities of *The Wire*.

Critics such as Liam Kennedy and Steve Macek argue that movies, television news, and other mainstream American media have persistently misrepresented inner-city neighborhoods in "economically depressed urban centers" like Baltimore as "landscapes of fear" which— along with their often non-white residents—are largely and perhaps irredeemably lawless and savage (Macek xii). Macek suggests in passing that "fictional television dramas like *NYPD Blue* and *Homicide*" (viii) have also contributed to this misrepresentation of inner cities as breeding-grounds for virulent criminality, but detailed attention to television series is conspicuously absent from his generally persuasive analysis. Macek's comment does less than justice to David Simon's earlier police series, *Homicide: Life on the Street* (1993–1999), and it also disregards the possibility that a series with story arcs that extend beyond the episodic—a feature *The Wire* inherits and develops from *Homicide*—may be particularly well-suited to explore the contexts and nuances of complex urban problems. The investigation of matters of housing, development, and environment is most intensive in Season Three of *The Wire*, but attention to these matters is built into numerous ongoing storylines throughout the series. This ongoing investigation identifies Baltimore itself as a collateral victim of indifference, unenlightened self-interest, and corruption among politicians, developers, and other powerfully-placed people. In linking the concrete local conditions of the city to the (apparently) more abstract economic, political, and ideological forces shaping its spaces and their uses, the series resonates with the work of urban geographer (and adoptive Baltimorean) David Harvey, who explores the material problems produced by a globalizing economic system under which "machinery, buildings, and even whole urban infra-structures and life-styles are made prematurely obsolescent" by the cycles of investment and profit-taking (*Urban Experience* 191). *The Wire* harmonizes not only with Harvey's indictment of finance capitalism and the spatial waste and disorder it creates, but also with his insistence that finding alternatives to this unsustainable system requires treating urban development and redevelopment as "fundamentally ecological processes" (*Justice, Nature* 392) and regaining an understanding of inner cities as vital parts of the environment, rather than as crimes against it.

As executive producer Nina Kostroff Noble notes in her DVD commentary on "Time After Time" (3.01), the Franklin Terrace implosion is accomplished with computer graphics. This piece of virtual redevelopment reminds us that *The Wire* creates its own version of Baltimore, but also illustrates that the series gets its construction materials from concrete details of contemporary cities. The modernist housing projects that Franklin Terrace represents were intended to design crime and other social ills out of existence, in the U.S. and elsewhere (see Vidler 63), but their shortcomings have been widely registered, and their demolitions have become spectacles both in reality and in fiction. *Homicide*, for example, contributes notable takes on the fate of Baltimore's projects. One of its key characters, Detective Meldrick Lewis, has grown up in "West Baltimore's Lafayette Courts . . . probably the most violent of the city's housing projects" (Hoffman 125), and two episodes from the fourth season address his ambivalent views about such places. "Full Moon" (4.10) centers on a dingy motel and its semi-transient residents, but ends with Lewis reluctantly witnessing the demolition, or as he terms it, the "murder," of the Courts—shown in footage of the actual event on 21 August 1995—and reflecting that his family's apartment there was "the last real home [he] ever really had." "Scene of the Crime" (4.21) explores another highrise project, where Lewis, investigating the fatal balcony fall of a drug dealer, must negotiate with the Black Muslim firm that has been contracted to provide security.[1] Rejecting their racial separatism, and provoked by their obstruction of his work, Lewis nevertheless recognizes a case for their presence, particularly since elsewhere in the same project (and the same episode), a white police officer has failed to intervene in an armed conflict that has left two young black residents dead. Together, the two episodes suggest that one measure of the failure of such projects is the gap between the potential progress they once represented and the intractable problem they have often become.

Farther afield, David Greig's 1996 play *The Architect* examines the final stages of a comparable failure in a Scottish council housing estate, whose demolition serves as a dramatic conclusion for the work. The play's 2006 film adaptation revolves around the impending implosion of a Chicago housing project. The fact that Season Three of *The Wire* employs an implosion as its departure point, rather than as part of a spectacular narrative climax, is a deft structural indication that such drastic measures do not in themselves represent solutions to ongoing housing problems, despite the promises delivered by Mayor Clarence Royce, as he presides over the demolition ceremony. The sequence's main commentators on the event are not public figures, but mid-level Barksdale gang members Malik "Poot" Carr and Preston "Bodie" Broadus. Both are established by this point in the series as individual personalities with their own ordinary concerns, and though the implosion is disrupting their livelihood, they talk of it in relation to everyday, noncriminal experience. Poot is nostalgic: for him the towers represent "people—memories and shit." Bodie takes a harsher view: "They gonna tear this building down, they gonna build some new shit. But people? They don't give a fuck about people." When Poot reveals that he lost his virginity in one of the towers, Bodie restates his point with characteristic sarcasm: "Man, why didn't you say something before—they probably wouldn't be tearing this tower down now!" But as Bodie continues to mock him, and dust from the implosion rises, Poot reiterates feelings akin to Lewis's response to the "murder" of Lafayette Courts: "Shit, I feel like I ain't got no home no more."[2] The vigor of the exchange emphasizes that the demolition sequence is not only a memorable visual metaphor for Season Three's theme of "reform," as creator David Simon describes it in his DVD commentary on the episode, but also a metonym for the close attention that *The Wire* pays to the physical spaces that Baltimore's people inhabit.

In his commentary on 3.01, Simon dwells on the derelict condition of many of Baltimore's distinctive row houses. As the camera, tracking the return of parolee and former Barksdale associate Dennis "Cutty" Wise to his old neighborhood, reveals an entire block of abandoned houses, Simon becomes uncharacteristically (yet eloquently) inarticulate on the subject:

I love this shot. This is what was at stake. This is the Baltimore that . . .
I mean, I love row houses, and if you're from around here you know
that they've . . . destroyed and gutted and bulldozed . . . a lot of the
vacant ones. And, even though they're vacant, you, you just wanna
think that one day they're all gonna come back, and . . . it's just so
sad . . . The city's been emptied of people. (Original ellipses)

The scale of the depopulation Simon refers to is assessed in Harvey's *Spaces of Hope*, whose longest chapter details the movement of industries, jobs, and people from older parts of the city into suburban and exurban areas. Harvey reports that as of 1998, Baltimore's vacant houses numbered "an estimated 40,000 out of a total housing stock of just over 300,000 units." He adds, "The idea of reclaiming older neighbourhoods— particularly those with a high quality housing stock—for impoverished populations has been abandoned even though it could make much economic and environmental sense" (135). A more recent account puts the number of vacants as high as 50,000 (Lanahan 25). Simon's hope that "one day they're all gonna come back" could refer to the rehabilitation of houses themselves or to the possibility that people will return to revitalize inner-city neighborhoods. The ambiguity of the remark reflects *The Wire*'s linkage of houses and people, a connection that is especially strong with row houses, which architect Vincent Scully, quoted in a 1999 *New York Times* article on Baltimore's losses of jobs, people, and buildings, praises for "their doors and windows showing the scale of human use" (Rozhon).

Baltimore is not just setting and backdrop, but subject and fabric for *The Wire*, and this is rearticulated in the opening exchange of Season Three's second episode, as a Barksdale corner boy tells colleagues about an irritating encounter with a tourist. The visitor is looking for the "Poe house" (the North Amity Street house near downtown Baltimore that was once lived in by Edgar Allan Poe and is now a museum). To the local, though, the request seems foolish: "I'm like, look around—take your pick!" The corner boy may interpret "Poe house" to refer to the Poe Homes, Baltimore's first public housing project, built in the 1930s adjacent to the Amity Street house, or to mean "po' [poor] house." Either way, the incident evokes the mutual incomprehension of the outsider seeking the Baltimore marketed to tourists (see Ward 272; Harvey, *Spaces of Capital* 142–143) and the insider to whom the city's heritage attractions mean little. As Simon's commentary on 3.01 suggests, moreover, Baltimore's neglected houses are "poor" in that they stand for communities once built in and around them but now hauntingly absent.

The play on "Poe" here hints at yet further key qualities of the vacant houses. Architecture scholar Anthony Vidler's *The Architectural Uncanny* builds on Sigmund Freud's 1919 essay "The Uncanny," noting that uncanniness arises "from the transformation of something that once seemed homely into something decidedly not so" (6). Unhomeliness thus designates a hostile environment that is all the more menacing because it could and should have been a place of safety. Such transformations recur both in houses in Poe's fiction and in the structures of his works, and *The Wire* pays tribute to Poe by developing its own distinctive form of structural or architectural uncanniness. The vacants are visible from the very beginning of the first episode of the series, which touches on the case of a decomposing body found in the Poe Homes (1.01). The full and startling implications of these "Poe" houses, however, emerge only in Seasons Four and Five, to which I will return.

During Season Three, meanwhile, *The Wire* addresses the linked destinies of Baltimore's urban space and its people in a way that is focused through two very different, yet comparably unofficial, redevelopment initiatives. Veteran police Major Howard "Bunny" Colvin attempts to clean up his Western District by experimentally confining the drug trade to a designated area of abandoned houses, while Barksdale lieutenant Russell "Stringer" Bell tries to abandon the drug trade by refashioning himself and Avon Barksdale as partners in a real estate development firm called B & B Enterprises.

The very neglect of the blocks that Simon laments helps to accommodate the location filming that grounds construction of authenticity in the representation of Baltimore in *The Wire*. The vacants are also central to Colvin's scheme: he selects one of the most completely desolated areas of his district, and on his own authority declares it a "free zone" where the day-to-day drug trade will be tolerated. After initial resistance and incomprehension both from Colvin's subordinates and from drug dealers and users, the area soon comes to be called "Hamsterdam," after Amsterdam's association with drug decriminalization. Ironically, in this bid to "keep the devil" of drugs "down in the hole" of a particularly dilapidated area, Colvin does on a small scale, and in a principled way, what the phenomenon often nicknamed "white flight" has done to entire areas of American inner cities. Ecocritic Michael Bennett describes government policies of "the Reagan-Bush years" that favored sprawling suburban areas, and their mostly white and middle-class occupants, at the expense of inner cities, which bore the economic and environmental brunt of deindustrialization (Bennett 176–177). More specifically, Harvey's *Spaces of Hope* surveys the particularly savage and polarizing version of this process that has taken place in Baltimore and the surrounding area (138–152), and goes on to suggest that it has resulted in the ideological construction of "the inner city as a hell-hole where all the damned (with plenty of underclass racial coding thrown in) are properly confined" (158).[3] This ideological coding of inner-city people as beyond redemption abets a material process whereby cities such as Baltimore—having been impoverished by the migration of capital and by government subsidy of this migration—are utilized as dumping grounds for toxic substances generated by rapid and wasteful development elsewhere. As an epigraph in Harvey's *Justice, Nature and the Geography of Difference* suggests, "The bourgeoisie has only one solution to its pollution problems: it moves them around" (366).[4] What distinguishes Colvin's Hamsterdam from such practices, and makes it readable as a response to the kind of large-scale environmental class-subjugation and racism that Bennett and Harvey challenge, is its status as a principled, localized, and supervised experiment.

One of Colvin's community contacts, the Deacon, calls drugs a "force of nature" (3.02), but Colvin's actions amount to a decisive rejection of the trope of the inner city as a naturally savage jungle. The environmental implications of Colvin's scheme are highlighted by the way the camera repeatedly frames him against backdrops of green vegetation—a literal and benign jungle. Many location-shot street sequences during the season, and throughout the series, show city blocks that, though crime-menaced, are also tree-lined. Such visual hints that the city itself is something other than an irredeemable toxic wasteland grow as Colvin's plan begins to take effect. In a key sequence, Colvin escorts ambitious, reform-minded mayoral candidate Tommy Carcetti, along with the viewer, on a tour of reclaimed, formerly drug-infested West Baltimore streets, where children play in the sun and ordinary people go about routine activities (3.11). Colvin's main achievement—and possibly the most optimistic feature of *The Wire* as a whole—is this vivid suggestion that most of the neglected city itself can be rehabilitated, along with, by implication, many of its drug- and poverty-damaged citizens.[5]

Colvin's experiment itself, however, leads to no direct leap forward. In insisting that Carcetti see Hamsterdam—the drug zone—as well as the reclaimed streets, he acknowledges that the latter are utopian and depend, for the moment, on the dystopia of the former. By the time of his tour with Carcetti, news of Hamsterdam has reached both Colvin's superiors and the media (hence Carcetti's interest), and Colvin is resigned to being disciplined for his initiative. Still, his efforts lead indirectly to the end of the Barksdale gang. His unconventional view of the drug trade attracts the interest of Stringer Bell, whose latent rivalry with Avon Barksdale has become increasingly active over matters such as Avon's lukewarm response to Stringer's interest in real estate. Stringer, alluding to his affinity with Colvin as would-be reformers, gives to the maverick police officer information that will lead to Avon's arrest. The cemetery setting of the meeting, however, is apt: Stringer's fate is even harsher than the demotion that Colvin endures.

Stringer's bid to redevelop himself as a businessman presents an intriguing mixture of ruthlessness and naivety. Detectives Lester Freamon and Jimmy McNulty and their colleagues have tracked Stringer's interest in real estate since Season One, but only in Season Three do they realize that Stringer is not merely accumulating property to flip as a means of laundering drug money: "worse than a drug dealer . . . he's a developer" (3.04). This mordant suggestion about relative orders of criminality is somewhat unfair to Stringer, who has been diligently taking community college business courses and reading Adam Smith. Though he makes sizeable unofficial payments to State Assemblyman Clay Davis (the iconic figure of political corruption in *The Wire*), he fails to grasp the extent of Davis's deviousness or the degree to which the development business, as conducted by figures such as Davis's glad-handing crony Andy Krawczyk, is founded on influence peddling and other forms of double dealing. Harvey remarks that it is only through such instances as "corruption within a system of planning permissions" that "the nonneutrality of the creation of space become[s] evident" (*Urban Experience* 187). In this light, Stringer's undoing plays partly as the result of a capitalist utopianism that has led him to assume that the redevelopment of downtown Baltimore is a more honorable and orderly industry than the one he is trying to leave behind. It is possible that *The Wire* is somewhat harsh here in its implicit characterization of the so-called "Baltimore model" of urban renewal. Urban development can be more complex even than it seems in *The Wire*. Harvey, for example, criticizes the municipally-sponsored redevelopment of central Baltimore for its focus on projects that have consumed public subsidies but brought more benefits to developers, investors, and promoters than to ordinary people (*Spaces of Capital* 150–156; see also Ward 184–185). However, he also judges that these failings exemplify "not corruption of the ordinary sort but circumvention of the democratic processes of government and of public accountability for the uses of public money" (156). Still, if *The Wire* caricatures developers, this treatment might be accounted a legitimate tactical response to the misrepresentation of inner cities, and a constructive use of fictional license to concretize actual problems of spatial inequity.

Near the end of the Season Three episode "Middle Ground," Stringer and Avon drink and reminisce together on the balcony of Avon's luxurious condo overlooking the redeveloped inner harbor (3.11). They recall that the area's upscale retail space was the site of some of their juvenile criminal escapades, and Avon reminds Stringer of one incident in particular: "I told your ass not to steal the badminton set! What you gonna do . . . with a fuckin' . . . net and a racquet . . . [when] we ain't got no yard?" Though the two men laugh at the memory, its implications are ironic and poignant. It is virtually the last thing they share as friends (Stringer has already betrayed Avon to Colvin, and Avon is setting up Stringer to be ambushed by old enemies), and it hints at the origins of Stringer's ambitions for spatial and class mobility. Criminal careers like those of Stringer and Avon do not derive solely from their lack of access to healthy urban space or to the constructive competition that sports can afford. Uneven distribution of recreational space is, nevertheless, one of the real iniquities *The Wire* depicts. Episode 1.04, for example, pointedly juxtaposes the suburban soccer match of McNulty's young son with scenes of children playing on inner-city sidewalks and using improvised basketball hoops on the grounds of Franklin Terrace. "Middle Ground" itself emphasizes recreational space by following the final meeting of Stringer and Avon with a sequence in the youth boxing gym that Cutty, Avon's former employee, has set up after opting out of the drug trade and tiring of casual labor in suburban landscaping. Avon, himself a former boxer, has provided funds to equip the gym, and Cutty endures various difficulties to sustain a constructive, if modest, presence in his neighborhood. The fact that it takes drug profits to support facilities to divert youth from the drug trade implies an indictment of official neglect of the importance of recreational opportunity.

The day after his reminiscences with Avon, Stringer meets his fate in a downtown property that B & B Enterprises is redeveloping (3.11). Arguing with Krawczyk over the project's delays and the way Davis has been stringing him along, Stringer is confronted by Omar Little and Brother Mouzone, freelance gunmen who have joined forces against him through Avon's management. Shooting a bodyguard but sparing the cowering Krawczyk, they stalk Stringer through the partly-renovated space, dismiss his claims to be done with "gangster bullshit," and gun him down. This end is payback for Stringer's extensive crimes. However, the final long shot of his body lying in an empty, sunlit room serves also to stress the unfulfilled potential of the city and its people, particularly because Stringer was among the most popular characters over the first three seasons of *The Wire*, and his death disappointed many viewers. Long after his death, though, the themes of Stringer's dealings with developers are revisited in the final two seasons, which feature a striking profusion of inventive references and allusions to houses and homes, especially at strategic moments.

The opening sequence of Season Four has Felicia "Snoop" Pearson, one of Marlo's top enforcers, shopping for a nailgun in a big box home improvement store, where she and a middle-aged white salesman join in admiration of the deluxe model she chooses. The tool proves instrumental in the macabre real estate strategy that Marlo uses as he consolidates power in the wake of the downfall of Avon and Stringer. At the bidding of the remorseless next-generation gangster—who is, interestingly, nearly affectless except while tending his homing pigeons— Snoop and her colleague Chris Partlow systematically repopulate vacant houses with the bodies of assorted rivals, unlucky subordinates, and bystanders. Thus the uncanniness of *The Wire* is brought home, and the vacants become "Poe houses" in new senses. Their use as hiding-places for corpses alludes to the various wallings-up and floorboard entombments in Poe's fiction (in "The Cask of Amontillado" and "The Tell-Tale Heart," for instance). Even more horrifically, their status as graves serves to animate the anthropomorphic qualities of the vacants. Anthony Vidler reads Poe's House of Usher as the "paradigmatic haunted house . . . its windows 'eye-like' but without life—'vacant'" (Vidler 18). The boarded, blanked-out windows of the houses represent the blind eyes of the victims within; the presence of the victims reinforces the sense that the houses, too, are suffering entities; in turn the houses take on new power as metonyms for the ordeals of the living neglected people of the area.

In the final two episodes of the fourth season, Freamon figures out Marlo's perverse repopulation strategy, locating the hidden bodies by finding doors that have been reboarded with distinctive nails from Snoop's gun. This detective work keeps the vacants in view as sites uncannily linking the state of Baltimore's physical structures and the fates of its people. Season Five brings complications as the city's new Mayor, Carcetti, refuses strings-attached financial help from the Republican state government, leaving the police unable to fund investigation of the vacants. McNulty responds with a fiction-making exercise that adds yet further ironic dimensions to the connections between unhomely buildings and unfortunate human beings: he obtains resources for the vacants investigation by fabricating evidence of a serial killer targeting homeless people. This invention is a version of the truth. The season implies that the city's homeless and working poor are being assailed not by an individual psychopath but by a social system that treats people, like much else, as disposable commodities. The series thus gains further resonance with Harvey's ideas and also those of Vidler, who explores how "[t]he resurgent problem of homelessness, as the last traces of welfare capitalism are systematically demolished, lends . . . a special urgency to any reflection on the modern unhomely" (12). Unhomeliness is not just a trope, but an all-too-literal condition prevailing in the Baltimore constructed by *The Wire*.

As McNulty's fabrication gains media attention, Carcetti, by this time campaigning for the Governor's job, makes much of the cause of homelessness. In pursuit of his political goals, however, Carcetti also gets co-opted into supporting Krawczyk's development schemes, including the conversion of 500 public housing units into office space (5.04) and the "New Westport" project (5.06) that is to occupy the site of some of the actual port facilities whose decline (and whose role as entry point for drugs) has been examined in Season Two. Ominously, this involvement associates Carcetti, albeit unwittingly, with Marlo Stanfield: thanks to Maurice Levy, the well-connected lawyer whose services he inherits from Avon and Stringer, Marlo escapes prosecution for his crimes, and in the final episode he is introduced by Levy to Krawczyk at a cocktail party overlooking "New Westport." The sharp lawyer vehemently cautions the remorseless murderer about the portly businessman: "Do not get in a room with him alone—you want me there with you, believe me, otherwise guys like that will bleed you!" Despite this echo of the suggestion that developers are worse villains than drug-dealers, Marlo—who has been shown earlier noting a lesser dealer's suggestion about the investment possibilities of gentrification (5.04)—appears positioned to move into the world of real estate and real power and to succeed where Bell has failed. Marlo remains enigmatic: following his introduction to Krawczyk he leaves the party and provokes a street skirmish that leaves him with a minor knife wound. Yet, precisely because he seems to be without Stringer's desire for legitimacy, his prospective involvement with real estate underlines the critique of urban redevelopment in *The Wire* as an industry driven by amoral pursuit of profit rather than by principle.

The fact that *The Wire* leaves both antagonistic characters and a flawed system thriving—while well-intentioned mavericks fare less well— suggests a bleak view of possibilities for long-term solutions to the urban problems the series dramatizes. Simon's "premonition of the American empire's future" reportedly includes "more gated communities and more of a police state" (Lanahan 31). Yet *The Wire* does construct some "spaces of hope" (to borrow one of Harvey's book titles). One of the subtlest of the trademark cross-seasonal allusions in the series comes in the final sequence of Season Four. Colvin, following his departure from the police, has become involved in programs for the city's under-resourced schools, and he and his wife take in one of the students he works with, Namond Brice, the son of an imprisoned Barksdale associate. The final shots of the season have Namond surveying his new, pleasantly ordinary environment from the Colvins' porch. The moment is disrupted as a hip-hop-blaring SUV passes and its driver and Namond exchange gestures of recognition, before the vehicle runs a stop sign and speeds off. The camera then lingers on the image of the leafy, sunlit, and peacefully populated neighborhood, as the faint ambient sound of wind-chimes blends into the slow introductory percussion of the downbeat closing theme. This evocation of the street as a living, breathing environment delicately remembers Colvin's hopes for the areas he temporarily improved with the Hamsterdam initiative. At the same time, the sequence hints that Namond's future is still in the wind, though we later see Namond succeeding at a school debating contest (5.09). At the debate, Colvin rebuffs the campaigning Carcetti for his compromises as Mayor, but politically astute compromise also allows optimistic potential: Carcetti's success in his bid to unseat the anti-urban Republican governor holds out the possibility that he will bridge some of the city's differences with its surroundings. Also far from hopeless is the final line of the series, delivered by a chastened McNulty as he retrieves the bewildered homeless man he has involved in his fabrication: "let's go home" (5.10).

The Wire insists that cities like Baltimore are still worth attempts at real renewal. Given that the city's tourist-oriented redevelopments have inspired similar projects in many other places (as Stephen V. Ward details), perhaps the success of *The Wire* in adapting television crime drama into a virtual space for the exploration of concrete, complex urban issues offers hope that its critique of short-sighted and corrupt development practices, and its hints for more sustainable alternatives, can also be influential.[6]

Notes

1. Many episodes in Season Four were broadcast out of order. As their numbers indicate, these episodes were originally intended to be separated by half a season; that they were broadcast in succession (on 5 and 12 April 1996) reinforces their emphasis on living spaces in Baltimore.

2. The debate here, like Lewis's comments in *Homicide*, reflects the complexity of actual residents' responses to demolitions of dysfunctional projects (see Cohen).

3. As used in *The Wire*, the title song, Tom Waits's "Way Down in the Hole" (1987), seems to be about the need to subdue the "devil" of drug-addiction, but Harvey's description of the ideology of "white flight" suggests alternative, ironic implications to the lyrics.

4. In his chapter "Inventing the Savage Urban Other," Macek traces the fostering of race- and class-based environmental discrimination by right-wing ideologues and complicit media (37–69). An illustration of the "urban othering" of Baltimore comes from the 15 September 2008 episode of the A&E "reality" series *Intervention*, which concerns Kristen, a young woman who regularly drives 90 minutes from her suburban home to buy and use drugs in the city. The episode dramatizes her fear of Baltimore, but the depiction of her activities suggests as much about the negative effects of suburban drug users on the city as vice-versa.

5. Colvin's experiment links the concerns of *The Wire* with those of Canadian series *Da Vinci's Inquest* (1998–2005), where Vancouver coroner Dominic Da Vinci advocates needle exchanges and other harm-reduction measures whose real-world implementation by the character's model (former coroner and Mayor, and current Senator Larry Campbell) continues to provoke debate in Canada.

6. For constructive influences on this chapter, I thank the editors, along with Daren Johnson, Katja Lee, Antje Rauwerda, Joanne Valin, and Sarah Winters.

3

Heroism, Institutions, and the Police Procedural

Alasdair McMillan

First of all, it seems, we must control the story tellers . . .

—*Plato,* The Republic *(377 b-c)*

Plato argued that for the sake of social order, storytellers needed to identify their heroes unequivocally with the highest moral ideals. Those who failed to do so would be exiled from his ideal Republic. While we have grown far more tolerant of anti-heroes and moral ambiguity in our narratives, the police procedural is a genre still dominated by an essentially Platonic moral framework. More often than not, these dramas depict police as heroes and unequivocal servants of the Good, while their criminal antagonists tend to be just as unambiguously villainous and evil.

The situation in *The Wire* is quite the opposite: David Simon hoped that "instead of the usual good guys chasing bad guys framework, questions would be raised about the very labels of good and bad, and, indeed, whether such distinctly moral notions were really the point" (Hornby). He goes on to describe the narrative as a "Greek tragedy"—in the same vein as those decried by Plato—but one in which the "Olympian forces" set against the protagonists are "postmodern institutions" rather than gods or Fate. By emphasizing the power of such institutional forces, Simon effectively rules out the independence and extraordinary virtue of traditional police heroes, along with the *ethos* of "catharsis

50

and redemption and triumph of character" which once governed their stories.

In this respect, an affinity with the social theory of Michel Foucault is evident. A philosopher best known for his critique of "disciplinary society" and its institutions, Foucault approached the question of power in a uniquely influential way. Philosophy from Plato onward, he argued, was a discourse of legitimation and "right" whose primary goal was the identification of political-legal power with goodness and justice. Foucault described his critical, "genealogical" approach instead as a concern with "the 'how' of power" (*Society* 24); in this general sense, the concerns of Foucault and *The Wire* are identical. Like Foucault, Simon casts aside cherished beliefs about the legitimacy of legal institutions in order to examine the concrete effects of their power on individuals.

Foucault interpreted the late-eighteenth-century transition from the punitive execution of criminals to the modern penitentiary system as a transition to a "new micro-physics of power" (*Discipline* 139). In this era, the feudal model of power—founded on public spectacles of royal grandeur and brutal torture—gave way gradually to the exercise of power by hierarchical institutions and through discipline: means of "correct training" and "gentle punishment" such as ranked progress, regular examinations, incarceration, and, above all, surveillance (*Discipline* 170–194).

Specific techniques of discipline and punishment have changed a great deal since their origins, but the general modes enumerated by Foucault remain pillars of institutional power, directly implicated in the contemporary questions raised by *The Wire*. This chapter considers the police procedural through the lens of Foucault's theory, with the intention of understanding specifically why heroes in the traditional sense must be absent from the narrative. It seems that at least since Plato, heroism has been closely associated with morality and the triumph of the individual; in *The Wire*, by contrast, we are shown a Baltimore where individuals are perpetually at the mercy of dysfunctional, amoral institutions.

Procedures of the Procedural

Emerging from the genre of detective fiction, the police procedural was developed first as a literary and then as a radio format. It came into its own on television, following the early success of Jack Webb's first televised adaptation of *Dragnet* (NBC, 1951–59). His formula was widely adopted by networks, giving rise to an enduring tradition of televised procedurals, from pioneers like *Columbo* and *Hill Street Blues* to the *Law & Order* and *CSI* franchises currently dominating prime time. In an overview of the genre, Stephen Stark deftly summarizes both its basic appeal and its moral character:

> Legal stories . . . feature clear winners and losers, stock scenarios, compelling characters, and recognizable villains and heroes. Moreover, the moral imperatives that television usually has injected into these melodramas—respect the law, good conquers evil, the system works—strike a responsive chord with corporate advertisers who sponsor network programming. (232–233)

The networks have long populated their police dramas with heroes modeled after the successful example of Joe Friday in *Dragnet*. Driven by their own virtuous nature, such characters stopped at nothing to root out crime and villainy. The validity of the laws they pledged to uphold was beyond question. Sustained by individual heroism, triumphing over evil time after time, the legal system was portrayed as a well-oiled machine in the service of justice. And just as the driving force for justice was the heroic police officer, crime was depicted as the work of a few "deranged or greedy" individuals; broader "social factors" giving rise to criminality were only rarely addressed (Stark 266). As David Marc puts it, "*Dragnet* was not merely a hit . . . it was an ideology" (74).

This depiction of discipline aims to leave viewers feeling secure and confident in the efficacy of their legal institutions. The ideology thereby continues to strike the same responsive chord with advertisers, for, as Stark quips, "in plain terms, a secure audience buys more Drano, Crest, and Miller Beer than an insecure one" (246). Network procedurals have consequently done little over the years to question the genre's proven formula: "valorous" police doing their "very best" to catch villainous criminals (Stark 275).

Without sponsors to please, the subscriber-based network HBO is more willing to experiment with subversive reinterpretations of old formats. Simon claims that the series was pitched to the network as "a rebellion of sorts against all the horseshit police procedurals afflicting American television" (Hornby). The genre's traditional formulas are certainly subverted: investigations are drawn-out, anticlimactic affairs, in which the valor of police officers is often uncertain and their best efforts are only rarely good enough. This is not a matter of emphasizing the corruption of a few "bad apples" in the department, or questioning the goodness of police officers in general. In the end, such moral notions are themselves placed in doubt: the narrative just isn't about good guys chasing bad guys.

As Simon emphasizes, *The Wire* is about "how institutions have an effect on individuals," and how "whether you're a cop, a longshoreman, a drug dealer, a politician, [or] a judge . . . you are ultimately compromised and must contend with whatever institution you've committed to" (1.01, DVD commentary). Individual heroism and morality are often simply irrelevant, while the "social factors" excluded from most procedurals are promoted to centrality. Leaving behind the isolated investigations and cathartic individualism typical of police procedurals, *The Wire* depicts crime and punishment within a troublingly realistic representation of their entire social context.

In *Discipline and Punish*, Foucault claimed that "the delinquent is an institutional product" (301); nowhere else in contemporary culture is the truth of this assertion so apparent as in *The Wire*. Criminality is depicted as an entrenched, systemic phenomenon, produced and shaped by the same institutions tasked with enforcing social discipline (or, as they would have it, "fighting crime"). Laws themselves are often portrayed—along with all other institutional dictates—as fundamentally misguided. The Baltimore Police Department and the other legal institutions of *The Wire* are machines in the service not of justice, but of short-term political interests. These are not bastions of heroism, but its most significant contemporary obstacles.

Each season, a new wiretap allows the narrative to "dig up the ways that legal and illegal Baltimore talk to each other every day" (Kois). What these excavations reveal is that neither side can claim the moral high ground. The police department and criminal organizations are depicted as structurally similar and highly interconnected. Connected not just by wires, but by flows of power, patronage, and profit, each demands similar compromises from the individuals caught up within.

Whether you're a cop, a drug dealer, or a politician, institutional discipline aims to make you into a docile and obedient subject, leaving very little room in the process for noble principles or heroic goals. *The Wire* thereby renounces the idealism of the orthodox procedural, bearing a far closer resemblance to modern social theory. Like orthodox political philosophy as interpreted by Foucault, orthodox police procedurals serve a legitimizing function: with very few exceptions, they equate institutional power with right, and Law with Good. In many respects, this grossly distorts the reality of discipline. As Foucault notes, such a "discourse of right" is in fact "an instrument of domination" (*Society* 27). By contrast, the essence of *The Wire* is critique: in each storyline and episode, viewers are confronted with the fact of institutional domination in all its arbitrariness, brutality, and secrecy.

Three Character Studies

McNulty. *The Wire* has no main character, and certainly no singular hero. A reasonable place to begin when considering its depiction of heroism, however, is with Detective Jimmy McNulty. The narrative initially sets him up as a heroic figure of sorts, when he pressures Judge Daniel Phelan to demand an investigation of Avon Barksdale's drug-trafficking organization (1.01). McNulty suspects the organization to be responsible for the murders of several witnesses, but his bosses operate under continual pressure from the Mayor's Office to reduce crime statistics, easier to do with "buy-and-bust" arrests rather than large-scale operations. McNulty makes it clear that, unless Phelan applies some political pressure of his own, McNulty's bosses will refuse to pursue any serious investigation of Barksdale.

This, in a nutshell, is law enforcement as depicted in *The Wire*: career-minded officers like McNulty's bosses do the bidding of career-minded politicians, working together to climb their respective ladders in an orderly fashion. An axiom of Foucault's theory of discipline is that its principal aim is to produce "subjected and practiced," "useful," and generally "docile bodies" (*Discipline* 138). Like any other disciplinary institution, the Baltimore Police Department can be interpreted as a mechanism for the production of such docility: the ambitious, career-minded officers are those who have internalized its regime of ranked progress, allowing it to "function automatically" within them (*Discipline* 227). Deeply invested in the status quo and unconcerned with the effects of their actions, high-ranking characters like William Rawls and Ervin Burrell are the culmination of the useful, docile bodies of the department.

The kind of lengthy, expensive, and occasionally embarrassing surveillance required to bring down a criminal organization would not take place, therefore, without the back-channel maneuvers of short-sighted and subversive types like McNulty.[1] The driving force behind the investigations of the first three seasons, he is indeed (as his supervisor Jay Landsman puts it) "natural police" (5.10). But the larger question remains: is he a hero? An officer who defies bureaucrats for a good cause is a common heroic figure in police dramas. Yet even when we disregard his obvious character flaws—like a propensity for driving while intoxicated (DWI) and self-destructive sex—he bears little resemblance to the police heroes of television past.

After the first investigation of Barksdale's organization, an incredulous McNulty asks himself a simple yet telling question: "What the fuck did I do?" (1.13). We might note, first of all, that he irritated his bosses enough to end up on the boat with the Baltimore Police Department (BPD) Marine Unit: precisely where he kept telling his colleagues he never wanted to be transferred. In situations like these, the disciplinary mechanism of ranked progress can serve equally as punishment. Insubordination and political machinations like McNulty's are shown to be the only ways to accomplish anything worthwhile in an institution as broken as the BPD as presented on *The Wire*, but even (perhaps especially) in service of a good cause they are portrayed as quick ways to destroy a career. This may also suggest why the bosses are so willing to ignore the real problems of the city: their unquestioning docility seems to be precisely the quality that earned them promotion.

Another cause of McNulty's incredulity is that at his investigation's premature end it is he himself, rather than the criminals, who seems to bear the brunt of the punishment. Thanks to defense lawyer Maurice Levy, Avon Barksdale receives only a few years in prison, and his second-in-command Stringer Bell avoids prosecution altogether. McNulty's career is left at an apparent dead end, for the sake of what amounts to little more than a speed bump in the continuing operations of a multi-million-dollar criminal organization. Unlike the simple homicide cases that are the staples of most procedurals, drug cases in *The Wire* offers no easy cathartic resolution.

Drug-trafficking organizations are deeply entrenched elements of this decaying system. Such delinquency is, as Foucault notes, not only a "product" of an institutional context, but "a part and an instrument of it" (*Discipline* 282). Discipline does not relate to delinquency in a purely negative or punitive fashion, but uses the delinquent for its own purposes. Their economic niche having been produced in the first place by the War on Drugs, the gangs' activities are organized in turn around police surveillance and potential prosecution. The politicians they bribe do their part to discourage investigations; lawyers like Levy create structured pleas to ensure that the gangs can continue their operations (and lawyers' practices can flourish). When a leader is imprisoned, someone quickly assumes his role. Even when an entire organization collapses (like Barksdale's does in Season Three) another is always ready to pick up the pieces (as does Marlo Stanfield's in Season Four). This kind of bleak social realism makes the Baltimore of *The Wire* a frustrating place for any would-be hero.

Yet all the while, McNulty seems to be guided by the same ideal of the hero called into question by his narrative. Following one of McNulty's rants about his own investigative prowess, he and Lester Freamon have this memorable exchange:

Freamon: Tell me something, Jimmy: how exactly do you think it all ends?

McNulty: What do you mean?

Freamon: A parade? Gold watch? A shining Jimmy McNulty Day moment when you bring in a case so sweet, everybody gets together and says, "Oh, shit, he was right all along, we should have listened to him!"

McNulty: I don't know. A good case . . .

Freamon: . . . ends. They all end. The handcuffs go click and it's over . . .

McNulty: Until the next case! (3.09)

The case "so sweet" that it would affirm once and for all his own superiority: Freamon recognizes that this imaginary triumph is what really drives McNulty throughout *The Wire*. McNulty is perpetually thwarted, however, by his own institution and the reality of his position therein. Baltimore's criminal institutions, moreover, are not the kind of villains which lend themselves well to such fantasies. McNulty is no Joe Friday, no principled defender of law and justice. His desire is to assert his dominance over Baltimore's criminal element, whatever the means and whatever the cost. As Foucault notes, not just the delinquent but the individual as such is an institutional product (*Discipline* 170, 194). What propels McNulty is ultimately revealed as little more than raw will-to-power channeled, organized, and individuated by discipline. As Nietzsche's infamous rebuttal to Platonism would have it, McNulty's motivations are beyond good and evil. He is driven not by an internal wellspring of the Good, but simply by a will "to grow, spread, seize, become predominant—not from any morality or immorality but because it is living . . . and because life simply is will to power" (Nietzsche 259). This is perhaps the deepest challenge of all within Simon's general project of challenging the paradigm of the police procedural. McNulty's investigations may initially seem like good causes, but over time it becomes apparent that these are merely outlets for this fundamental drive.

We may respect his courageous defiance of the bosses, but eventually his motives and principles become altogether suspect. Insofar as he never really puts his ideal scenario of pursuit and triumph to the question, his principles are deeply problematic. His motive, on the other hand, becomes self-evident in Season Five, when he fabricates a serial killer to cover for an illegal and ultimately futile wiretap of Marlo Stanfield's organization. Unmistakably, this becomes more of a vendetta than a quest for justice. The conclusion of McNulty's story thereby knocks the biggest hole of all in the heroic image suggested by the early episodes of Season One, revealing his readiness to discard ethics and law in pursuit of a fantasy of domination. Without altogether negating his heroism, this constitutes an obvious divergence from the Platonic heroic archetype.

Colvin. Major Howard "Bunny" Colvin is another officer who demonstrates a willingness to think outside the box, also defying both his superiors and the law. Where McNulty limits himself to devising creative ways to provoke and prolong investigations of drug traffickers, Colvin takes a much broader view. Eventually, he steps outside the "good guys chasing bad guys" paradigm altogether, coming to question the law and the very premise of the War on Drugs. He decides, in effect, to legalize drugs in three of his district's abandoned neighborhoods. As he puts it,

> Dozerman gets shot for some bullshit . . . and that's when the idea of the free zone, of Hamsterdam, come to me. 'Cause this drug thing, this ain't police work. Naw, it ain't . . . I mean you call something a war and pretty soon, everybody gonna be running around acting like warriors . . . Soon the neighborhood that you supposed to be policing, that's just occupied territory. (3.10)

Once the dealers are convinced to use Colvin's free zones, crime is virtually eliminated in the district's residential neighborhoods. Predictably, Colvin's creative policy-making greatly improves ordinary citizens' quality of life. Just as predictably, once press and politicians learn of the scheme, the free zones are dismantled, the dealers arrested, and Colvin forced to resign.

Colvin doesn't just pursue some heroic fantasy within the same old framework. Instead, he tries to effect positive change the only way he can in such a broken system, by an outright refusal to obey or enforce its dysfunctional brand of discipline. Colvin recognizes that Baltimore's problem with drugs calls for harm reduction: a public health solution, not an interminable project of incarceration. The Hamsterdam storyline thereby makes David Simon's "unalterable opposition" (Hornby) to the War on Drugs quite clear. It leaves us asking, however, whether principles like Colvin's can have any lasting effect. Though most every character recognizes the effectiveness of his free zones and the futility of the punitive War on Drugs approach, the status quo is quickly restored in Baltimore. The discipline of the BPD ultimately renders Colvin's heroism—like McNulty's—both wholly ineffectual and ruinous for his career.

After his forced resignation, Colvin decides to participate in a University of Maryland pilot program with Dr. David Parenti at Edward Tilghman Middle School (4.03). Their class seems to be a positive influence in the lives of its at-risk students, and is reasonably successful in keeping them in school and out of the drug trade. After a formal review, however, the Mayor's Office cancels its funding, citing vague concerns about segregation and the program's failure to teach material for federally-mandated tests. Such examinations (both in the academic and political context) are, as Foucault notes, an essential and "highly ritualized procedure" of disciplinary power (*Discipline* 184). Not only does an examination of the program's political usefulness lead to its cancellation, but the cited concern is that the program itself somehow interferes with other regimes of mandatory examination. While Parenti remains optimistic about the attention his study will receive from other researchers, Colvin is dismissive, offering a parting jab at academia: "Academics? What, they gonna study your study? When do this shit change?" (4.13).

The project may have proven inconsequential from Colvin's point of view, but it leads to one of the more inspiring storylines of the series. Colvin bonds in the class with Namond Brice, son of Wee-Bey Brice (an incarcerated member of Barksdale's now-defunct organization). No longer receiving funds from the Barksdales, Namond's mother De'Londa pushes him to follow in his father's footsteps by getting his own corner. Here, at the level of families and communities, we can begin to recognize a counter-discipline which sets itself against the law, driving individuals from poverty into an institutionalized delinquency. When Namond proves ill-suited for the violent life of a corner boy, De'Londa throws him out of the house to "harden him up" (4.10). He ends up staying with Colvin and his wife, and eventually Colvin takes the remarkable step of visiting Wee-Bey in prison. Colvin tells him that Namond just "isn't cut out for them corners" (4.13); eventually, Wee-Bey is persuaded that Namond would be better off with Colvin and his wife than with De'Londa and on the corner.

The effects of institutional forces on the paths taken by individuals are especially prominent in the stories of Namond and the other students at Edward Tilghman Middle. But they also illustrate how individuals can offer resistance to discipline. Significantly, it is only by having the courage to step outside the battle lines drawn by institutions and connect on a basic human level—with a convicted murderer no less—that Colvin is finally able to effect an enduring, positive change. Although this is change on a small scale, his and Wee-Bey's actions in this storyline stand out as some of the most individually heroic in *The Wire*.

Daniels. While demonstrating such flashes of heroism, McNulty and Colvin are continually thwarted by institutions. Cedric Daniels, by contrast, seems to be one of the few officers in the department able to sustain a commitment both to real police work and to his career. Balancing principles with pragmatism and political savvy, he ascends quickly through the ranks over the course of the series. From the beginning, however, it is suggested that Daniels's record is less than spotless. McNulty learns early on that Daniels was once investigated by the FBI and found to have "a couple hundred thousand dollars more in liquid assets" than a police lieutenant really should (1.03). Police Commissioner Ervin Burrell kept the investigation's findings quiet, partly to avoid scandal, but also to keep the knowledge in reserve. As Daniels puts it, "He's got me if he wants me. Thing is, I don't think he wants me. Too much stink, too much mess" (1.13). But after lingering in the background for years, Daniels's enigmatic misdeeds come back to haunt him, indicating how "whatever institution you as an individual commit to will somehow find a way to betray you on *The Wire*" (Simon in Havrilesky). In due course, discipline proves itself capable of neutralizing even the most promising of potential heroes.

Daniels' rise through the department is meteoric: in five seasons, he goes from Lieutenant to Deputy Commissioner. Burrell uses his knowledge as leverage throughout, occasionally pressuring Daniels to hold off or end troublesome investigations. In this disciplinary use of information, we may recognize yet another of Foucault's well-known axioms: "power and knowledge directly imply one another" (*Discipline* 27). When Daniels threatens to replace him in Season Five, however, Burrell is no longer in a position to deploy this knowledge as power. Nerese Campbell, the city councillor to whom he reveals the secret, quietly tucks away the dossier on Daniels. Later, when newly-elected mayor Tommy Carcetti is attempting unsuccessfully to persuade Daniels to "juke" the statistics, Campbell sees a way to curry favor with her knowledge. Unless Daniels agrees to "come to his senses" or step down for "personal reasons," she threatens to leak the dossier, simultaneously preventing his appointment as Commissioner and ruining his wife's political career (5.10). After successfully negotiating the delicate balance between career and principles for five seasons, and precisely when he would have been in a position to effect substantial change in the BPD, Daniels is forced into the very same compromising position as his predecessors.

The critical difference is that given the choice of preserving the status quo or stepping down, he makes the heroic decision to step down. Even after keeping quiet about McNulty's invented serial killer, the institutional pressure to present artificial statistics proves too much for Daniels. As he puts it, neatly summarizing the fundamental problem with the BPD:

> I'll swallow a lie when I have to. I've swallowed a few big ones lately. But the stat games? That lie? It's what ruined this department. Shining up shit and calling it gold, so Majors become Colonels and mayors become governors. Pretending to do police work, while one generation fuckin' trains the next how not to do the job. (5.10)

The "stat game" is a lie that he simply can't live with. Daniels has come to recognize what this lie means and how it reproduces itself, and he can't allow himself to be complicit. Not only would he be upholding a dysfunctional system of ranked progress by helping to elect a governor who accomplished little in his term as Mayor, as Commissioner he would be in Campbell's pocket. From then on—as Mayor—she would expect docility. Like Burrell before him, Daniels would be responsible for keeping the BPD captive to political interests. McNulty's lies were intended (at least in his mind) to serve some useful purpose; the lies Campbell asks Daniels to tell would have him participating directly in the undermining of his department and destruction of his city.

Organizations and Discipline

As J. M. Tyree observes, "*The Wire* is in the business of telling America truths about itself that would be unbearable even if it were interested in bearing them" (38). The series is by no means optimistic about individual heroism: this is one of the most essential of the unbearable truths it tells. When Daniels decides to resign, for instance, we may respect his courage and the importance of the principles at stake. As his wife notes, however, the gesture is futile. Burrell "played the game" before him and "Rawls or whoever" will do it afterward (5.10). Guided by a considerably more realistic view of society and its institutions than orthodox procedurals, *The Wire* disavows the idea that a few heroic individuals could solve the entrenched problems of a city like Baltimore.

Analysis of the narrative in terms of discipline indicates a chief reason for this disavowal: the would-be heroes' chief antagonists are their own superiors. Like much of David Simon's work—notably *The Corner* (HBO, 2000) and *Generation Kill* (HBO, 2008)—*The Wire* is simultaneously very sympathetic in its portrayal of individuals forced into compromising positions by institutions, and very critical of the ones doing the forcing. But although we ought to find the bosses' callousness reprehensible, we can hardly blame them for having internalized the discipline of their institutions by keeping their careers firmly in mind. Just as there can be no singular hero in *The Wire*, no individual villain can be considered responsible for Baltimore's decay. What we are shown instead is a hierarchy of docile bosses achieving the same effect by enforcing discipline's countless small compromises and training their successors to do likewise.

Thus we have arrived at a fundamental distinction between *The Wire* and the "horseshit police procedurals" against which Simon set out to rebel. Its hero/villain distinction is not mapped on to the opposition police/criminal, "good guys"/"bad guys," or any such facile dualism. The dialectic of heroism plays out instead in the complex relationships between institutions, bosses, and those subject to their discipline. In contrast with the docile, obedient ones "willing to play the game without regard to the effect on others or society as a whole" (Simon in Havrilesky), the heroes of *The Wire* are the rebellious, insubordinate characters who resist compromising when it matters most. McNulty and the others may not embody an abstract ideal of goodness the way Joe Friday once did, but given the questionable status of this ideal in itself we may at least regard their heroism as considerably more realistic.

In the narrative of *The Wire*, heroes aren't necessarily good, and they aren't necessarily police, while the law and its institutions are in no way linked with goodness or justice. More importantly, however, the natural scheme is inverted in Foucauldian fashion. Discarding the idea that the character of an institution is somehow derived from the nature of the individuals within—good or evil, heroic or villainous—*The Wire* dramatizes how the natures and actions of individuals are produced and used by impersonal institutions. While the series takes the form of a police procedural, it does so only to rebel against their traditional legitimizing function. Ultimately, this provides us with a far more critical examination of contemporary legal institutions and their discipline.

Note

1. Of course, police surveillance is itself a disciplinary technique. In this respect, we may see McNulty's storyline—and much of the series—as being about the discipline of disciplinary institutions: disciplinary mechanisms within the BPD determine the targets of its external discipline.

4

The Narrative Production of "Real Police"

Ryan Brooks

In its treatment of the institutions of the American city, *The Wire* dramatizes the effects of power while simultaneously denying its own power, as a literary entity, to regulate the behavior of its viewers. On one hand, the show is practically a catalogue of the mechanics by which these institutions maintain discipline (the two groups on display in Season One are the Barksdale drug organization and the Baltimore Police Department, both of which rely on often cruel tactics—prescriptive and proscriptive, official and unofficial, covert and overt, violent and normative—to control their members). On the other hand, the show also disavows its own rhetorical strategies by contrasting this rigid discipline with its own authentic knowledge or truth. The experiences of cops and criminals play out in front of the camera, which appears to watch passively and nonjudgmentally. Even though the "first season of *The Wire* was a dry, deliberate argument against the American drug prohibition" (Simon, "Introduction" 12), the force of the argument is made possible by a position of ostensible detachment: "The show's point of view was that of the insider, the proverbial fly on the wall" (22).

D. A. Miller has suggested that this detached narrative technique is one of a collection of practices first used by the nineteenth-century novel to carve out a supposedly power-free zone: "The *knowledge* commanded in omniscient narration is thus opposed to the *power* that inheres in the circumstances of the novelistic world" (25, italics in the original). Extending Michel Foucault's analysis of social control in *Discipline and*

Punish to a consideration of the novel, Miller suggests that the apparent disavowal of power is actually a tactic used by the literary form to covertly reclaim disciplinary power. As Miller puts it, the gesture of disowning power in some ways defines

> the basic move of a familiar power play, in which the name of power is given over to one agency in order that the function of power may be less visibly retained by another. Impotent to intervene in the "facts," the narration nevertheless controls the discursive framework in which they are perceived as such. (25)

The goal of this discursive framing, Miller suggests, is to normalize certain characters and behaviors and to marginalize others. I argue that the normalizing function of the narrative in *The Wire* is to produce what its characters call, alternatively, "good" or "real" or "natural police."[1] My point is not simply that the show tells us what it means to be a good police officer, but rather that this definition privileges certain tactics of crime-prevention and order-maintenance over others.

Even though *The Wire* opposes knowledge to power, it simultaneously creates a world in which knowledge is equated with power. Prosecutorial success demands clear recordings, legally obtained evidence, and hours of surveillance work. The content of this good policing comes into focus when we consider that knowledge-power is not restricted to characters in positions of institutional authority. The rank-and-file detectives most effective at disciplining the drug gang are those who can analyze and articulate—in convincing narratives and bulletin boards of photographic evidence—the mechanics by which the gang disciplines itself and the territory it controls. This ability to analyze goes hand in hand with the ability to manipulate, reversing the flows of power. The docile bodies of gang members are turned into docile bodies for the police, as scared or hostile "citizens" are convinced to go undercover, or lower-level drug runners are convinced to "flip" and testify against their higher-ups. What makes this mutually reinforcing chain of power and knowledge possible is constant surveillance, the ability of the police to monitor zones of disorder without being monitored themselves. What makes this surveillance possible, in turn, is a flexible attitude toward crime, the patience to wait until the root cause of the crime is exposed before acting to correct it. This attitude is squarely at odds with the political pressures presented in the show (for improved crime statistics or for high-profile busts that are seen as newsworthy), leading to recurring conflicts that demonstrate the authority of the police is itself subject to disciplinary control.

The fact that "good police" are subject to discipline does not mean, however, that the object of the show's critique is disciplinarity as such. (Indeed, what I am suggesting is that "good police" is itself a form of disciplinary power.) Yet some critics have interpreted *The Wire* in precisely these terms. In Alasdair McMillan's account, for instance, the point seems to be that disciplinarity leads inevitably to a dysfunctional, dehumanizing world of self-policing insiders and penalized outsiders. He describes *The Wire* as "one of the most profound artistic statements since Kafka of the individual condition—the conditions of individuation—in a society dominated by dysfunctional institutions" (50). Rather than a humanist critique of bureaucracy (or of the techniques of analysis and articulation that make bureaucracy possible), I argue that the show is instead a critique of two competing modes of policing, what I will call the statistical approach and the paramilitary, "War on Drugs" approach. These modes depend on a logic of visibility and representation, in which order is maintained partially through messages sent to the public: messages guaranteeing police accountability, strict enforcement of the law, and swift and severe punishment for infractions. In *The Wire*, these competing forms are recast as games of pure power, technologies for preserving the institution rather than ensuring public order. As I have already suggested, however, these treatments should be understood as part of the narrative power game of *The Wire*, which is an attempt to train viewers to critically question these hierarchies and which, like a police surveillance unit, must remain hidden in order to have its coercive effect.

"Good Police, Good Police Work"

Season One of *The Wire* is founded, in part, on a failure of institutional discipline. Thanks to a bribed witness, a Barksdale gang member is acquitted of murder. Following the verdict, Homicide Detective Jimmy McNulty violates a department taboo by complaining to an outsider, the judge in the case, about the police failure to stop or even investigate Avon Barksdale. Under pressure from the judge, the police hierarchy sets up a special detail to investigate the Barksdale organization, but also takes various steps to restore and maintain control over McNulty and the rest of the detail. In fact, the staffing of the unit represents, in itself, a form of control, specifically designed to guide its actual investigative approach. The unit's commander, Lieutenant Cedric Daniels, reasons that by assigning him "dead wood," the Deputy Commissioner "sent me a message on this . . . Don't dig in, don't get fancy. Put a quick charge on this Barksdale and then get out. If he sends me good police, I might get it into my head to do good police work" (1.02).

As Daniels's comments indicate, the characterization of different officers is the most immediate way the show privileges certain forms of policing—"good police" do "good police work," which is linked to "digging in"; all the rest is "garbage." In fact, the narrative framework for ranking characters ultimately displaces the rankings—both official and unofficial—established by the organizational mechanisms in the first two episodes. Ellis Carver and Thomas "Herc" Hauk, for instance, are handpicked by Daniels, but prove to be violent, bumbling "War on Drugs" cowboys, who play "bad cop" even when trying to play "good cop." Detective Roland "Prez" Pryzbylewski, meanwhile, becomes an effective investigator only after his gun and car, traditional visible markers of police authority, are taken away from him. This chapter will focus on the supporting character who undergoes the most drastic change in status and who is most indicative of the privileging of disciplinary power: Detective Lester Freamon.

At first, Freamon seems to deserve his unofficial bureaucratic designation as "dead wood." He comes from the Pawnshop Unit, a paper-shuffling job, where he has been for 13 years—and "four months," he stresses—and for the first few episodes, he sits quietly at his desk, building miniature furniture, peering archly over the top of his glasses like a librarian. When McNulty complains to his partner, Bunk Moreland (still on regular assignment in Homicide), about Freamon, Bunk cautions him: "Jimmy . . . Don't let Lester fool you . . . he's natural police" (1.04). McNulty confronts Freamon, later in the episode, touching off a punchy, hard-boiled exchange that confirms Freamon is no "cuddly housecat," as Daniels describes him at first. After adjourning to a bar—where "real police" like McNulty and Bunk hang out—Freamon explains that he was reassigned to the Pawnshop Unit from Homicide as punishment for doing what he describes as simply "police work": arresting the son of a newspaper editor, a fence for stolen goods, despite his commissioner's orders. Like McNulty, Freamon is made delinquent, by departmental standards, after disrupting the *quid pro quo* that protects the department from outsider (media, legal, public) scrutiny. Freamon is disciplined precisely for his commitment to public rather than institutional security, a tension that will recur through the season. Now, purely by virtue of a bureaucratic short-circuit, Freamon has been taken "off the shelf."

The show's implicit claim, of course, is that punishing a "natural police" simply for doing "police work" represents a violation of the natural order, the elevation of appearance over performance. More specifically, the writers also use Freamon to naturalize a style of policing in which the watchful eyes of professionals must see without being seen. One of his early investigative breakthroughs provides an example of this narrative tactic. In the aftermath of a police raid on a drug "stash house," Freamon spies a phone number, accompanied by the initial "D" faintly inscribed on the stash-house wall. This will turn out to be the pager number for D'Angelo Barksdale, Avon's nephew, a find that will allow the detail to start "cloning" the gang's pagers (so that whenever gang members get beeped, the cops do, too) and later to install wiretaps in the pay phones of the housing projects controlled by the gang (1.04).

In order to check out his hunch, though, Freamon must first return to the housing projects, where D'Angelo and Preston "Bodie" Broadus, a low-level dealer, are throwing rocks at a security camera high up on a wall. Just as Bodie hits the camera, cracking its lens and causing it to pivot downward—which we see, in black-and-white, from the camera's perspective—D'Angelo's pager goes off. We watch as Freamon, sitting in his car, observes D'Angelo walk over to a pay phone and make a call; when the phone rings in Freamon's hand, he does not answer but merely chuckles in satisfaction. In the background, at the payphone, D'Angelo looks around in confusion. In this scene, the drug crew has successfully disrupted one form of control, the security cameras, only to be ensnared by a less visible but more effective form of control—the detective who has secretly tapped into their communication network.

The image of the smashed camera is also one of the few images to be used in the credit sequence for all five seasons of the show, forming a kind of recurring reminder of the need for nimble-minded detectives to ensure order. In this sense, the scene points to a tension between the show's discourse of "natural police" and the ideals of panopticism: power works to produce docile subjects who have internalized the gaze of the police (or of disciplinary institutions more generally), which thereby reduces the need for actual enforcement (Foucault, *Discipline* 201). As McMillan writes, the shot from the perspective of the broken camera "typifies the ease with which panopticism is subverted by delinquency in *The Wire*. Surveillance alone can never guarantee discipline" (46). The point of this scene is that surveillance must be supplemented—not only by material force and power over bodies, as McMillan suggests, but also by detectives with specialized skills, experience, and abilities.[2]

In fact, Simon suggests, the proliferation of cameras and other surveillance devices—"watched with a certain indifference"—has actually created new challenges for these detectives. Instead of dramatizing a desperate search for "little nuggets of information," Simon says the show's creators were

> trying to create a world in which there was almost too much information being thrown at the detectives, and it was their job to sift. It was almost as if there was so much garbage coming in, and the detectives' challenge was to separate the wheat from chaff. (DVD Commentary, 1.01)

This shift from the capturing of precious "little nuggets of information" to the sifting of "too much information" is enacted, temporally, in the narrative as well. After the wiretap is up and running, Freamon's function shifts from digging up bits of evidence to sifting through the "garbage" coming in over the phones, a job made even more difficult by the fact the calls are delivered in code.

Of course, these two skills, panning for "little nuggets" and sifting through "too much information," are, as the metaphors suggest, two sides to the same activity—the production of knowledge. And, again, in either case, it takes the right detective to do the job. After Freamon and Prez listen in to a seemingly innocuous call between Bodie and one of his higher ups, Prez marks the call as "non-pertinent." Freamon corrects him:

> Freamon: Non-pertinent? How do you log that non-pertinent?
> Prez: No drug talk.
> Freamon: They use codes that hide their pager and phone numbers. And when someone does use a phone, they don't use names. And if someone does use a name, he's reminded not to. All of that is valuable evidence.
> Prez: Of what?
> Freamon: Conspiracy.
> Prez: Conspiracy?
> Freamon: We're building something here, detective. We're building it from scratch. All the pieces matter. (1.06)

Like his hobby of building tiny furniture, Freamon's ability to turn the "non-pertinent" into the pertinent, to make "all the pieces matter," is a signifier of the micro-physics of power, power that extends its control over the minutest details. As this chapter argues, the point of *The Wire* is that when other modes of policing prevent these "natural police" from "building something" with their knowledge-power, the machinery of the disciplinary society grinds to a screeching halt.

"The Man Upstairs Wants a Circus"

Sheer bureaucratic dysfunction is not what ultimately threatens the detail's case, although (as we have seen with Lester Freamon) it will be in terms of such dysfunction that the show recasts its real villains, the rival law-enforcement tactics I am calling the statistical and the paramilitary. The flipside of *The Wire*'s production of good police is its production of bad police: it stages a series of conflicts between the rank-and-file and the brass as the conflict between "good police work"— which connotes pursuing order in reality, the position of the "real" rank-and-file detectives—and pursuing order in appearance only, a narrative designed merely to send messages to specific audiences.

What I am calling the statistical approach is represented by Major William Rawls, head of the Homicide division, obsessed with improving the clearance rate, "the percentage of crimes that a police department feels it has closed," which, however, "need not result in a conviction in court" (Wilson, *Cop Knowledge* 146). Rawls demands that McNulty arrest and charge D'Angelo Barksdale with three counts of murder, even though this will cripple the ongoing effort to build a conspiracy charge against Avon Barksdale. Moreover, McNulty complains, the evidence against D'Angelo is not even strong enough to convince a grand jury to indict. Outside the courthouse, while the detail ponders its next move—and while hands roam over outdoor chess sets in the foreground—Freamon explains Rawls's game to a narcotics detective: "He can charge anything he wants and get credit for the clearance. Grand jury doesn't indict, he drops the case, keeps the stats" (1.06).

The plotlines involving the clearance rate allude to a broader context in which Baltimore and other cities have attempted to prevent crime by promoting police accountability at both the district (geographic) and divisional (functional) level. In their case study of Baltimore police management in the 1990s, James Clawson and Gerry Yemen attribute this approach to the influence of New York City's widely publicized COMSTAT statistics-based accountability process model, credited by some as key to the drop in that city's crime rates during the 1990s. This model involves computerized mapping of crime and regular performance reviews in which commanders are held accountable for the crime rates in their districts or their investigative category (Clawson 11).

The kind of number fudging and "bureaucratic territoriality" (Clawson 16) that can result from such approaches, as well as the more explicit treatments of the COMSTAT model, play an even larger role in Seasons Two and Three. In Season One, though, we see that this statistical mode of policing, represented by the clearance rate, is privileged over other forms because of its ability to send certain messages to higher-ups and to the public at large. As Christopher Wilson writes, "Many police departments in our time, of course, have become fully cognizant that effective crime busting can actually lead to the appearance of higher crime rates, which can then be used against them by a cost-conscious public and publicity-conscious mayors." Wilson suggests that the "in-house emphasis on clearance rates" emerges in response to this "public pressure for greater efficiency and productivity" (146). The show's point, however, is that this emphasis merely substitutes the message of "efficiency and productivity" for actual efficiency and productivity, and thus substitutes career and institutional security for public security (all ironically in the name of public security).[3] In the pursuit of a single, mid-level perpetrator who can give him "three paper clearances," Rawls is willing to jeopardize an investigation into the gang leaders who have, according to McNulty, "dropped 10 or 12 bodies in as many months" (1.01).

The detail's opposition to the paramilitary or "War on Drugs" approach (as the characters describe it) represents the same basic conflict—the tension between the disciplinary tactics of the "real police" and a set of tactics that are, or have devolved into, ineffective spectacle. Deputy Commissioner Ervin Burrell repeatedly pressures Daniels to set up short-term, undercover drug deals ("buy-bust"); follow them up with highly visible raids and arrests; and then shut down the investigation. His tactics are to "send a message": "Tomorrow, on the six o'clock news, we put a lot of fucking dope on the table. A lot of it! . . . We need to let them know who we are. We can't let them think for one minute that this will stand" (1.11). The show's ironic treatment of this press conference suggests that the "message" is primarily designed to promote the department itself—by invoking its ongoing "war," as the commissioner describes it. It is primarily aimed at the public rather than the dealers themselves, who quickly regroup. Throughout the season, this approach is counterpoised to the long-term surveillance techniques advocated by McNulty, the slow, quiet "digging in" that actually gets to the root of the problem.[4] "Not just the shooters," as Daniels puts it, "but the ones who make the dirt happen" (1.12).

Of course, one implication of these depictions is that public pressure is an obstacle, leading to the elevation of means over end. At the same time as the show's producers employ a populist rhetoric, the show consistently depicts methods designed to guarantee visibility and transparency as impediments to the "real police." This disagreement over the effectiveness of high visibility versus other forms of control is, in fact, a debate as old as modern policing itself. "Because police cannot be everywhere, the calculating criminal is thus offered an advantage by an all-uniformed force; the accountability and protection of liberty thought to be associated with the uniform in a democratic society comes at a cost" (Marx, *Undercover* 21). An implicit message of *The Wire*'s critique of the statistical and War on Drugs models is that the cost of visibility and democratic "accountability" is simply too high. Arguably, the show asks us to concede that, to be effective, cops should be able to move in secret (less obstructed by the rules of the juridical "game," as characters call it) in order to effect the penalization of criminals like Avon Barksdale. Ironically, we are able to recognize the truth of this claim—within *The Wire*'s narrative—precisely because the show itself aspires to fill this need for visibility and transparency.

As I have already suggested, one of the show's chief mechanisms of truth-telling is its omniscient narration, which makes these tactical disagreements rather one-sided. The hierarchy of information is such that, while we sometimes know more than the gang members, and sometimes less, we almost never know less than the investigative unit and usually know more; thus there is almost always more delinquency to uncover, an imbalance generating the suspense that drives the narrative. Such omniscience clearly works in McNulty's favor, suggesting all of his hunches are right; as D. A. Miller makes clear, however, an omniscient narration is still shot through with power. As when Lester Freamon fits a Barksdale employee with contact lenses so she can gather information for the detail, the narration offers the "gift of corrected vision" (1.12). The gift is knowledge (or "corrected vision"), given in exchange for the possibility of control. In this case, "corrected vision" is also corrective: it will help discipline Avon Barksdale, and will train the viewer to understand urban conflict in a specific way.

We get a snapshot of this knowledge-production in the episode fittingly entitled "The Wire" (1.06). The episode opens with the same image with which it closes—the dead, mutilated body of Brandon Wright, a "stick-up boy" who robs drug dealers, spread out on the hood of a car in a crucifix-like pose. The first image is from a crane shot, the omniscient narrative gaze, looking down on the body as morning breaks in the housing project. The closing image is a police photograph of the body, taken from eye-level; Daniels sets the picture down on his desk, sighing, then turns off his desk lamp, signaling the end of a long, frustrating work day. In between these two images, the detail is finally able to get a wiretap installed in the projects' payphones; before that, they were merely registering the numbers going in and out, with no sound. Because of bureaucratic delays concerning surveillance, the police discover the murder plot only after it is too late. As McNulty puts it, slamming the photo down on Daniels's desk in fury:

> He's on you. We're up on those pay phones Tuesday night we catch that murder. Shit, we get there before the murder. It's all here on the pen register . . . We're up on those pay phones when we should be, and we have him cold. But we're not up in time, are we? *In this case, we're never where we need to be.* (1.06, emphasis mine)

The repetition of the image of Brandon's body makes McNulty's point explicit: where the police need to be, in order to function effectively, is where the narration is. This means, in other words, being everywhere, even before the crime takes place, as the viewer is when we see the genesis of the plot to kill Brandon (1.05). To do this, of course, the police also have to see like the narration sees—invisibly, without being seen itself. Other tactics amount to foot-dragging, effectively allowing such murders to happen.

Tolerated Illegality

In *The Wire*, high visibility not only works against the apprehension of the calculating criminal, but actually leads to corruption, defeating the whole point of the visible demarcations (from the uniform to the drug raid) that are supposed to show "a moral separation of police from criminals and a visual separation of police from everyone else" (Marx, *Undercover* 21). Burrell's model not only threatens to let Avon Barksdale slip free, but also allows the politicians who accept his drug money to avoid prosecution. That is the real meaning of the "message" Burrell sends to Daniels—"Don't dig in, don't get fancy"—through his paramilitary tactics, through his assignment of personnel. He demands "dope on the table" because he does not want the money passing under the table brought to light. After the detail intercepts a state senatorial aide leaving the high-rises with $20,000 in a drug money, Burrell rebukes Daniels and makes him give the money back. Later, in the privacy of his home, Daniels fumes to his wife, invoking the cynical rhetoric of the open secret:

> See, this is the thing that everyone knows and no one says. You follow the drugs, you get a drug case. You start following the

money, you don't know where you're going. That's why they don't want wiretaps or wired C.I.s or anything they can't control. Because once that tape starts rolling, who the hell knows what's going to be said? (1.08)

Thus, Burrell's reprimand—"I told you no surprises, remember?"—suggests that Daniels's "surprise" consists not of new information but of moving into an area that should be off-limits, one that undermines institutional control. Daniels has overstepped a boundary of "tolerated illegality, the non-application of the rule" which is a "condition of the political and social functioning of society" (Foucault, *Discipline* 82). In this case, keeping certain things off the tape and following the drugs rather than the money is the condition of the functioning of the police administration, which depends on the cooperation of the political order for self-preservation.

Of course, "tolerated illegality" is just as central to the style of policing that hides itself. In Freamon and McNulty's approach, order is maintained only when criminals are actually convicted, not just arrested, and only when the person who orders the crime is also brought to justice. In the pursuit of this more totalizing form of power, the detail will decide when and why to arrest, creating long intervals of unpunished violation and effectively changing the meaning of certain criminal acts, even murders, making them merely the building blocks for the larger conspiracy charge. A degree of lawlessness on the part of both the uncorrected criminal and the cop who exempts himself from strict application of the law is the condition of possibility for the detail's pursuit of justice.[5]

My point in making this comparison is to reiterate that "good police" and "bad police" can be understood as competing discourses, with, for instance, different methods of arranging zones of accepted criminality. This redescription is helpful, in turn, for reconnecting the show to some of the broader claims that have been made about it. As David Simon insists, "it isn't a cop show" ("Introduction" 2)—not only because it devotes screen time to other institutions, but because "real police" is more than a name for the actions of certain Baltimore police officers. In *The Wire*, "real police" is really a form of knowledge-power, a whole way of thinking about how social order should be interpreted and enforced.

This mode thus denotes both a theory of knowledge—that objective truth is produced only by observers who follow the action yet remain invisible—and a theory of action, in which change can happen only through expert intervention at the level of the institutional structures shaping people's lives. In *The Wire*, the content or knowledge revealed "once that tape starts rolling"—even Season One's "dry, deliberate argument against the American drug prohibition" (Simon, "Introduction" 12)—should be understood as, above all, a prop for this specific discourse.

Notes

1. In the Baltimore accent, noticeable in several of the show's characters, "police" is pronounced "POE-leese"—making the compliment "real POE-leese" seem all the more authentic and distinctive.

2. This professionalized model could be read as an implicit rejoinder to the idea of community policing, which, like panopticism, would ostensibly "privatize" policing by giving more authority and responsibility to citizens themselves. In Season Four, Commissioner Burrell briefly adopts the "broken windows" approach, in which police crack down on minor, quality-of-life offenses, which Steve Herbert identifies as the other major contemporary model of police reform (446). Once again, McNulty dismisses this tactic as simply "juking stats" (4.10).

3. In July 2003, the *BJA (Bureau of Justice Assistance) Bulletin* published an article by Ed Burns, a former homicide detective and "policy visionary" (Talbot), who is also co-creator of *The Wire*, in which he criticizes the statistical model and implicitly calls for a zone of tolerated illegalities: "BPD generated large numbers of arrests to maintain statistical indicators of its impact. Unfortunately, this caused street-level information to dry up because the frequent interruptions made offenders wary. Thus, the department was without data that had been routinely obtained from offenders and informants and that was necessary to assess gang problems and initiate solutions" (Burns).

4. Specifically, McNulty calls for "Surveillance teams. DNRs. Asset investigation. Keep gathering string until we can find a way in. Either a wired C.I. or a Title III. It's what makes this case" (1.01). A "DNR" is a "Dialed-number recorder used to intercept the telephone numbers called from a phone and, if the caller ID is installed, to record incoming numbers. A preliminary step to any wiretap" (Alvarez 256); "Title III" is "A legal term for a federally sanctioned wiretap" (262); a "wired C.I." is a "Confidential informant who is wearing a concealed recording device" (262).

5. In Season Three, this effective truth is made literal when Major Howard "Bunny" Colvin, a true cop's cop—clearly "real police"—attempts to reduce drug-related violence in his district by designating areas where dealers will be allowed to sell drugs without being arrested. This *ad hoc* approach has mixed consequences, but, true to form, it is ultimately the public spectacle of the drug zone, rather than any internal problems, that lead to its demise. The best efforts of a group of professionals are undone by politicians who exploit this spectacle to further their careers.

5

"I Got the Shotgun, You Got the Briefcase": Lawyering and Ethics

Lynne Viti

Among the expansive cast of *The Wire*, two lawyers on opposite sides of the adversarial system, Rhonda Pearlman and Maurice Levy, confront, navigate, evade, and resolve ethical issues, either by conforming to the written code of professional responsibility and disciplinary rules, or by skirting these rules and inventing an entirely personal code. Though neither Pearlman nor Levy is a model of ethical perfection, Pearlman sticks closer to the accepted mores of the profession, while Levy strays from the code and transgresses. Through these characters, *The Wire* challenges the existing criminal justice system and the efficacy and meaning of the Law itself, as well as the many campaigns the law undertakes, most notably the American War on Drugs. Although at first glance Assistant State's Attorney (ASA) Pearlman appears to be a stereotypical prosecutor-heroine and Levy, a standard-issue sleazy criminal defense attorney, over five seasons, the stereotypes are at times destabilized, portraying depth and change in Pearlman, caricature and stasis in Levy. Yet we question whether either lawyer believes that the legal system is truly capable of meting out justice, or alternatively, whether the criminal justice system is merely a stage on which the attorney enacts certain rituals that are no longer really meaningful. Together, the characters of Pearlman and Levy convey a broader cultural anxiety about the "confused and sometimes even contradictory" face of the law in Baltimore (Kronman 226).

In *The Wire*, viewers experience the justice system in large part through Pearlman and Levy, both of them white and Jewish in this majority African American city.[1] Pearlman is young and ambitious, beginning the series with a curious mixture of idealism and street-smarts. She is an experienced prosecutor, having worked her way up from bail hearings and minor crimes to prosecuting major drug crimes. She intends to rise in the State's Attorney hierarchy or become a judge, and, to that end, fights what *The Wire* paints as a losing and never-ending war, one that cannot even be called a war, because as Detective Ellis Carver says to Thomas "Herc" Hauk, "Wars end" (1.01). Pearlman's foil is Levy, counsel and mentor for three generations of Baltimore drug dealers: Proposition Joe Stewart, the Barksdale organization, and Marlo Stanfield.

Both Pearlman and Levy have, upon their admission to the Maryland Bar, sworn to uphold the standards and ethics of the legal profession. Each must decide on a daily basis how to balance professional ethics with what Richard Zitrin and Carol Langford call the "moral principles of our society" (4). As a prosecutor, Pearlman must determine whether police evidence has been lawfully obtained, and whether there exists an adequate basis for the government to bring charges against alleged wrongdoers. For his part, Levy must decide whether to remain loyal to "client[s] who insist on acting illegally" (Zitrin and Langford 4). Each lawyer approaches—and at times crosses—the line between zealous representation of a client within the bounds of the law, and questionable and unethical professional behavior.

Individual episodes of *The Wire* often evoke images of the classic American Western, with gunfights in the street, quick draw contests, holdups, sniping, and shooting from behind buildings. Pearlman and Levy are Baltimore's courtroom and conference room versions of gunfighters, using as weapons wiretap affidavits, motions to suppress evidence, plea bargaining sessions, and exquisite manipulation of the law. Pearlman strives to secure convictions, send shooters and dealers away for long prison terms, and advance in the State's Attorney's office. Levy, while fulfilling the defense attorney's ethical obligation to defend his clients zealously, goes far beyond this: he advises them on how to launder and hide the fives, tens, and twenties from the corners, and how to expand into legitimate businesses such as downtown real estate ventures.

Morals, Ambitions, and Cogs: Rhonda Pearlman

In Pearlman, the audience is offered a complex and realistic portrayal of a prosecutor. Ambition drives her; her work consumes her life. She is fueled by a need to immerse herself in paperwork, routine court appearances, plea bargaining, and strategy sessions. It is not only professionally fulfilling, but also seductive to Pearlman, and not surprisingly her work obsession spills over to fuel sexual encounters, first with Jimmy McNulty and later with Cedric Daniels, with whom she eventually forges a permanent relationship. Pearlman crosses the ethical line at times, relentlessly pursuing what she knows is a "career case." Whether her goal is a Circuit Court of Baltimore judgeship—where we see her land at the conclusion of Season Five—or a more prestigious prosecutor's job, like that of Maryland State's Attorney or first assistant counsel, she labors not only for the good of the Baltimore community, but also for the rush of the conviction. She is not above flirting with the cynical, savvy Judge Phelan to get a wiretap order renewed for sixty days (1.07). At times she will stretch the truth in an affidavit to get what she wants. She has moments of uncertainty and doubt and repeatedly faces moral and ethical dilemmas as she lawyers on.

We first meet Pearlman—or rather, Pearlman's chic and expensive black briefcase—in the sterile office of the Drug Unit (1.01). Her left hand, a plain silver ring on the little finger, slips a small notebook out of the briefcase. The camera tilts upward to reveal Pearlman, in gender-neutral attire, a brown pinstriped suit and tailored white blouse; she silently takes notes as she observes the members of Daniels's detail, who are told "Buy-bust, quick and dirty." McNulty advocates for DNRs (dialed number recorders) and wiretaps, but Daniels orders, "No mikes, no wires . . . We do this fast and clean and simple." As the two argue, Pearlman intervenes, and her first words are explosive and pointed: "You all don't need a prosecutor, you need a fucking referee . . . When you know how you're playing this, give a yell." She is more in control than anyone else here, including Daniels.

We next see Pearlman in a cluttered and cramped office when Daniels asks her to intercede with her boss for better police for his wire detail

(1.02). Pearlman appears at a distance in the frame, walking with Daniels in a narrow hallway. The institutional yellow walls and a cluttered bulletin board frame the two. They discuss Daniels's ragtag team, most of them hapless rejects from other departments. In these scenes we are given all the signs of a workaholic lawyer on the public payroll: no wedding band, stacks of files, small cubicle, lunch at her desk. Evidence of her personal life is scant—two framed photos on a bookcase, too small and far away for the viewer to make out. Pearlman is married to the job; she has neither time nor inclination to reflect on the work's purpose or meaning.

Still, she is not one to pick a fight unnecessarily with the powerful forces in Baltimore's legal community. Near the end of Season One, Pearlman and McNulty visit the Barksdales' criminal defense lawyer; they want Levy to persuade his client Savino to turn himself in for shooting Kima Greggs when she went undercover (1.11). McNulty, fueled by guilt over Kima's injury, threatens Levy with an ethical investigation, and forces Pearlman to back him up. Levy seems surprised to see Pearlman violating the unspoken fellowship of officers of the court. On the sidewalk outside Levy's office, Pearlman refers to Levy's power in Baltimore legal circles. He is "a past officer of the Monumental Bar Association," one of those "people who matter" and whom she dare not cross unless she wants "to spend the rest of . . . [her] life as a fucking ASA." McNulty casts blame on Pearlman, Levy, and virtually all the lawyers of Baltimore. "Everybody stays friends," he spits out. "Everybody gets paid. And everybody has a fucking future." Though Pearlman responds by turning it all back on McNulty's self-aggrandizing obsession with solving cases, there is a ring of truth to his accusations. Levy wants to feather his nest with fat legal fees and feel satisfied about securing his clients' constitutional rights, but Pearlman is driven by a different kind of self-serving professional ambition.

At the end of Season One, we see Pearlman's prowess at plea bargaining. When D'Angelo is arrested on his way back from a quick drug run to Manhattan, we see McNulty, Bunk Moreland, Pearlman, and D'Angelo's New Jersey public defender at a proffer meeting (1.13). At first, the African American woman public defender seems to be running this session, but McNulty, Bunk, and Pearlman take over. They outline the many potential charges against D'Angelo—22 of them by now. Pearlman does not let empathy deter her. "What are you looking for?" she asks. D'Angelo wants to live "like regular folk. You give me that and I'll give you them," he tells her. The camera is tight on D'Angelo's face, then shoots from just behind Pearlman's head, creating a shadow that gradually eclipses him. In the plea bargain that emerges, Pearlman gains convictions (Wee-Bey Brice pleads guilty to several open murders, even though it is clear he did not commit all of them), and gains some Barksdale assets as well, but this falls short of her goals in this deal, and Pearlman's victory is only bittersweet. Still, she keeps her shoulder to the justice system's wheel, not yet able to step back to assess whether her actions are genuinely connected to doing justice, or merely to a series of career moves.

In the Season One finale, Pearlman is in her glory, presenting plea agreements to the judge. Shown in a wide shot looking down on the prosecution and defense tables, a row of Barksdale thugs seated on the bench directly behind her, Pearlman is barely able to conceal her triumph as she recites the names of Avon Barksdale and his crew. The scene ends abruptly *in medias res*, and we move to Wee-Bey's plea bargain session. Immediately we move back to the same courtroom, as Pearlman presents the terms of another plea bargain. These scenes imply that though Pearlman may think she is accomplishing justice and making "Bodymore, Murdaland"[2] a better place, she is in actuality a cog in a justice system that grinds everyone down, from cold-hearted thugs like Wee-Bey to lost souls like D'Angelo. Far from creating change in West Baltimore, Pearlman is only going through the motions as the state's lawyer, though she does not yet understand this. At this stage, she has only inklings that her work is Sisyphean.

Sex, Law, and Ambition

Pearlman's unhealthy sexual relationship with McNulty early in the series is presented as a distraction, a chance to pull away from files she has brought home. Alone in her townhouse, she accedes to McNulty's needs because with him she can at least complain about her job. On the way back from interviewing D'Angelo in New Jersey, Pearlman tells McNulty breathlessly, "This is a great case . . . because of how deep it goes . . . the murders, the money. Jesus, I feel like I've been drunk ever since that kid [D'Angelo] started talking to us." She begins talking about "going federal with it", and calls the Barksdale prosecution a "career fucking case" (1.13). In a comic scene, Pearlman climbs all over McNulty in the police garage. The prospect of a "career fucking case" is a heady aphrodisiac, reducing her for the moment to a hormone-fueled adolescent.

Less comically, Pearlman is also willing to use her sexuality for the pursuit of a case. When Daniels comes to Judge Phelan's chambers to ask for a new wiretap order, Phelan resists initially:

> Let me understand. You want to sell drug traffickers a series of cell phones that are pre-approved for telephonic intercepts. And you want me . . . to sign off on court-ordered taps on a bunch of phones that, at the time I'm signing the order, have not been used for any illegal activity whatsoever. (3.10)

He is more than skeptical. Pearlman admits, "If you're looking for precedents, your Honor, there aren't any. It's circumstantial PC at best." She methodically recrosses her legs, encouraging him to accede. He laughs, "What the hell, let's do it. Let the Court of Appeals sort it out, if it even gets that far." In the corridor, Daniels ribs her, calling her "Quite the legal mind." Pearlman is unapologetic for using her sexual charms to secure the judge's cooperation. She knows what everyone knows: that attractive lawyers are more successful than their less attractive colleagues (Biddle and Hamermesh).

Pearlman is also competent, and aware of the practical limits within which she operates. When the wire detail first turns up evidence that the Barksdale money has found its way into the pockets of elected officials, Pearlman is reluctant to build a case against Senator Clay Davis and developer Andy Krawczyk. When Lester Freamon follows the money from Avon Barksdale and Russell "Stringer" Bell to developers with close ties to the State House and City Hall, she is aghast: "You want to do this now? . . . Four weeks before the Baltimore city primary, you hand me a stack of drug subpoenas that hit a dozen key political figures?" (5.02). She plans to sit on the subpoenas until after the election, in part because her chances for advancement would be destroyed if she rushed into the political fray. When Freamon protests that he's "just following the money," a wary Pearlman promises him that she will do just that— "after the polls close."

Pearlman's "career fucking case" transforms into a prosecution of Clay Davis for bribery and fraud. She skillfully presents her case, but Davis is acquitted, and as Davis and his lawyer raise their clasped hands in victory on the courthouse steps, another lawyer asks Pearlman, "What the fuck just happened?" Pearlman responds sagely: "Whatever it was, they don't teach it in law school" (5.07). Pearlman's case falls to a crooked politician's popularity. In this moment, Pearlman begins to admit to herself that justice is seldom achieved in court. Near the end of Season Four, Pearlman gets another go at a career case, this one tied to the two dozen decomposing bodies in the vacants. This leads Pearlman, unawares, into the most complex ethical dilemma of her career, and the audience into a fuller understanding of the politics of what is supposed to be a neutral legal system.

In Season Five, Pearlman must endure McNulty and Freamon's conspiratorial shenanigans, especially the imaginary serial killer they create to maintain their wiretap on Stanfield. McNulty's deceit pushes Pearlman into a complex series of ethical dilemmas. When Daniels reveals the ruse and informs Pearlman that the wiretap for which she has argued is nothing but a tap on a cell phone in the Police evidence control room, she is despondent (5.09). She has worked with McNulty and Freamon in good faith, and they have kept her in the dark. She fears that Daniels will be punished for the sins of McNulty and Freamon, "and they'll fire me . . . This is my career. This is everything . . . All those years in that courthouse." We root for Pearlman, and forgive even her request that Daniels accept the mayor's suggestion to participate in a cover-up. Her public legal persona is offered redemption, though, when Freamon provides Pearlman with a way to salvage the tainted case against Stanfield, identifying Levy's courthouse mole for her, and documenting the man's "gambling problem and a bank of drug lawyers" (5.10).

In a final showdown with Levy, Pearlman has one more go at that career case (5.10). She visits his office, intending to batter him into a plea deal. She plays the tape of his conversation with the courthouse mole, then lays out her demands: "Partlow pleads to all the bodies in the vacants and takes life, no parole." When Levy protests that Pearlman is out of line—"blackmailing an officer of the court . . . guilty of obstruction of justice"—Pearlman doesn't bat an eye. Though Levy may be technically right, she tells him he could be on the hook for ten to twelve for bribery of a state's attorney and violation of grand jury secrecy.

Pearlman relaxes, easing back into her chair: "I'll be out a couple years before you, Maury. You come home, first round's on me." She meets Levy almost halfway; Stanfield will walk, but his case will be held undismissed on the "stet docket." Pearlman insists that Stanfield leave the drug game: "He's done. We even get the scent of him on the street ever again, this comes off stet and goes to trial." She does the best she can with a damaged case, weighed down as it is with the fruit of the poisonous tree.[3] In the series finale, the loose ends of five seasons are tied up in a montage, where Pearlman gets her reward as a Circuit Court judge.

Imperfect though the court system is, and imperfect as she has shown herself to be, Pearlman is a point of light. She has moved from pure idealist to seasoned realist. Her hands are not entirely clean, but she does her best to shut down Marlo Stanfield's operation. Yet we have a nagging feeling that nothing has changed in the Maryland criminal justice system. Pearlman has inherited Judge Phelan's slot. A new female prosecutor has taken Pearlman's place. *Plus ça change. . . .*

Maurice Levy for the Defense

Levy is a perplexing character in his own right, one who also develops against stereotype at times, as we move from season to season. At first, he is a clever defense attorney. And like Tom Hagen in Francis Ford Coppola's *The Godfather* (1973) Levy is more than a mouthpiece for his drug clients; he is *consigliere* to the likes of Avon Barksdale, Stringer Bell, Proposition Joe Stewart, and Marlo Stanfield. He is financial advisor, business strategist, entrée to the legitimate world of business in Baltimore, and in a strange twist, even becomes a mentor to Herc Hauk, after Herc is cashiered from the BPD. Choosing still to see himself as a genuine detective, Herc works with Levy as a private investigator, providing critical inside information on the illegal wiretap against Stanfield. In the series finale, Levy praises Herc for "taking this law firm to a whole new level." He invites Herc to the Levy preserve for Shabbat dinner—his wife Yvette's brisket: "You're *mishpocha* [family] now" (5.10). By taking Herc on first as an employee, then as a source of valuable tips, then as a protégée, Levy benefits from this arrangement, even as he likes to believe that he has altruistically helped the dim Herc in finding him a career after police work.

Despite these suggestions that he has some good in him, Levy remains a Dickensian villain, a mercenary defense lawyer comfortable manipulating the law. Levy wants to win cases, or secure the best possible plea bargain for his clients, not so much to vindicate their constitutional rights, but for the money, to get his business card "in the front pocket of every self-respectable drug trafficker." He condescends to his clients: "How many times do I have to tell you people?" he admonishes D'Angelo, with racist dismissal. "Kiddo, there's not another lawyer who could get better for you," he puffs, after he informs Stanfield he will go free, but must leave the game (5.10). Levy is happy to take drug merchants' money, and to put his name as clerk on incorporation papers for their front businesses. He is hard to like, a fact not lost on actor Michael Kostroff, who reports being accosted in the supermarket by a fan calling him "you mother-fucking son of a bitch" (cited in Murphy).

Levy embodies the antithesis of all that the *Maryland Lawyer's Rules of Professional Conduct* represent. The Preamble states, "As advocate, a lawyer zealously asserts the client's position under the rules of the adversary system" (*Rules* [2]). Levy frequently chooses not to exercise the required "moral judgment guided by the basic principles underlying the Rules . . . the lawyer's obligation zealously to protect and pursue a client's legitimate interests, within the bounds of the law." For example, by suborning perjury in D'Angelo Barksdale's first trial, Levy violates Rule 3.3, which prohibits a lawyer from "offer[ing] evidence that the lawyer knows to be false." Levy bends, stretches, and skirts the ethical rules (1.01). After the first eyewitness to the shooting, William Gant, nervously identifies D'Angelo, the high-rise security guard, Nakeisha Lyles, takes the stand. As the camera pans across three Barksdale lieutenants, Lyles recants her earlier statement, though the prosecutor helplessly attempts to rehabilitate the witness. The hard-core members of Avon Barksdale's crew—Stringer, Wee-Bey, Bird, Orlando—glare at Lyles just before she contradicts her earlier identification of D'Angelo as the shooter. A few scenes later, the jury returns with its verdict, not guilty on all counts. Levy opens his hands in a gesture that says, "Didn't I promise I'd get you off?" Disorder erupts; Judge Phelan bangs his gavel in vain. Levy knows the Barksdale crew has intimidated Lyles into recanting. If he has not actively suborned perjury (a clear violation of the Maryland Rules), the scene suggests that he fully understands what Stringer Bell and his

thugs have done to make Lyles change her testimony. Levy has knowingly tolerated perversion of the criminal justice system by acceding to
the witness intimidation that is so widespread in the Baltimore of
The Wire. He is what Preston "Bodie" Broadus disdainfully calls "a paid
lawyer" (4.03).

Levy's transgressions of the ethical canons do not stop here. The
Maryland Rules prescribe against counseling "a client to engage . . . in
conduct that the lawyer knows is criminal or fraudulent" (*Maryland
Rules* 1.16(b)(2)). Repeatedly, we see Levy meet with his drug clients to
advise them on how to limit their exposure: Who can hurt you? Have
you gotten rid of the guns? Who can you rely on to take the years for
murders and keep his mouth shut? Can we run the money through the
families to hide it? Levy conforms to the Rules of Professional Conduct
only when it is convenient or when it protects his clients. And when the
law bears down upon them, he secures the best deal he can. Indeed, he
acts with what the Rules term "reasonable diligence and promptness"
(*Maryland Rules* 1.3) in representing his criminal clients, but to this
mix he adds aiding and abetting criminal enterprises, bribery, and
conspiracy.

Levy, in fact, is not above fabricating a case out of whole cloth. In one
case, he tells a juvenile court judge that Bodie has simply fallen in with
a bad crowd (1.06). Bodie has been arrested for selling narcotics and
assaulting a police officer, earning him a "delinquent petition." He has
also walked away from a juvenile detention facility. Levy spins, "My client
acknowledges that he was involved for a time in the sale of a small
amount of drugs." He claims further that Bodie was never paid for his
work, and was "manipulated by older traffickers in his neighborhood."
When the judge asks how Bodie can afford two well-prepared lawyers,
Levy asserts that they are doing the case *pro bono*, as part of a program
to identify troubled youth. Levy speaks so convincingly that even Bodie's
grandmother believes this fairy tale. Levy first exaggerates ("Preston
was the victim of a brutal police beating") then lies to the judge, saying
Bodie "was heavily medicated" when he walked out of the detention
center, "simply trying to get back to his grandmother." Even Bodie is
impressed with his lawyer's rhetorical talents. Here, Levy never goes so
far as to suborn perjury, but he steps to the outer boundaries of what the
disciplinary rules permit; his twisting of the facts and his attempt to

portray Bodie as merely a misguided youth ready to "be good," as Bodie puts it, are concurrently legitimate and unethical. As far as Levy is concerned, he is doing nothing wrong, merely fulfilling his obligation to his client. Soon, however, Levy will cross the line from zealous advocacy to assisting the Barksdales, and later to explicitly instructing Marlo Stanfield on how to evade and subvert the law. At this point he will offend the Maryland Rules' prescriptive maxim, that lawyers must "use the law's procedures only for legitimate purposes" (*Maryland Rules* 2.5).

Levy's self-satisfied mien is particularly maddening to Jimmy McNulty. Levy promises that if the drug dealer Savino contacts him, Levy will advise him to turn himself in. McNulty is impatient: "I'm willing to let you little ratfuckers suborn perjury . . . and blow smoke up a judge's ass and jury tamper your balls off . . . and fuck me if I don't let you structure your cash into briefcase fees, either" (1.11). The only signs of Levy's discomfort at McNulty's badgering are a slight roll of the neck, the trace of an impudent smile, and a slight rocking back in his leather chair. McNulty threatens Levy with "a target letter from the state's attorney's office followed by subpoenas for every bank account in your name, to see whether the cash deposits match the income reported on your returns." Levy looks to Pearlman to stop McNulty's fulminations, but keeps his cool; he has no desire to open his books or expose himself to an investigation by the state's attorney. "I'll see what I can do," he tells them, outfoxed, but only temporarily.

Where Pearlman's motives are hard to read, Levy is transparent. Where Pearlman is all superego, Levy is all id. He is a master of supercilious gesture, the ironic smile, the smart comeback couched in legal clichés or terms of art. In a Season Two court scene, Levy accuses Omar Little, the stickup man who robs other drug dealers: "You are a parasite who leeches off the culture of drugs." Omar agrees, drawling, "The way I see it, I got the shotgun . . . you got the briefcase" (2.6). Sometimes directly, sometimes comedically, *The Wire* suggests that the law is more than an ass, to paraphrase Dickens: it is a sham, and it cheats, and in the case of juries, it co-opts the citizens of Baltimore in that deception. What makes Levy so worthy of our disdain is his manifest awareness that the law has devolved into an empty ritual in which judge, defense attorney, prosecutor, and jury enact predetermined, circumscribed roles.

His cynical approach to lawyering is a far cry from the ideals embodied in the professional code of ethics, whose goal is to "seek improvement of the law, access to the legal system, the administration of justice" (*Maryland Rules*, Preamble [6]). The Rules set a high standard; lawyers should lead American society to be more just, more equitable. They should "further the public's understanding of and confidence in the rule of law and the justice system . . . in a democratic society" (*Maryland Rules*, Preamble [6]). Levy's indiscriminate and overly zealous advocacy for Avon, Stringer, Prop Joe and Marlo is, at its heart, a moneymaking enterprise, a business—not the furtherance of this ideal judicial system in a representative democracy.

Thus, in the end, *The Wire* gives us a legal universe in which defense lawyers are cynical and mercenary; in which prosecutors are engaged in a task that eventually will use them up; in which judges know there is miscarriage of justice but can only tweak the system. At the end of five seasons, we know that the War on Drugs is not about to end, that even as Marlo leaves the game, there will be another to take his place. Another energetic prosecutor will step into Pearlman's shoes. As the Deacon says to Bunny Colvin, "Drugs . . . that is a force of nature. That's sweeping leaves on a windy day" (3.02). The exquisite tension between Pearlman and Levy, two representatives of a culture that claims to live by the written and spoken word of the law, defines the wearing away and degradation of justice in our oldest and most precious institutions against the backdrop of a seemingly perpetual war.

Notes

1. In Season One, Levy rushes in to police headquarters after D'Angelo Barksdale has been brought in for questioning about the death of a witness. Levy complains that he has been dragged "from the Levy preserve on a Friday night," a reference to the Jewish Sabbath. In this scene, McNulty refers to Pearlman as "another member of your twisted little tribe," with "tribe" explicitly referring to lawyers, but also perhaps to her being Jewish. Curt Schleier notes in an interview with David Simon, "There are two regular characters with Jewish names: Rhonda Pearlman, a conscientious assistant state's attorney, is one of a handful of generally positive characters in the show. The other, Maurice Levy, is a venal, amoral drug lawyer." See also Nora Lee Mandel's "Lilith Watch," on images of Jewish women in popular culture, which includes an entry on Pearlman.

2. This phrase, referring to Baltimore's high murder rate, appears in graffiti in the Season One title sequence. It is also sometimes found as "Bodymore, Murderland".

3. The Fruit of the Poisonous Tree doctrine is an established extension of the exclusionary rule. Evidence derived from a search and seizure that violates the Fourth Amendment is inadmissible in court (*Silverthorne Lumber Co. v. United States*, 251 U.S. 385 (1920)).

6

Posing Problems and Picking Fights: Critical Pedagogy and the Corner Boys

Ralph Beliveau and Laura Bolf-Beliveau

HBO's *The Wire* constructs complex relationships between people and the institutions in which they live. The series tells stories of how cops and criminals "game" the judicial system, how unions contend with the threats of a changing economy, and how politicians navigate governing. In Season Four, *The Wire* focuses on the stories of adolescents as they interact with various institutions of learning. None of these constructions offer simple narratives, however. As David Simon says of the series, "to be perfectly honest, we are not only trying to tell a good story or two. We are trying in our own way to pick a fight" (4). What makes these fights so compelling is how each one opens up a space to critique the gaps among individual and group ideologies.

The show's discussion of education is both formal, within the confines of traditional schools, and informal, within the confines of the corner and the game. In both cases, the situations offer a rich understanding of how relations of power control characters and their circumstances. This chapter focuses on two corner boys, Namond Brice and Michael Lee, who are reaching the age where they must negotiate between the seemingly oppositional forces of the school and the street. This season resists reducing each boy's story to a simple tale of good and evil. Because of this complexity, each character's progress can be illuminated by ideas of critical pedagogy.

Critical pedagogy offers a way to examine various contexts of education. It interrogates the conditions of power that give knowledge value, as well as analyzing the control of traditional institutional structures. A critical pedagogy approach encourages the development of self-consciousness in both the learner and the teacher, a process which is called "conscientization . . . a power we have when we recognize we *know* what we *know*" (Wink 37). This approach argues that self-determination is only possible through raising the consciousness of the individual, replacing the acceptance of conventional standardized learning with a critical, reflective perspective. Critical pedagogy struggles against allowing someone's identity and goals to be replaced by the definitions and goals of others.

Critical pedagogy is grounded in the ideas of Paulo Freire, initially explored in his landmark book *Pedagogy of the Oppressed*. Freire argues that educational systems traditionally impose a "banking model" of education, which reinforces traditional power relationships, affecting the student from outside and above. Students are seen as passive receivers of knowledge, and educational power structures reinforce their passivity. In this model, students play no role in determining the value of what is learned and are discouraged from questioning the validity of the process. This approach is used by public schools in Season Four of *The Wire*. State-wide testing drives the way students are taught—through drill and practice. One of the continuing characters in the series, teacher and ex-cop Roland "Prez" Pryzbylewski, tries to resist this model, but he is quickly admonished into reinforcing standard power relationships (4.09).

Freire works against this process by arguing for a type of education grounded in the individual. Rather than maintaining the status quo and reinforcing oppressive power relationships, Freire argues for education that enhances the power of the learner. In Freire's revisionist model, the banking concept is rejected and replaced by a problem-posing method that "consists in acts of cognition, not transferals of information" (79). Such a process could lead to "a constant unveiling of reality . . . and the *emergence* of consciousness and *critical intervention* in reality" (81). This can be seen, for example, in Pryzbylewski's class prior to state testing preparation, where students are actively engaged in lessons on probability. Understanding that the students needed to explore their own worlds, Pryzbylewski uses the "real world" example of gambling with dice (4.07). As a result, the boys are briefly able to see the relationship of math to their world.

Ultimately, Freire focuses on a concept vital for understanding this second type of education:

> In problem-posing education, people develop their power to perceive critically *the way they exist* in the world *with which* and *in which* they find themselves; they come to see the world not as a static reality, but as a reality in process, in transformation. (83)

A static reality is reinforced through the banking model of education. Grasping reality-as-process happens when learners understand that they can intervene in the construction of reality, as a result of problemposing. Learners are able to resist the oppressive use of power from outside and seize the productive possibilities of their own power (Gore 67). Rather than accept an imposed idea of themselves, learners become participants in the construction of their identities, thus turning the focus from static being to a dynamic of becoming.

Namond and Michael engage in this "reality in process," and both characters offer insight into the possibilities of transformation. Caught between institutional and ideological demands and the desire to form their own identities, they work through these tensions between traditional social institutions (and other contexts like family life, race, class consciousness) and the presence of "the game." As such, the trajectory of these two characters demonstrates the tensions inherent in teaching and learning. Neither boy's story provides a generic solution for the myriad problems inherent in educational institutions; instead, each highlights the nuanced ways in which *The Wire* presents a fight to the audience.

The Education of Namond Brice

When Namond is introduced at the start of Season Four, he appears to be just another corner boy. Under the tutelage of Preston "Bodie" Broadus, a long-time Barksdale soldier, Namond asks to leave the corner early to prepare for the upcoming school year. Bodie comments, "If it wasn't for social promotion . . . your ass would be in preschool and shit" (4.01). Yet Namond is different from a typical corner boy. His father, Roland "Wee-Bey" Brice, is a loyal soldier in the Barksdale organization. In Season One, he confesses to nine different murders—some he committed and some he did not—to protect his leader, Avon Barksdale (1.13).

In return, his family is promised financial security by the Barksdale family. Raised in the game, Namond uses his father's reputation to receive special treatment. This worries his mother, who demands that Wee-Bey discuss the situation with his son. Wee-Bey tells Namond, "Either you real out there or you ain't" (4.02).

Almost immediately, Namond must prove himself real or not when Brianna Barksdale cuts off financial support to the family. Enraged, Namond's mother De'Londa insists he "step up" and earn his way on the street. However, Namond is ill-prepared for the real demands of the game: his mother is infuriated when he brings drugs into her home, rival Stanfield corner boys beat him, and no matter how hard he tries, he cannot get suspended from school to work the package. Namond's sense of being exists in the tension between the expectations of the role he should play and the possibility that he may not fit that role. So much of the game is based on credibility and reputation, yet Namond falters and second-guesses himself. De'Londa and corner culture enact a banking model of education; both insist on a passive reenactment of the status quo so that the expectations of Namond's role are reinforced without any recognition of his own consciousness.

This is perhaps best seen when Namond and Michael confront young Kenard about a missing drug package (4.12). Kenard calls Namond a "gump," but Namond refuses to hit him, so Michael, along as muscle, severely beats Kenard and then insists Namond take his package back. Namond only replies, "I don't want it." Knowing he has crossed a line, Namond flees to the boxing gym and talks to Coach Cutty and Sergeant Ellis Carver, a local cop who once arrested him.

> Namond: What am I gonna do?
> Carver: I'll run you home.
> Namond: I can't go home. She expect me to be my father, but I ain't him. I mean, the way he is and shit. It just ain't me.
> Cutty: What's between you and Michael?
> Namond: Mike ain't Mike no more. He went hard on this boy last night. Fucked his shit up. I can't go home. I can't.

In choosing not to enact the codes of the street by beating Kenard, Namond knows he cannot meet his father's expectation that he be "real out there." His sense of being turns into a new becoming as his "emergence of consciousness" allows him to consider the possibility of "critical intervention in reality" (Freire 81).

Namond's newfound critical consciousness seems at least in part a result of the special school-within-a-school program. University of Maryland personnel and Howard "Bunny" Colvin, the former commander of Baltimore's western district, have funding for a special eighth grade class. Middle school teacher Grace Sampson says that students like Namond could "benefit from the special curriculum and the smaller class size" (4.08). When students balk, she responds, "every one of you has proven time and again that you're not ready for a regular classroom. But this is a new program that if you work, it is going to make you ready." Namond, one of the ten students, responds, "Ready for gen pop. This is prison, yo. And we in solitary an' shit." As he names this new world, Namond takes a first step toward critical consciousness. Freire and Macedo describe the naming process by explaining that students must read both words and worlds and must eventually write and rewrite them in order to transform: "Words should be laden with the meaning of the people's existential experience, and not of the teacher's experience . . . We then give the words back to the people inserted in what I call 'codifications,' pictures representing real situations" (35–36). In *The Wire*, the students continue to name their world as they codify the rules of the street:

Colvin: So you saying you don't ever give anybody a break?
Namond: Nah . . . 'cause if you let him slide for a dollar, it's a sign
          that you're weak. Today's dollar is tomorrow's two.

The adults listen as the students insist they must "mess up" those who are responsible for spillage or snitching to the police. Colvin asks why they must act with such decisiveness. One student responds, "There always people watching." Another agrees, "Watching, watching you."

Colvin then asks them to write down these rules, and it is then that Namond sees connections to the larger world:

Like you all say: don't lie, don't bunk, don't cheat, don't steal, or whatever. But what about y'all, huh? What, the government? What it—Enron? . . . We do the same thing as y'all, except when we do it, it's like, "Oh my God, these kids is animals." Like it's the end of the world coming . . . 'Cause it's like—what is it—hypocrite—hypocritical. (4.08)

These scenes imply that the students are more engaged when discussing what they know, in this case the game. Once they give words to the world they know, they can connect it to the larger society. Zenobia, another student in this special program, realizes, "We got our thing, but this is just part of the big thing." The school-within-a-school activities offer the corner kids a variety of opportunities to change their educational experience. In one direction, the students' lives outside the school are presented and discussed inside the school. Students are encouraged to affix words, descriptions, and understandings of the system of the streets, experiences that are usually excluded from institutional context. This offers the students the opportunity to author and own their experience within the classroom, and at the same time to establish a legitimate connection between the students and the people in the institution—especially Colvin.

While Colvin's students are discussing their real-world experiences, they are presented with practices in the classroom that have an abstract relationship to the pedagogy of the streets. These are more abstract because the lesson to be learned is implied; hence they represent Freire's notion of problem-posing. The students use a traditional large group trust exercise, where one falls backward blindfolded and trusts the others to catch him or her. Another is a competitive group exercise where students in small groups are charged to assemble a building from a kit without the printed instructions. Tensions exist between the experience-based knowledge and the abstract lessons; one is so familiar, and the other has the potential of reproducing typical school alienation. Such a tension is necessary and compels the students to combine ownership over the terms of their world with more abstract understandings of how they as individuals and groups work within it.

But the success of the program is tempered. The combination of the authorship of real-world experience and the gaining of insights from abstraction is not sufficient to empower the students to rewrite their world. As Freire and Macedo explain, the experience of literacy—the writing of the world—is only part of the triggering mechanism for empowerment. Rewriting the rigid social hierarchical order for the corner kids requires the literacy of writing their world as a necessary condition, but it is only a sufficient condition when it triggers other social responses (Freire and Macedo 107). The corner kids are still likely to feel out of place in the face of rigid hierarchical structures, whether that means the return to the "gen pop" world of the typical classroom, or the social protocols of an upscale restaurant. As Colvin argues to Baltimore school personnel, "They're not learning for our world. They're learning for theirs" (4.10).

Namond appears to be the only student actively to question the world of the corner. When he is arrested (4.10), he is afraid to go to "baby booking". He calls on Colvin to save him from that fate. And, as mentioned earlier, when he must step up and face Kenard, he refuses. In the last episode of Season Four, Colvin convinces Wee-Bey that his son will not survive on the streets. Later, Wee-Bey tells De'Londa, "Man came down here to say my son can be anything he damn please" (4.13). She insists that Namond can still be a soldier, but Wee-Bey asks why anyone would want to end up like him. Namond is taken in by Colvin and his wife, and he briefly appears in Season Five: participating in the Baltimore Urban Debate League, Namond gives an award-winning speech about HIV and AIDS in Africa. Colvin says, "I tell ya, if I had that boy's gift to talk, I'da really caused a stir" (5.09). It is intimated that Namond will do just that—cause a stir in this new world.

Namond's ability to join the new world and his inability to follow the script of the street are interrelated. To understand his character's arc in terms of critical pedagogy, we need to study his developing sense of power because it tracks with his sense of becoming. But he has already demonstrated a deep understanding of the world of "the game." His inability to be a soldier should not be taken as a lack of understanding of the situation. His move away from the street is not an oversimplified moral tale of the evil found there and embodied by those that belong. The strengths of *The Wire* trade on complicating the struggles of people living in urban centers. This means that any judgment about the moral position of a character is tied to his or her situation. This becomes evident as Michael also transforms in Seasons Four and Five.

The Education of Michael Lee

Michael takes a very different path toward critical consciousness. Responsible for his younger brother Bug and weary of his drug-addicted mother, Michael is forced to take on adult roles at an early age. As such, he has a rigid set of codes. We see him stand up for another boy, Duquan "Dukie" Weems and take on the Terrace boys, unafraid of the violence that ensues. He also refuses Marlo Stanfield's handout saying, "That ownin' niggas for shit, man. That ain't me" (4.02). It seems as though Michael has already read the world of the game. But unlike other television shows, *The Wire* allows the characters continually to evolve, and Michael's sense of self is first challenged by Marlo's interest in his ability to stand up for himself; Marlo sees Michael's strength of character as something useful to his drug organization. Second, Bug's father returns, and it quickly becomes clear that he has molested Michael in the past. Although Michael has grown considerably and boxes fairly well, he is not "big enough" to take his stepfather. Concerned with his own safety and desperate to protect Bug, Michael turns to Marlo for help, telling him, "I got a problem I can't bring to no one else" (4.09). Marlo responds by calling for a hit on the stepfather, and Chris Partlow and Felicia "Snoop" Pearson brutally kill the man.

From this point forward, Michael becomes schooled in the game. Chris and Snoop teach him the rules of the street beginning with a chilling scene where Michael is chased into a deserted building. Michael turns the tables and shoots them with paintballs (4.12). Reminiscent of the drill and practice preparing for state-wide testing, Chris and Snoop grill Michael about what he should do next. He responds, "One to the head. I keep it quick." They approve, and later in that episode, both Michael and Namond approach Kenard. This turning point for Namond becomes one for Michael, too—as Namond later says, "Mike ain't Mike no more." The institutions of the street and the game ironically become similar to the institution of the school. Michael is educated to become a passive follower of Marlo and his crew; he is taught to follow rules without question. Michael seems to become another passive loyal soldier, killing when Marlo says. Whereas Namond has the school within a school and Bunny Colvin to provide a chance at another path, at the end of Season Four, Michael seems to adopt a new state of being, one ingrained in the rules of the street. We are left to wonder if he will transform somehow.

As Season Five begins, however, we see that Michael is striving to understand his world (5.02). As with Namond, Michael will pursue the Freirean process of gaining power in his environment through renaming that world. As they are about to carry out a hit on June Bug, a boy who has badmouthed Marlo, Chris continues teaching Michael the code of the streets.

Chris: Why you think we sitting here?
Michael: See who home and who not, who on the block, police and whatnot.
Chris: That's right. You don't ever want to be the last man to a party . . . That's why I show up to a job an hour before, sometimes two. I don't want nobody settin' up on me while I'm settin' up on them.
Michael: Why we doin' June Bug anyway?
Snoop: Heard he called Marlo a dicksuck. Talkin' shit like that.
Michael: You heard? You ain't sure?
Snoop: People say he said it.
Chris: Don't matter if he said it or not. People think he said it. Can't let that shit go.
Michael: Why not? . . . What the fuck he care what June Bug say? What anybody say? Why this boy got to get dead, just for talking shit?
Snoop: 'Cause he got a big motherfuckin' mouth, that's why, and you need to stop runnin' your own mouth, young 'un.

Michael is told to shoot anyone who leaves through the back door. However, when a child of five runs from the violent scene of the hit, Michael points the gun at him but cannot pull the trigger.

Thus begins Michael's new trajectory of learning. Later in Season Five, Chris and Marlo are arrested, and Snoop is sent to take out Michael, who may have leaked information to the police (5.09). But Michael has been schooled well. Sensing a set-up, Michael comes prepared and pulls a gun on Snoop. She asks, "How you know?" His reply is, "Y'all taught me. Get there early." When Michael presses her about why he must be killed, she tells him, "it's how you carry yourself . . . always apart. Always askin' why you should be doin' what you told. You was never one of us. You never could be." Michael shoots her, leaves the car, and prepares to go into hiding. After taking his little brother to safety, he prepares to drop off Dukie, who asks him if he remembers when they took on the Terrace boys with "piss balloons." Michael pauses and then says, "I don't" (5.09). Although we are not sure if Michael speaks the truth, it is clear that he is neither a naïve corner boy nor a seasoned soldier.

Michael ultimately transcends both of these institutional contexts; he essentially fails at both by succeeding in becoming the agent of his own power. Michael is able to determine his own course, and he becomes an echo of Omar Little by the end of the series. In Michael's final scene, he holds up a rim shop and takes whatever he wants (5.10). As he steps into such a role, viewers come to a deeper understanding of Omar's circumstances, perhaps finally realizing why Omar's character has represented something the audience finds engaging, moving, and compelling. Viewers connect with Omar because of his complete individualism. Like the traditional anti-hero archetype, he embodies characteristics that would seem unheroic but become admirable and even attractive in the world of *The Wire*. The challenge of understanding Omar lies in the question, "How did he become this way?" Michael's transformation provides an answer.

Michael's path through the series is both complex and disturbing. Early on, he shows Mr. Pryzbylewski that he is quite capable of succeeding at school. He also demonstrates a loyalty to Dukie, Namond, and Randy Wagstaff, willing to take a beating for these friends. But these corner boys are reaching a level of maturity where they will either succeed at school or move into the game. Pryzbylewski's class demonstrates the integration of street lives into the classroom. In the terms of critical pedagogy, Freire would call this a dialogic relation, where lives outside are brought in to the school (Murrell 42). Despite his demonstration of an aptitude for schoolwork, Michael is alienated both by the banking model of education and by Mr. Pryzbylewski's model inviting street life into the classroom. Michael is forced by his circumstances to reject both versions of schooling, while at the same time, through doing homework with his brother, demonstrating his understanding of the fundamental value of an education.

Michael's process of becoming is grounded in the material circumstances and responsibilities of his life, as well as his own traumatic upbringing. The street emphasizes a version of masculinity that prevents Michael from doing anything about his problems through the institution, which could offer very little in any event. His little brother's potential exposure to sexual molestation is a danger that requires a more radical and antisocial sort of help. By asking Marlo to kill Bug's father, Michael incurs a debt that moves him into the ruthless social matrix of the criminal organization. For Michael, school has failed, both as a place where social values are taught and as a place that can offer a working alternative to the street. The result is a dark and disturbing realization of conscience as Michael takes for a time the path of a successful soldier.

To understand finally how ideas of critical pedagogy illuminate Michael's path, we need to see the street as another kind of institution. Michael is taught to take orders, not to question, and thereby to help the organization to demonstrate another kind of banking model. This form is more effective in creating empowerment of a different sort, still capable of realizing material gains and social status, but working a game on the other side of the law. Judging this banking model requires a suspension from the mainstream middle class world, and a connection to the measures of success in the specific terms of the street and the game.

Ultimately, however, Michael's sense of social responsibility, damaged though it is by his own trauma and the choices that followed, puts him in confrontation with the rules of the street. His path of becoming is not as destructive and free from conscience as the street requires. Michael is unable to carry out ruthless action without questioning the injustice of the situation. Marlo's gang becomes oppressive, and Michael moves closer to a revolutionary state; he identifies the myths of Marlo's gang and rewrites his understanding of the game. Michael then rejects that path. Our last images of him directly connect to Omar, a character who has acted outside of the rules of the game and acted on his code. Michael adopts Omar's *modus operandi*. He remains recognizable but becomes unpredictable. He hides yet acts with such boldness that he will no doubt be noticed. Michael even repeats one of the first actions we see from Omar back in the first season of *The Wire*, when he has to shoot a leader of a street crew in the knee to demonstrate his conviction (1.03).

The Education of the Audience

The Wire presents a complex and nuanced portrait of American urban culture that transcends cynicism with a faith in the complexity of people and circumstances. It picks a fight with the oversimplistic suggestion that the failure of education happens only because of a lack of resources, or worse yet because of incompetent teachers and administration. Instead, the show suggests that education can only begin to make sense if the formal institutions are seen in the context of the other social forces that also educate students. Forces like the economy of the street, the ways of manipulating the application of rules or laws, and the competition to find one's place provide a matrix of forces that situate the formal and informal processes of being educated.

The stories of Namond and Michael are thought provoking when seen against this complexity. In the same way, a critical pedagogy approach offers a way for the audience to see the fight between the top-down style of education and the more progressive problem-solving method. Educators who write about critical pedagogy are usually teachers and teacher educators trying to enhance the classroom by focusing attention on the way power works in culture. By becoming more conscious of the way power and money interact with categories like race and class and gender, critical pedagogy tries to tie the teaching and learning of skills and knowledge with the contexts that give them value. The stories of Namond and Michael show that critical pedagogy can illuminate the ways of teaching and learning wherever they take place.

Namond and Michael both succeed in arriving at an alignment between what they are and what their education, in all its forms, has allowed them to become. But even this realization has more complexity in the telling. Namond succeeds through escaping the oppression of the game and arrives at a more stable, traditional, middle class life. His intellectual skills, recognized by Bunny Colvin, find their expression in Namond's eloquent debate performance. Michael also succeeds, but in a way that is much more difficult to align with traditional middle class values. By the end he has stripped away the trappings of friend and brother, but he has also transcended the role of mere soldier. He becomes the agent of his own power by gaming the game. He is violent and aggressive, but he has learned to use his own power. Exploiting the exploiters is a choice that reaches the most critical possibilities of learning.

Audiences may find themselves facing an awkward combination of reactions to this notion. The success of Namond is also the confirmation of middle class values, which in some ways are the very historical and material source of the inequalities inflicted on the poor. Will his critical consciousness one day lead him to see the flaws in the unequal distribution of power and money? The success of Michael is even more problematic. He is the thug's thug, so bad he comes back on the radar on the good side. Just as the audience has seen with the example of Omar, Michael's independence is admirable, and his reputation for being his own agent will secure his power. He becomes the anti-hero: he may have a short life ending violently, but it will follow his own terms rather than those set by oppressive systems.

Simple answers are never a part of the experience of *The Wire*, and Season Four's discussion of education certainly furthers this idea. David Simon suggests that the series contains "stories that, in the end, have a small chance of presenting a social, and even political, argument" (4). Simon understates the case. Studying the fight between Namond and Michael's wants and beliefs and the educational institutions that demand antithetical ideologies provides the audience with a complexity often hard to find in the overprocessed television diet, more recently over-stuffed with "reality" stories easy to see through. Seeing into *The Wire* is a fight worth picking.

II

On the Corner

7

Corner-Boy Masculinity: Intersections of Inner-City Manhood

James Braxton Peterson

In *Blues, Ideology, and Afro-American Literature,* Houston Baker analyzes the intersecting matrices of lack and desire for the enigmatic bluesman. These crossroads of lack and desire, according to Baker, became a foundational intersection for the formulation of African American identity. Fast forward to the postindustrial economic conditions of the twenty-first-century inner city and this foundational intersection finds an extraordinary consistency with the lack of economic opportunity available to generations of inner-city youth who are (through various media) exposed to many of the most desirable outposts of capitalist society, and the corollary to this desire-producing exposure: an utter absence of the structural and civic resources necessary to transcend abject poverty. The spectacle of this society notwithstanding, various verbal and visual discourses generated in popular media seek to construct original models of masculinity for these generational constituents. In this chapter I engage emerging theoretical conceptions of black masculinity (à la Mark Anthony Neal and others) and juxtapose these ideas with several specific constructions of black masculinity articulated and visualized and exemplified through the characters of *The Wire.* Of significance to this discussion is a collaboration between the rapper Common and the Last Poets, aptly entitled, "The Corner," which brilliantly articulates the urban corner as a master site for the both the production and representations of black masculinity. "The Corner" in many ways reflects the complex intersections of black male identities depicted on the corners of the television version of Baltimore, Maryland. My focus then is on the proliferation of various complex representations of urban black masculinity detailed in *The Wire*.

The Wire reveals a dramatically realistic Baltimore where corner boys formulate an inner-city 'juvenocracy' based on the unchecked drug trade.[1] Yet even within this hyperviolent world of man-children, extraordinary models of black masculinity emerge. "[M]asculinity is a social fact produced through a set of both educational and social practices that function to regulate and circumscribe the lives of young men, as well as reinforce dominant social norms at a time of transition and uncertainty" (Davis 292): the models of masculinity in *The Wire* (most notably here in Seasons Four and Five) intersect and/or converge on the proverbial corners of the inner-city experience. Preston "Bodie" Broadus is raised, comes of age, thrives, and dies on the corner. Omar Little makes his name in the street by terrorizing those same corners, even though his sexual identity should preclude him from the legendary street status he attains. The various types of masculinity performed in *The Wire* provide incisive depictions of a wide range of black male being. The corner is merely the nexus through which this cornucopia of black manhood is expressed.

I

The opening epigraph for the "Corner Boys" episode of *The Wire* cites Zenobia as saying: "We got our thing, but it's just part of the big thing" (4.08). Corner boys are the youngest initiates or entrants into the illicit drug "game." From Avon Barksdale to Marlo Stanfield, drug bosses on *The Wire* exploit their allure with the youngest denizens of inner-city neighborhoods in order to compel them to work the corners. The drug lord thereby accomplishes (at least) two objectives: first, since the majority of the corner boys are younger than the age of legal responsibility they function as buffers for the bosses, automatically circumventing the criminal justice system; and second, by recruiting the youngest of the youth, the drug organization indoctrinates them into the central "code of the street". In his ethnographic research conducted in inner-city Philadelphia, Elijah Anderson draws the following conclusions:

> It must be continually underscored that much of this violence and drug activity is a reflection of the dislocations brought about by economic transformations . . . [W]here the wider economy is not receptive to these dislocated people, the underground economy is. . . . [T]he facts of race relations, unemployment, dislocation, and destitution create alienation, and alienation allows for certain receptivity to overtures made by people seeking youthful new recruits for the drug trade. (Anderson, *Code of the Street* 120)

Thus Zenobia's words take on powerful meanings in the context of the classroom scenario in which she makes this claim.

Although Zenobia is an African American girl, she is, in the context of this episode and from the viewpoint of her alternative educators, a corner boy.[2] This status is marked by her posture, attitude, and vocal outbursts in class. She, like several other junior-high school students, is forced into a program where they are studied and in some ways further alienated from their classmates and traditional classrooms. As a group they face extraordinary challenges that include neglect, abuse, violence, and their resultant psycho-social trauma. Over the course of the "Corner Boys" episode, the researchers, mostly led by former police officer Howard "Bunny" Colvin, make what is termed a "breakthrough." They have been trying for weeks to establish a genuine connection with the students in this recently isolated research project. Their work will eventually fall under the scrutiny of various political interests, but in this episode they are still relatively free to explore the possibilities of an educational experiment that removes the most troubled and troublesome youth from the traditional classroom—so that students in those classrooms can work relatively free from distraction—and uses nontraditional pedagogies to harness the dysfunctional social attitudes common among the corner-boy students.

The "breakthrough" occurs in this episode when Colvin intercedes during one of the other researchers' exercises. Colvin has become somewhat flustered with their efforts to have a genuine interaction with the corner-boy students and it dawns on him suddenly that even in this nontraditional, less school-like setting, the corner-boy students are consistently trying to get over on their teachers and the researchers. Colvin then confronts the class on this fact. He unveils their in-school hustle as a mere training ground for the streets—where they are the corner boys and the teachers, administrators, and researchers are the police. Here Zenobia (through body language, visage, and subtle commentary) underscores the fact that this is true in less metaphorical ways since Colvin actually has been a police officer. Ultimately Colvin gives them various opportunities to reflect on, discuss, and write about their lives as corner boys. He even invites them to develop a code for corner-boy life, lists of rules, the do's and don'ts of corner-boy livelihood.

These scenes are powerful moments for educators who watch *The Wire* and know the challenges, possibilities, and failures of inner-city classrooms overrun by children of the drug trade. As James E. Davis notes,

> [t]he interaction of school context and masculine identities and socialization is important to consider . . . These performances of masculinity are not necessarily linked to troublemaking but to how teachers and other adults interpret these performances. (Davis 298)

Davis's insight sheds light on the interaction that ensues in the corner-boy classroom after Colvin radically reinterprets the educational proceedings. Once the corner-boy students accept the interpretation of their classroom as a training ground for their involvement in the illegal drug trade—as well as their own limited life experiences and truncated opportunities on the mean streets of Baltimore—they become willing participants in the educational process. The idea that masculinity is directly linked to economic prowess (and possibility) is especially relevant and particularly compelling to dispossessed African American youth (Davis 296). Therefore the corner-boy students almost instantly become excited and engaged in their classroom. They participate in discussions, work together in groups to construct the code of streets from the corner-boy perspective, and even talk about their learning with peers outside of the classroom.

Zenobia's claim, "We got our thing, but it's just a part of the big thing," is delivered in the midst of one of these engaging dialogues. Essentially, she situates the drug trade within the context of the dislocating power of the global economy. From the corner-boy perspective, at the crossroads of lack and desire, selling drugs is no different from selling cigarettes or alcohol except that some trades are arbitrarily deemed legal and others are not. This suggestion and these scenes unveil an abiding intersectionality with respect to how black masculinity is conceptualized and operationalized on *The Wire*. That girls can be corner boys is important to recognize here, but the youths' acknowledgment of the relationship between aspirational masculinity, global capital, arbitrary illegality, and the possibility of public education as a means to overcome socioeconomic and violent challenges are also powerful intersecting messages in these scenes.

Alycee J. Lane states that "[i]ntersectionality calls into question the construction of monolithic identities and forces one to consider how one is positioned by the intersecting and multiple hegemonies that structure American culture" (325). If black masculinity was or is in any way monolithic, the corner-as-metaphor in *The Wire* represents numerous attempts to deconstruct the monolithic notion of black manhood. Since the corner is literally an urban intersection it is a fitting metaphor for the deconstructive work necessary to unpack, dismantle, and reformulate notions of black masculinity in the twenty-first century. Some of the socioeconomic forces that rigidly construct black masculinity are the material lack and ad-induced desire that collude to produce the collective willingness to engage in the underground economy. Poor public education, crumbling postindustrial residential neighborhoods, and the inherently violent communities that result from these structural challenges all work to obscure the full range of black masculine possibilities. It follows that the literature, film, and music that represent black masculine behavior tend toward these monolithic depictions. *The Wire* departs from this monolithic morass and dwells comfortably within the spaces of intersectionality that the real-life geography of an urban corner subtly reflects.

The quintessential corner boy of the series is Bodie Broadus. Bodie works corners for the Barksdale cartel as well as Marlo Stanfield's cartel. He even attempts a brief stint on his own as the power struggle within the drug trade shifts from Barksdale to Stanfield, but for most of *The Wire* he is the most hard-working, loyal, and dedicated hustler on the corner. Technically speaking, he has younger corner boys and/or hoppers working for him, but the preponderance of Bodie's scenes in *The Wire* are set on a corner or at some urban intersection where he hustles drugs. Bodie's determination and loyalty allow him to thrive within the Barksdale drug organization, but after the cartel crumbles, he is quickly absorbed by Marlo's organization. Bodie's work ethic is indefatigable over several seasons. He is a worker bee and thus he debunks stereotypes about black male laziness. Moreover, Bodie challenges the Horatio Alger narrative of drug dealing and hustling. His hard work, loyalty, and heart do not allow him to achieve the economic spoils of his bosses. In fact, Bodie seems to live a fairly meager, working class existence. He usually eats in bodegas or cheap corner store shops. He never wears expensive clothes or jewelry and he never really flashes or flosses his cash. Bodie lives at the intersection of working class and hustler black masculinities and is not permitted to live through to the conclusion of *The Wire*. In one of his last extended dialogues of the series, he analyzes his years in "the game" with police officer Jimmy McNulty and concludes that the "game is rigged" (4.11); he is and has been just a pawn. McNulty is ultimately able to convince Bodie to consider providing some information to police. Through a series of somewhat random events, Marlo is made aware of the possibility that Bodie will become an informant. He is murdered by Marlo's assassins, Chris and Snoop. He may well have had a chance to escape, but he refuses to leave "his" corner. Bodie's murder is a poignant moment: although he is murdered like so many other victims in *The Wire*, he is in fact an emblematic figure of a murdered generation of corner boys.

More than any other character on *The Wire*, Bodie reflects the cacophony of voices in one of the rapper Common's most popular singles, "The Corner." (2005/*BE*) "The Corner" features contributions by Kanye West and The Last Poets. Lyrically, "The Corner" has three vocal and conceptual perspectives—three trajectories representing the concept of the urban corner intersect through the vocal performances of the artists. Common rhymes verses that suggest the hopelessness of urban environments centered on the street life that corners have come to represent:

> Corners leave souls opened and closed, hoping for more
> With nowhere to go, rolling in droves
> They shoot the wrong way, 'cause they ain't knowing they goal
> The streets ain't safe cause they ain't knowing the code

In addition to constructing the mosaic and internal rhyme schemes of these lines, Common is also one of the most skillful practitioners of enjambment, a technique in which rappers/MCs break poetic lines in the midst of a sentence.[3]

> Got cousins with flows hope they open some doors
> So we can cop clothes & roll in a Rolls
> Now I roll in a "Olds" with windows that don't roll
> Down the roads where cars get broke in & stole
> These are the stories told by Stony & Cottage Grove
> The world is cold the block is hot as a stove
> On the corners

The total poetic effect of Common's repeated use of enjambment throughout his verses is to sound as if he is rhyming around corners. Thus the form of Common's delivery reflects the culturally intersecting space of the song's subject while the content of the lyrics reveals the working class aesthetics inherent in Bodie's characterization as the quintessential corner boy on *The Wire*.

Kanye West and The Last Poets represent two distinct but likewise intersecting examples of "The Corner." West's hook can be interpreted as a both a subtle critique and tacit glorification of the violent ways and means of the underground economy.

> I wish I could give ya this feeling
> I wish I could give ya this feeling
> On the corners, robbing, killing, dying
> Just to make a living (huh)

The rapper wishes that he could somehow give his listeners the feeling of the corner. In fact by wishing it he likely does provide his listeners (many of whom do not live in inner-city neighborhoods) with some sense of the allure that the drug trade produces at the crossroads of lack and desire. West's voice and conceptual thread are limited to the hook or refrain of the song but his lyrics clearly intersect and confront the general thematics of Common's more somber, less glorified verses.

The Last Poets proffer a distinct yet intersecting trajectory into this song. They are relegated to the ad-lib portion of the song, but their presence is remarkable for at least two reasons: first, the Last Poets are the artistic progenitors of all rappers/MCs, but they are rarely recognized as such. Second, their verses produce a completely new conceptualization of the corner as a nostalgic historical monument of inner-city existence:

> The corner was our Rock of Gibraltar, our Stonehenge
> Our Taj Mahal, our monument,
> Our testimonial to freedom, to peace and to love
> Down on the corner.

By positioning the corner as a monument, The Last Poets have further fleshed out an intersecting discourse on the ultimate point of urban existence. The 'corner' depicted in Common's lyrics, Kanye West's refrain, and The Last Poets' ad-libs is the foundational component of Bodie's demographic identity. He says as much in his last extended dialogue on the series. He represents the underground economy's working class aesthetics depicted by Common's verses; Bodie lives and dies on the corners gently glorified in West's refrain; and he spends much of his life paying homage to a historicized version of those corners that at the point of his murder no longer exists.

II

Corner-boy masculinity exists and conceptually thrives at the intersections represented by several pairings or groupings of characters in *The Wire*. Like the ways in which Bodie's narrative can be compared to Common's lyrics or Zenobia's complex encapsulation of the cog-like existence of the corner boy, corner-boy masculinity is enmeshed in the public sphere through lived experiences, artistic production, and various social theories. In *New Black Man*, Mark Anthony Neal traces some of these intersecting theories and experiences and suggests that a "New-BlackMan" [*sic*] exists "for those willing to embrace the fuzzy edges of black masculinity that in reality is still under construction" (Neal 29). According to Neal, our uncritical allegiance to the "Strong Black Man," forged in the crucible of racial hatred and historical oppression, obscures the multifaceted range of black masculine expression in reality, in the media, and in artistic production. My argument here is that *The Wire* (almost by default) challenges the rigid conceptualizations of the "Strong Black Man" and offers the broader range reflected by Neal's sense of the "NewBlackMan":

> NewBlackMan is about resisting being inscribed by a wide range of forces and finding a comfort with a complex and progressive existence as a black man in America. As such NewBlackMan is not so much about conceiving of a more positive version of black masculinity . . . but rather a concept that acknowledges the many complex aspects, often contradictory, that make up a progressive and meaningful black masculinity. (29)

Corner-boy masculinity is only one of many intersecting and socially intertextual models for understanding how black masculinity is fleshed out through the various characters depicted in *The Wire*. Complex aspects of black masculinity are studiously rendered throughout the series. Both police officers and drug dealers can be cruel and unforgiving. They can also be altruistic and compassionate. Characters like Sergeant Ellis Carver, Stringer Bell, and Bodie all fluctuate between these binary oppositions. Their development as characters through various story arcs are an important aspect of the realism of *The Wire*. Corner-boy masculinity then fits into the series' fleshed out paradigm for depictions of black male identity that are consistent with Neal's NewBlackMan model.

Over the course of Season Four, Namond Brice becomes a corner boy under Bodie. Namond's parents overdetermine his identity, and through his character audiences bear honest witness to the struggles that young men face every day with the brutality of urban inner-city life, with nothing less than their manhood hanging in the balance. Namond's father Wee-Bey Brice is an enforcer for the Barksdale drug cartel who will spend the rest of his life in jail for his crimes (and for not ratting out the Barksdales). Namond is thus confronted with the credible reputation of his father, but also the awesome weight of his violent legacy. These challenges are only exacerbated by his mother, De'Londa, who, after enjoying the spoils of Wee-Bey's affiliation with the Barksdales, fully expects her son to carry on in his father's footsteps. De'Londa is an easy-to-demonize maternal figure that seems to have stepped right out of the 1965 Moynihan Report. As S. Craig Watkins summarizes,

> The report concluded that the structure of family life in the black community constituted a "tangle of pathology . . . capable of perpetuating itself without assistance from the white world" . . . Further, the report argued that the matriarchal structure of black culture weakened the ability of black men to function as authority figures. This particular notion of black familial life has become a widespread, if not dominant, paradigm for comprehending the social and economic disintegration of late twentieth-century black urban life. (Watkins 218–219)

De'Londa is certainly a powerful and at times physically imposing matriarch. At one point she "bitch-slaps" Namond when he makes yet another attempt to express his unwillingness to be the man that she wants him to be (4.13). Namond's mother does all that she can to instill him with a materialistic set of values—in fact amongst the four young men on whom Season Four centers (Namond, Duquan, Michael, and Randy), Namond is always the best dressed. He also lives in the most economically sound household, a middle-class by-product of his father's work with the Barksdales. Even though he appears to be the most economically comfortable, his mother eventually coerces him to sell drugs with Bodie. Thus the Moynihanian notion of pathology in the black family is not a default by-product of fatherlessness. For the Brice family, Namond's pathological behavior is the desired result. Explicitly because of his absence due to incarceration, Namond's father is actually a dominant presence in Namond's life. His mother, De'Londa consistently compares Namond to Wee-Bey, and Namond always comes up lacking. De'Londa's materialism drives her to push Namond toward the underground economy of the drug trade and, at least initially, Wee-Bey's limited sense of the world beyond his prison cell and the streets of Baltimore make him likewise complicit in the parental push to turn Namond into a criminal.

De'Londa's influence on Namond utterly shapes his sense of himself as a man. Although he is ultimately saved from her by his father's decision to relinquish custody to Bunny Colvin, De'Londa represents the signal role that mothers play in the construction of black masculinity (4.13). By focusing so effortlessly on the deleterious effects of her materialism and general affinity for the trappings of the drug trade, *The Wire* puts into bold relief the awesome potential of the single parent household to mold and negatively impact the young black male. Through Namond, the audience of *The Wire* experiences the emotional trauma of becoming a black man in a nihilistic material environment. We are often invited to critique his emotional responses in certain brutal scenes (notably his confrontations with Kenard, Michael, and his mother; 4.12), but ultimately viewers pity Namond and appreciate the fact that at least he (of the four corner boys in Season Four) will have an opportunity to live. The series does not simply proffer a middle-class existence over an impoverished one as a panacea for all that ails the corner boys. In fact Namond's life with his mother is not much different from his new life with Colvin, especially in terms of class. If anything Namond would have more access to the material trappings of middle-class status with his mother. Instead the series suggests that a stable household with attentive, caring, and compassionate parents makes the signal difference in Namond's life. The potential opportunities of this new life with Colvin and his wife are powerfully reflected in the closing scenes of Season Four (4.13). Namond finishes his homework on the porch as he is eating his breakfast. One of his homies from his corner-boy days drives by in a stolen vehicle. Both boys appear visibly older than at the outset of the season. As the boy in the stolen car speeds through the intersection he nearly causes an accident. Namond stares thoughtfully at the intersection and the corners. The camera view lingers on the intersection, emphasizing the difference in this neighborhood. Namond notices this difference as well: there are no corner boys on these corners.

On the opposite end of Namond's emotional character is Michael Lee's stoic, brooding demeanor and budding violent nature. Unlike Namond, Michael does not have any parents to push him into being a corner boy. Even though his mother is an addict who regularly sells their groceries and otherwise makes life impossible for Michael and his little brother Bug, Michael distinguishes himself from his peers by not taking ostensibly free money from Marlo at the beginning of the school year (4.01). Marlo takes an instant interest in Michael and soon Chris Partlow, Marlo's lieutenant and all around enforcer, begins to court Michael. For the most part Michael refuses these advances. He does not have any natural, contrived, or coerced affinity for the underworld. However, Chris makes it clear to him that if ever he needs Marlo's help, it is available. Of the four boys in Season Four, Michael most represents the traditional "Strong Black Man." He is the natural leader of the four: he is fathering his younger brother; he protects Dukie, Randy, and Namond at different points throughout the season; and he at least attempts to be his own man by resisting the offers from Marlo and his crew.[4]

Eventually Michael does need the help of Chris and Snoop, two of the most ruthless murderers in television history. When Bug's father returns home from prison, Michael is agitated and upset. He blames his mother for the man's return and after only one interaction, it is clear that Michael has been sexually abused by him (4.09). Michael walks with Chris and Snoop in order to identify Bug's father for the hit (4.10). They mark him coming up to a corner to buy drugs for Michael's mother. Snoop asks him, "What the fuck did he do to you?" to which Michael offers no reply. However Chris gives him a knowing look. When Chris and Snoop return to that same corner to escort Bug's father to his death, Chris asks him questions about sexual assault along the way. Throughout the season Chris and Snoop have murdered multiple people with guns, usually a gunshot to the head. But Chris brutally beats Bug's father to death. He punches and kicks him repeatedly and then spits on him to punctuate his hate for this man he does not know. Snoop can only look on in surprise, but a plausible interpretation of this brutal slaying is that Chris identifies with Michael based on a common past as victims of sexual assault and rape. That two men bond over being rape survivors is a singular achievement in this series—one of many. Yet this bond is formulated over the series's most brutal murder and it will require Michael's wholesale (if temporary) capitulation to the Stanfield organization. He is, after the brutal beat down of Bug's father, all in. Michael's circumstantial decision to join the Stanfield crew allows him to graduate quickly from corner boy to captain of his own corner. Among the four youths central to Season Four, Michael distinguishes himself, so it is not surprising that he ascends in the underground economy of the illegal drug trade. However, the conclusion of the series suggests that Michael becomes a figure similar to Omar Little in that he is depicted as robbing one of the drug dealing hubs (5.13). Thus Michael's character intersects with Omar's character albeit after Omar is murdered by Kenard (5.11). This intersection is a poignant and powerful point in the show's imagining of corner-boy masculinity. Michael's brutal beating of Kenard is just one step in the nihilistic socialization of Kenard that largely takes place off camera and in the background of the series' narrative. Kenard continues to work for Michael as a corner boy throughout Season Five and his striking nihilistic persona is all the more present in the series as a result of his age. His age is never clearly revealed but he appears to be about 9 or 10. That he ends up killing Omar Little is one of the more striking turns of events on *The Wire*, but the action is particularly significant in that it paves the way for Michael to inherit Omar's legacy. Thus the corner-boy masculinity model in this case incorporates an intersection of three characters whose violent ways and specific roles within the world of *The Wire* are all the more pronounced through their complex interrelated story arcs.

One final example to consider here by way of conclusion is the extraordinary character, Omar Little. Technically speaking Omar is not a corner boy: that is, he does not sell drugs and he is older than any of the corner boys described so far. He is much closer in age to the drug bosses, detectives, and politicos that populate the world of *The Wire*. However, Omar is one of the most feared figures in this world. After playing a pivotal role in crippling the Barksdale organization by assassinating Stringer Bell (3.12) he spends much of Seasons Four and Five robbing the drug "co-op" and hunting members of Marlo's organization whom he holds responsible for the torture and murder of his friend and mentor, Butchie (5.03). Omar is an urban Robin Hood whose sartorial presentation reflects the aesthetics of the wild west. The duster, vest, and shotguns notwithstanding, however, Omar is also gay. This fact remains somewhat unremarkable throughout his reign on *The Wire*, but the creators allow him to express his love for Brandon (Season Three) and for Reynaldo (Seasons Four and Five). Omar is not the first gay character or black gay character to appear on film or television. He is, however, the first black gay character to so readily and regularly empower himself through the phallic symbolism of the gun.

Omar's homosexuality only becomes remarkable as it intersects with his character's persona as a violent vigilante. His character is then a repository of what Mark Anthony Neal refers to as "black meta-identities," various and varied identities that exist beneath the surface of the American public sphere (Neal 28). Through Omar's various identities—vigilante, gay man, feared and respected underworld figure—the corner-boy masculinity model also becomes visible. When Omar emerges from his hideouts during the day, corner boys spot him from a distance and warn all of the dealers and people in the vicinity that "Omar is coming! Omar is coming!" (4.04). In a silk pink bathrobe and bearing an enormous silver-plated pistol Omar walks and stalks the corners, embodying the intersectional nature of corner-boy masculinity, his reputation for violence somehow utterly obscuring homophobic perspectives of black manhood. This kind of confrontation with traditional notions of black masculinity centers on the contestation between Omar's sexuality and his fearless wielding of the most pronounced phallic symbol in American society—the gun. This character is an anomaly amidst the depictions of the black manhood in television history. Note well though that Omar's positionality in *The Wire* is a function of a wide range of black masculinities portrayed through a diverse group of African American actors.

Yet the corner-boy masculinity model distinguishes itself from Neal's studious portrait of the NewBlackMan as well as other scholarship dedicated toward fluid conceptualizations of black masculinity. Corner-boy masculinity lends itself to the narratological intersections of characters complexly situated within the labyrinthine world of inner-city Baltimore. Here, the setting, with its near claustrophobic enclaves, narrow streets, and countless intersections, suggests itself as an environmental model of the ideological expression of one of the most complex identities in the world. The wide-ranging and intersectional nature of black masculinity as it is depicted and portrayed on *The Wire* directly engages organic and or authentic notions of identity in our own realities. Although Omar Little likely does not walk among us, the pathways of black masculinity expressed through his character intersect with our own sense of ourselves as African American men.

Notes

1. Michael Eric Dyson coins the term "juvenocracy" in *Race Rules*. It refers to urban communities that are dominated by youth who are emboldened and empowered by their status in various nefarious underground economies.

2. At various points in the season the corner-boy students are referred to as "corner kids," especially notable when Bunny Colvin theorizes that corner kids distinguish themselves from stoop kids based upon their domestic situation and how that situation (drug-addicted parents, neglect and the like) translates for them in the school system. More often than not, though, this group of students is referred to as corner boys.

3. Technically speaking, enjambment is the continuation of a syntactic unit from one line or couplet of a poem to the next without pause. This is an intriguing and perhaps perplexing technique to discern within rap music since we rarely see or know how an artist actually writes and organizes his/her lines.

4. He protects Dukie from Namond throughout the season; he fights on behalf of Randy when their schoolmates believe that Randy is a snitch (4.11); and he beats Kenard when Kenard tries to hustle Namond out of some drugs (4.12).

8

Stringer Bell's Lament: Violence and Legitimacy in Contemporary Capitalism

Jason Read

In *The Wire*, the illegal drug trade acts as a sustained allegory for capitalism. It is at once the outside of the world of legitimate business, governed by different rules and principles of loyalty, and the dark mirror of business, revealing the effects of a relentless pursuit of profit on the community and lives of those caught in its grip. Nowhere is this tension between "the game" (the drug trade) and the larger world of capitalism illustrated with greater clarity than in the life and death of Russell "Stringer" Bell. Stringer is often presented as the character most enamored of the legitimate world of business, taking economics classes at community college and applying the lessons to the world of the drug trade. Stringer is also presented as the character who desires not only wealth, but the legitimacy of the world of legal business. His story offers a brutal retelling of the classic "rags to riches" story in which murder, addiction, and betrayal are as fundamental as hard work and business acumen. His story ends tragically as well: while Stringer is able to accumulate money, he is unable to acquire security and legitimacy, and he remains caught between the semi-feudal loyalties of the drug trade and the ruthless world of capital, until the contradictions between the two eventually kill him.

What Stringer's story reveals is not only the unstable nature of the border that separates the drug trade from the world of legitimate business, but the way in which the relationship between the two is sustained as much by narratives and fictions as by their actual material relations. The connection between material relations and the narratives and fictions that sustain them is at the center of Karl Marx's critique of capitalism, most famously in his concept of ideology, which reveals the way in which particular social relations of production are sustained by particular ideas, narratives and fictions. More specifically, and more relevant to the matter of the drug trade, is Marx's critique of primitive accumulation.

So-called primitive accumulation is the narrative that classical political economy offers to account for the historical origins of capitalism. In order for capitalism to exist, there must be an original difference between capitalists and workers, between those who have money to invest and those who have only their labor power to sell. Within capitalism this situation is always presupposed. Political economy solves this problem by transforming this difference of class into a moral difference, and the economic distinction of workers and capitalists is transposed into a difference between the wasteful and frugal. As Marx writes,

> This primitive accumulation plays approximately the same role in political economy as original sin does in theology. Adam bit the apple, and thereupon sin fell on the human race. Its origin is supposed to be explained when it is told as an anecdote about the past. Long, long ago there were two sorts of people; one the diligent, intelligent, and above all frugal elite; the other lazy rascals, spending their substance, and more, in riotous living. (*Capital* 873)

Marx's irony indicates that such a moral difference is insufficient to account for the historical emergence of capitalism. It is not enough to save money, because the saving of money will not produce the other necessary condition, the existence of workers. The morality of thrift does not produce the dispossessed that can be put to work. In order for this to happen, there must be a corresponding dispossession of peasants from the land, a destruction of the old feudal system. This destruction takes place through a complex list of factors that includes the laws that convert the commons to private property, the accumulation of wealth made possible by colonialism and slavery, and practices of debt and usury, previously outlawed due to religious restrictions.

Marx's point here is twofold. First, he replaces a moralizing fairy tale with a historical genealogy that stresses a multiplicity of conditions: capitalism is the product of a series of historical transformations, reshaping Europe and the world, and not the simple effect of a moral difference. Capital is not the cause of this process, but the effect: "The knights of industry, however, only succeeded in supplanting the knights of the sword by making use of events in which they had played no part in whatsoever" (*Capital* 875). Second, whereas the first narrative stressed the importance of morality, painting the worker as lazy and the capitalist as thrifty, Marx's counter-history underscores the importance of violence and force. In order for capitalism to exist, peasants had to be violently expropriated from the land. Workers are not born, they are made: "Force is the midwife of every old society which is pregnant with a new one" (*Capital* 915). On first glance it would appear that Marx is simply inverting the terms of the narrative of so-called primitive accumulation: where the first saw the clear victory of moral intention, Marx sees the hazy effects of unintended consequences tainted with violence. However, Marx does not simply oppose one narrative to the other, juxtaposing the image of the capitalist with blood on his hands with that of the moral hero of thrift, because the story of primitive accumulation, the idea that we could all become rich with a little more thrift or the right investment advice, is a functioning element of contemporary capitalism. It is not enough simply to displace the false, ideological account of the formation of capitalism with the true account, because the false account continues to linger on in the fantasy life of most people in capitalist society. Unlike previous modes of production (such as feudalism, in which people were born into specific paths for life), capitalism undoes previous conditions of social hierarchy, replacing the motley ties of birth and title, with money, which is available to everyone. Capitalism does not spread the wealth, just the idea that we could all become wealthy.

Marx's critical engagement with primitive accumulation provides the schema from which much of the central allegorical dynamic of *The Wire* can be unpacked. It outlines the constitutive elements of myth, violence, and unintended consequences that make up day-to-day life in capitalism.

Right and Money

The connection between the drug trade and a certain ideal of capitalism is firmly established early in the series. In interrogating D'Angelo Barksdale, Detective Jimmy McNulty, in an attempt to play off of Barksdale's guilt over the murder of a "citizen" (i.e. someone not in the drug trade), clearly states the line of demarcation that separates the drug trade from legitimate business. As McNulty argues, "Everything else in this country gets sold without people shooting each other behind it" (1.02). Later D'Angelo repeats McNulty's description to his underlings in "the Pit," modifying it slightly: "Shit, everything else in this world gets sold without people taking advantage. Scamming, lying, doing each other dirty. Why does it got to be that way with this?" (1.03). The world of legitimate business stands apart from the drug world precisely because of its moral basis. For D'Angelo, guilt-ridden and torn over the human cost of the drug business, this moral difference constitutes an ideal. D'Angelo initially seems to believe in the ideals and narratives of the world of business, taking its maxims and slogans, "the customer is always right," as moral maxims rather than just advertising type (1.03). D'Angelo believes that the world of business is a moral world, in that one can survive while doing right, and that moral behavior is rewarded. As with the narrative of so-called primitive accumulation, the distinction between the rich and the poor is a moral distinction, between good and bad.

The break between the world of business and the world of drugs is never clean; however, they are both constituted by the same fundamental economy and the same drive for profit. They are unified by the fact that in each economy it is money, and not morals or any other measure, that stands as the highest value. Despite his idealization of the business world, D'Angelo recognizes this with darkly humorous clarity. This is reflected when D'Angelo corrects Poot Carr and Wallace about the workings of the world of business in a discussion about the inventor of the Chicken McNugget. Against Wallace's and Poot's naïve claim that the "genius" inventor of the McNugget "got paid" for the idea of serving chicken in nugget form, D'Angelo argues that the corporate hierarchy dictates that the man who invented the McNugget would still be working in the basement of McDonald's, "figuring out a way to make the shakes taste better" (1.02). Against the ideal of equal and just compensation, D'Angelo asserts the harsh reality of the rule of money: "Fuck right. It ain't about right, it's about money." As much as D'Angelo eventually wants to escape the game, he recognizes that the same hierarchy and harsh pursuit of profit exists in the legitimate world as well. The world of business and the drug trade are thus two different manifestations of the same chessboard, of the same structure, in which the pawns remain pawns, slaving away, and the king stays the king. They may be separated by means, legal and illegal, but are ultimately unified by ends, by the pursuit of profit.

In *The Wire*, money is presented as what Marx terms the "abstract equivalent," not only because it can be exchanged for any commodity, but because it effaces its condition of origin. Once money is made, once the drugs have been sold, the money is as good as the money from any other enterprise, legal or illegal. By definition money overspills its specific condition of origin. As Lester Freamon sums up the show's narrative itinerary, which extends from the streets to the corridors of power, "You follow drugs, you get drug addicts and drug dealers. But you start to follow the money, and you don't know where the fuck it's gonna take you" (1.09). As money ties together the various businesses and human endeavors (traveling in garbage bags of stacked and counted bills from the hands of junkies to politicians such as Clay Davis), it carries with it the ability to transgress borders as well. Though money crosses borders, it does not always take its earners or holders with it: when D'Angelo takes his girlfriend Donette out to dinner at one of Baltimore's upscale restaurants in the inner harbor, he wonders if its high-class clientele knows "what he is about"; Donette is quick to remind him that the distinctions between legal and illegal fall apart in the face of money's indifference to its conditions, saying, "You got money, you get to be whoever you say you are" (1.05). Donette's remark echoes one of Marx's fundamental points regarding money: money is not just a means of payment, it is a means of transformation. Money transforms the desire to have something into the possession of that thing; money actualizes desire, including the desire to be someone.

In the tension between D'Angelo's desire to escape the world of drugs, gaining legitimacy through an enterprise governed by moral rules, and the recognition that, in our society money is legitimacy, we see the contours of Marx's critique of the fundamental division of capitalist society: a division between its values, which are opposed to drugs and murder, and its measure of value, which is primarily if not exclusively economic, recognizing only money. For Marx, capitalist society is schizophrenic, divided between two standards:

> The ethics of political economy is *acquisition*, work, thrift, sobriety— but political economy promises to satisfy my needs.—The political economy of ethics is the opulence of a good conscience, of virtue, etc.; but how can I live virtuously if I do not live? . . . It stems from the very nature of estrangement that each sphere applies to me a different and opposite yardstick—ethics one and political economy another; for each is a specific estrangement of man and focuses attention on a particular field of estranged essential activity, and each stands in an estranged relation to the other. (*1844 Manuscript* 151)

This is the split that plagues D'Angelo. He has all that society values—a closet full of fine clothes, an SUV, and meals at fine restaurants—but it comes at the cost of a good conscience. D'Angelo recognizes that he can only make money by devaluing human life, by selling his own conscience. Against this split existence, which poses a division between the value of money and the values of morals, D'Angelo dreams of a unified existence. For D'Angelo the world of drug trafficking is not some sort of refusal of the norms and ideals of society, crime as some kind of rebellion, but it is an attempt to possess the very dream that has been denied to him. This is why when D'Angelo is arrested, and offered an opportunity to be a witness against his uncle and the Barksdale organization, he sees this as a chance to escape not only jail time, but his life. His fantasy is that the police will make it possible for him to live like "regular folks" (1.13).

The Soldier and the CEO

The ambiguous relationship between the drug trade and the world of capitalism reaches its point of maximum tension and outright contradiction in the relationship between Avon Barksdale and Stringer. In the beginning Stringer is simply Avon's second in command, the queen to his king, to use the chess metaphor from the opening of Season One. As such he is more directly tied to the day-to-day and brutal aspects of the drug trade. Stringer orders the initial hit on Omar's crew (1.05), and the murder of Wallace. These killings are presented as purely rational, governed by a strict logic of cost and benefit. By Stringer's estimation, letting Omar's crew get away with the robbery of the Barksdale stash would expose them to future robberies; similarly, Wallace has proven himself too weak, a likely candidate to become an informant. At the same time that Stringer orders these murders, revealing his ability to utilize violence, he also dissuades Avon from engaging in an out-and-out war with Omar. In Stringer's mind, a war is too expensive, risking not only loss of life but the increased police scrutiny that comes with bodies. The logic underlying Stringer's initial acts of brutality is governed by a rational assessment of risks versus benefits. It is this ability to calculate costs against potential profits that eventually pits Stringer against Avon.

From the beginning, Avon is presented as a "soldier," as someone whose control of the drug trade is less about turning a profit than it is about controlling territory and respect. For Avon, conflict and violence are not subject to calculations that measure cost against benefits, but to a tradition that establishes the rules and conditions of respect. Conflict takes place within particular rules and traditions. These traditions include the truce that limits conflict and violence on Sundays, and the annual Eastside/Westside basketball game, in which rival gangs put aside violence in order to compete for bragging rights on the court. These rules provide no instrumental purpose; they do not serve the ends of profit or even dominance. The rules reveal that violence is not just a strategy, but it is constitutive of reputation, inseparable from the ends it serves.

In Season One, Stringer is Avon's loyal second in command, whose shrewd calculations maintain Avon's power at whatever cost. As Avon's organization faces the dual threats of Omar and an aggressive police investigation, Stringer is willing to employ deception, murder, and a fundamental restructuring of the organization, in order to protect

Avon and maintain territory. When Avon is incarcerated at the end of Season One and the drug connection dries up, Stringer continues his pursuit of power. This is at first a question of pure survival. The incarceration of D'Angelo and Avon has left the Barksdale crew severely crippled and without access to a product. Stringer, however, recognizes this problem to be as much a problem of economics as a problem of street-level warfare, asking his economics professor at the community college how to deal with "an inferior product in an aggressive market place" (2.05). After attempting to simply rename and thus rebrand his product, Stringer turns to his rival, Proposition Joe, in order to cut a deal, exchanging territory in the Towers (the housing projects) for access to Joe's supply at wholesale prices. In the conversation in which Proposition Joe and Stringer make their deal, the ideal of running drugs like a business is opposed to the work of being a soldier: they are two fundamentally different strategies, and ultimately two different perspectives on the game. From this conversation, the business strategy emerges. Rather than deal with conflict through violence and the struggle over territory, the agreement makes it possible to convert every possible conflict into a shared enterprise. This is the ideal behind the "co-op" in which formerly rival drug gangs are unified through shared access to a wholesale supply of drugs. The co-op ultimately becomes its own end, the idea of the drug trade as pure business, separate from street-level conflicts. As Stringer relates this ideal to Avon, the co-op makes possible a new business plan, based on product rather than territory: "Nothing but cash. No corners, no territory, nothing" (3.06).

When Avon is released from prison in Season Three, Stringer's reorganization of the drug trade into a business comes into direct conflict with Avon's ideal. Avon responds to Stringer's drug trade without violence, saying, "Yeah, I ain't no suit-wearing businessman like you. You know I am just a gangster, I suppose. And I want my corners" (3.06). Despite Avon's increasing militarization over the course of the sustained wars with Marlo and Omar (evident in his army-fatigue hat and increasingly lethal arsenal), his disdain for the ideal of running the drug trade as a pure business is not just based on some crude street-level mentality, or a simple identification of masculinity and violence. Being a soldier, or a gangster, is not just about using violence to solve problems: it requires restricting that violence with specific rules in order to gain respect. Avon is enraged when Stringer orders a hit on Omar on a Sunday: "Sunday truce been there as long as the game itself" (3.09). In order to gain respect, to earn a name, it is necessary to maintain territory within certain respected traditions and rules. When Stringer and Avon come to a direct conflict over their respective strategies, Avon angrily states that the difference between the two of them is in their blood, touching the core of their humanity: "I bleed red and you bleed green" (3.08). For Avon the rules of the game are the very conditions for recognition, for the constitution of a reputation. In the world of a businessman, there is only one rule—to accumulate money. The conflict between Avon and Stringer is not just between different means, violence or negotiations, but between the ends those means serve, reputation or accumulation.

For Marx primitive accumulation is not just an argument about the violent foundation of capitalism; it is an argument about the transformation of violence. Both of these apply to the situation of Stringer. Just as Marx argues that capitalism was made possible by the wealth generated through slavery and colonial plunder, economic relations that would become illegitimate under capitalism itself, Stringer utilizes the money gained from the drug trade to start a legitimate business, to invest in real estate, and even to have his own business cards printed. The drug trade does not just make Stringer wealthy; it carries the possibility of making him a capitalist, someone who not only has wealth, but legitimacy as well. Whereas it first appears that Stringer is not concerned with reputation, discarding the rules that govern the game, this is only because he has switched games, moved to the point where it is accumulating wealth, rather than maintaining territory and upholding the codes of the street, that dictate reputation. The businesses that Stringer runs, copy shops and condo developments, initially function as a front; but eventually they make it possible for him not only to print business cards, but to hand one to McNulty.

Stringer's struggle for legitimacy can be contrasted with Bubbles's story. Bubbles, the informant who works closely with Detectives McNulty and Greggs, begins a legitimate enterprise in Season Three, selling t-shirts and other consumer goods from a shopping cart he dubs "Bubble's Depo [sic]" (3.07). While such an endeavor is in many respects more legitimate than Bubbles's other activities such as scavenging or stealing scrap metal and selling information to the police, he does not pursue it as an attempt to become a legitimate member of society. For Bubbles, money is money; any endeavor that makes enough money to provide the next high is equally legitimate. This puts him into conflict with his "boy" Johnny for whom there is a certain point of pride in making money from "capers." It also puts him into conflict with Stringer's world-view in which there is a fundamental dignity to the ideal of becoming a legitimate businessman. Bubbles does not subscribe to the code of the streets or to the moral ideal of capitalism. He neither romanticizes "capers" nor idealizes business, grasping instead what Marx referred to as the "ethics of political economy" (*1844 Manuscript* 151): the funda-mental idea that what is good is what makes money. It takes an addict, the ultimate consumer, to see the truth of money's indifference to its causes or conditions.

At first glance the narrative of primitive accumulation, whether on the individual or social scale, would seem to bring an end to violence, as legitimate means of exploitation take the place of plunder. For Marx, however, primitive accumulation is not so much an end to violence, but a transformation of it; the overt violence of slavery is replaced with the day-to-day violence of the factory floor: "The silent compulsion of eco-nomic relations sets the seal on the domination of the capitalist over the worker. Direct extra-economic force is still of course used, but only in exceptional cases" (*Capital* 899). Capitalism is not an end to violence but a codification of it, a normalization of it to the point where it becomes invisible. A similar transformation of violence takes place in *The Wire*. For Avon, all violence is caught up in the drama of recognition; it is visible and overt, functioning as a sign as much as the simple elimina-tion of an adversary. In contrast to this, Stringer utilizes a different mode of violence when he arranges the murder of D'Angelo. The motivation is based on a simple calculation: the 20-year sentence that D'Angelo received for transporting drugs is, in Stringer's view, more than he can be reasonably expected to carry. When he becomes a risk to the organization he is eliminated. Since he is family, his murder is made to look like a suicide, rendered invisible. Violence is transformed from an activity to what is at once a strategy and a symbol, to a way of dealing with the risks of doing business.

Man without a Country

As Avon and Stringer come into conflict, they each find others who embody their particular side of the contradiction between soldier and CEO: Avon turns to the fiercely principled Brother Mouzone, while Stinger finds an unlikely ally in Police Major Howard "Bunny" Colvin. Stringer admires Colvin's "Hamsterdam" experiment not for its effect on the quality of life in West Baltimore or for its effects on the crime statistics, but because it emulates the ideal of drugs as business, removing crime from the picture. Stringer reveals the location of Avon's hideout to Colvin, in a betrayal that he defines as "strictly business" (3.11). At the same time Avon turns to Brother Mouzone (and, less directly, to Omar) in order to eliminate Stringer. Mouzone and Omar personify the ideal of a life governed by the rules of respect, by a code.

When Avon and Stringer turn on each other, betraying each other to the forces that will see the other arrested or murdered, it is not out of personal animosity; they still regard each other as brothers (3.11). They have come to represent two sides of an uneasy duality—the soldier and the CEO—that has been torn asunder. While this particular duality reflects the drug trade, it is not without its resonances within the culture at large. When McNulty searches the apartment of the recently deceased Stringer, it is no accident that he stumbles upon a copy of Adam Smith's *The Wealth of Nations* alongside a pair of samurai swords (3.12): this represents the ideal of the CEO as "knight of industry," as one who conducts business while consulting Sun Tzu for strategy. Stringer's identification with the idea of the CEO is made clear in Season Two, when he struggles with the collapsing market and increased violence of the Barksdale organization in decline. As an exasperated Stringer states, "That's why they be payin' these CEOs so much damn money, 'cause when the shit fall bad it fall on them" (2.09). Stringer believes in the American ideal, right down to the justification of the extreme inequality of current pay scales, and this turns out to be his undoing. The deadly conflict between Avon and Stringer is a conflict between two ways of establishing a reputation, violence and money, which come into such bloody conflict because they are so intertwined.

Although the conflict ends poorly for both the incarcerated Avon and the murdered Stringer, there is a fundamental asymmetry in this tragedy. It is not just that Stringer is dead, paying the ultimate price for his ambition, but that he is, as Avon says, "a man without a country" (3.06). Stringer's attempts to become a legitimate businessman are in part thwarted by Clay Davis. Davis, a State Senator, is hired by Stringer to negotiate the complex world of city and state permits. However, this is actually a scam, playing on Stringer's credulity, inexperience, and desire for legitimacy; Davis is simply milking Stringer for money, scamming him for hundreds of thousands of dollars, a point that he eventually brags about (5.09). Stringer's search for legitimacy is doomed from the start; he fails to see the way in which drugs and business overlap. Stringer views the world of the drug trade to be a world of brutal survival, a world to be escaped as quickly as possible. In contrast to this, he sees the world of business to be governed by different rules, to be less bloody and thus more moral. He proves to be wrong on both counts: the drug world is more moral than he thinks (Avon, Brother Mouzone, and Omar are all governed by a code) and the business world is more ruthless than he imagines.

Stringer's demise illustrates the difference between the story that capital tells about its origins, stressing the moral basis of the distinction between the rich and the poor, and Marx's understanding of primitive accumulation, which stresses the role of violence and the primacy of conditions over intentions. The first is the narrative that Stringer believes in; it is why he thinks that his intelligence and hard work will translate into not only wealth but also legitimacy. In subscribing to such a narrative, Stringer fails to perceive the divided nature of capitalist society, in which, as Marx argues, the "ethics of political economy" are separate from the "political economy of ethics" (*1844 Manuscript* 151); each comprises a separate measure. Stringer's story is thus not just a retelling of the fundamental narrative of capitalism, in which the game stands in for the violent and honor-bound world of feudalism, but it becomes an allegory for life under capitalism. Stringer has proven to be too good a student, taking seriously capital's lessons about the virtues of the market and the idealization of the CEO—all of which proves to be his undoing. Stringer's lesson, learned too late, is the lesson learned by every employee who has been downsized, or anyone who has fallen for the latest get-rich-quick scheme: the only value capital respects is money. What *The Wire* reveals is not the inner workings of the dangerous underworld of drugs, but the nature of our world and the narratives that sustain it.[1]

Note

1. This chapter benefits immeasurably from countless conversations with Jackson Nichols.

9

Networks of Affiliation: Familialism and Anticorporatism in Black and White

Stephen Lucasi

Mark Bowden's profile of David Simon, creator of *The Wire*, begins not with Simon's successes, but by enumerating his disappointments and professional grudges. Chief among these are experiences reporting for *The Baltimore Sun*, experiences rendered lamentable by "the editors and corporate owners who have . . . spent the last two decades eviscerating a great American newspaper" (Bowden 51). *The Sun* certainly receives its fair share of critique throughout the series, especially in its final season. Among the most nefarious characters introduced in Season Five is *Sun* Executive Editor James C. Whiting, who refers and defers to "Chicago" (the paper's corporate headquarters), who engineers the departures of veteran reporters in favor of younger, cheaper talent, and who parrots the corporate mantra "Do more with less" as a solution to the paper's escalating economic crises.

While Season Five of *The Wire* contains the most acerbic commentary on the corporatization of local economies and cultures, this same strident anticorporatism weaves its way throughout the series, intersecting often with another of its central themes: the deformation of traditional familial networks under conditions of socio-economic privation. The series of divorces, detentions, and deaths that shape the many familial narratives mirror an equally robust catalog of mergers, acquisitions, and hostile takeovers in the commercial narratives. If Mark Bowden is correct that Simon rails against the corporate-capitalist evisceration of "a great American newspaper," then it seems appropriate to argue, as I do here, that *The Wire* rails against the eviscerating effects of globalization and corporatization on a (formerly) great American city. By tracing the juxtapositions of familial and commercial strands in the narratives of Avon Barksdale, Russell "Stringer" Bell, and the Sobotka family, I argue that *The Wire* critiques the neoliberal economic practices of globalization that dissolve communities into little more than markets and families into little more than competitive consumers therein.

Before exploring how *The Wire* illustrates the shift toward a globalized economy, it is necessary to map a few competing perspectives on the ways global capitalism affects localities and families. In capitalist fantasies disseminated by corporate media outlets, communal tensions are alleviated by transnational flows of capital, which in turn make diverse geographic and cultural sites seemingly equal participants in global economies. As Fernando Coronil notes, corporate images of globalization offer "the promise of a unified humanity" divided neither by "the rich and the poor" nor by racial, national, or regional differences; such optimistic projections suggest "that the separate histories, geographies, and cultures that have divided humanity are now being brought together by the warm embrace of globalization" (351–352). Of course, scholarly accounts of globalization present vastly different perspectives on the possibilities enunciated in this rhetoric, illustrating how the flow of capital across national borders merely intensifies pre-existent inequalities. Spurred by U.S.-based transnational corporations' interests in eliminating blue- and white-collar occupations, corporate globalization has affected all sectors of the U.S. economy, but African Americans often are more adversely affected than others (Johnson *et al.*; Okazawa-Rey; Persuad and Lusane).

That it intensifies America's pre-existent (racial) inequalities on national and transnational scales does not mean, however, that globalization's more local effects on specific urban centers have not been equally intensified during the last half-century. Arjun Appadurai argues, for instance, that "not all deterritorialization [the severance of cultural tradition from its original geographical moorings] is global in scope"; it affects "even small geographical and cultural spaces," including cities, towns and villages (61). David Wilson concurs that "globalization does not uniformly affect all cities and all economic sectors within them" ("City Transformation" 31); rather, it creates "global cities" of exorbitant capital investment while instituting policies "that explicitly [fragment] cities into mosaics of 'deserving' and 'undeserving' terrains" (36). The depictions of Baltimore in *The Wire* reveal precisely these polarizations between, for instance, the Inner Harbor (a "deserving" terrain) and predominantly black neighborhoods ("undeserving" terrains), where an estimated one-third to one-half of black men are jobless (Chaddha *et al.*).

Such economic trends clearly weighed on the minds behind *The Wire*. In a 2006 interview, David Simon comments on the thinking behind Season Two's focus on the ports, describing this shift as an effort to illustrate "the death of work and the death of the union-era middle class" (O'Rourke). After considering Baltimore's ailing General Motors and Bethlehem Steel plants, the producers settled on the ports since they so clearly depicted what Simon sees as a fundamental truth of life at the turn of the twenty-first century: the "triumph of capitalism over human value." Asked to sum up *The Wire*'s themes, Simon offers "the very simple idea that, in this Postmodern world of ours, human beings—all of us—are worth less. We're worth less every day, despite the fact that some of us are achieving more and more" (O'Rourke).

The family and its evolution under globalizing economies offer a trenchant example of this worth-less-ness. Cultural critics continually disagree about the effects of globalization on families. While some find that "globalisation cannot . . . be seen as responsible for any *major* departure from conventional family living" (Ziehl 334), others conclude that "the spread of global capitalism is undermining the strength of the underlying societal and familial values," including both marital and child-rearing patterns and arrangements (Harbison and Robinson 52). Anthony Giddens even claims, "The traditional family is under threat, is changing, and will change further" with the influence of current economic shifts (4). If *The Wire* is any indication, though, such evolution in familial structures is well under way. To envision this trend, one need only recall, for instance, the symbolic destruction of the domestic arrangement of Poot Carr and Wallace in Season One. Though only a "young'un" himself, Wallace provides a rudimentary home for a small group of what Simon calls Baltimore's "unparented" youth ("*The Wire*: It's All Connected"). In a series of sentimentalized scenes, Wallace feeds the children, readies them for school, and helps them with their homework. This vision of potential domestic stability proves fleeting, though, when Wallace runs afoul of Stringer's operation. After Wallace's departure following his involvement in the slaying of a stick-up boy, Stringer orders Poot and Bodie Broadus to execute Wallace, a telling example of the ways that capital corrupts the most fraternal connections visible in Season One. Thus, when they lure Wallace back to his makeshift home, the series's familial and commercial narratives intersect with brutal clarity. Framed by the bleak rowhouse, another ubiquitous symbol of the city's failing economy, Wallace playfully warns the absent children, "When I find y'all, I'm beatin' y'all asses. Don't let me find y'all." As Bodie pulls out his gun, though, Wallace's tone quickly shifts; he frantically struggles to dissuade Bodie and Poot: "Y'all my niggas, yo. . . . We boys! Why it gotta be like this?" (1.12). Set in the abandoned domestic space, the scene portrays the dual betrayals of the drug game; neither the fraternal connections between the young men nor the affective paternal connections with the young children can survive the game. Only transactional arrangements devoid of affect, such as Stringer's relation to Bodie and Poot, remain viable.

Similar examples of familial realignment abound throughout the series, but *The Wire* also employs familial narratives for contrasting purposes. The family continually operates as a guardedly optimistic site for the (re)valuation of human life against capitalism's global march, especially through the immediately established juxtaposition of Stringer's corporate ethos with Avon's more thoroughly local-familial ethos. Stringer enters the series as an observer at D'Angelo's trial, sporting a business suit and intimidating witnesses. In his next scene, Stringer informs D'Angelo of the consequences of his trial. When D'Angelo arrives for work, Stringer tells him, "You goin' out on point, pickin' up business in the Pit. . . . You the man in the low-rises." An incredulous D'Angelo asks, "Why you gonna put me in the low-rises when I had a tower since summer?" Stringer ends the conversation by explaining, "You show us you can run the Pit, and you'll be back uptown soon enough" (1.01). The symbolic spatial language Stringer employs here is equally as important as his organizational restructuring. The contrast between the uptown tower, which symbolizes financial success, and the low-rises or the Pit, a less profitable compensatory site, corresponds quite readily to the language and visual symbolism of modern capitalism's vertical financial structure. This economistic thinking inflects Stringer's handling of Barksdale crews and his aspirations eventually to transcend the drug trade. For Avon, however, a genuine interest in family and community mitigates financial discourse. After the trial (1.01), Avon tells D'Angelo, ". . . you family, okay? But that shit cost money. It cost time and money." Before D'Angelo leaves, Avon kisses him on the head, repeating, "You family, all right? You know it's always love." Though he dwells on the financial costs of the trial, Avon's introduction emphasizes his moral complexities. More than a heartless thug, he simultaneously runs a violent business and maintains affective familial connections. Avon's subsequent emergence, where he dons an apron and cooks at a community gathering, again emphasizes almost comically the commitment he upholds to his family and community (1.02).

This contrast structures much of the Barksdale-Bell narrative, including the final conflicts that dissolve their control of the Baltimore drug trade (3.06; 3.08; 3.09; 3.11). Importantly, their contrasting commitments materialize in discourse and deeds, especially through their interactions with D'Angelo. When together, D'Angelo and Avon often speak of and participate in familial activities, and financial matters materialize only tangentially. Among the most significant portrayals of Avon's commitment to family is a scene when he brings D'Angelo to visit an uncle in physical decline. There, Avon reflects on the human costs of his family business, expressing simultaneously the importance of maintaining familial ties and fear of becoming the uncle he evidently cares for: ". . . you about to see your uncle, you understand me? This family. . . . Family is what counts, family is what it's about. Family gonna always be there 'cause it's blood." Avon then shifts his focus to what his uncle has come to represent: "He scares me. See, if he dead, you know, I could carry it better. Comin' up the way we did, you know, you kinda expect that. . . . You can't plan for no shit like this, man. It's life" (1.05). The blocking of the scene emphasizes further Avon's affective connection to his family. While D'Angelo shares Avon's fears and stands away from the hospital bed, nervously shrugging his shoulders, Avon sits comfortably beside his uncle, continually patting the man's hand and affectionately touching his face. The ironic doubling of the scene— Avon models for his nephew the proper connection between uncle and nephew—affirms the significance for Avon of traditional, non-commercial familial relationships.

Despite Avon's seemingly good-faith efforts, the gulf separating Avon and D'Angelo widens throughout Season One and, by the final episode, threatens to destroy both the family and their business. Following D'Angelo's arrest, his mother, Brianna, visits him in a New Jersey jail, attempting to dissuade him from testifying against Avon and Stringer. Not surprisingly, a distraught D'Angelo questions the very commitment to family that Avon has touted throughout the season. He tells his mother, "You know, he always talking family. 'Family is the heart,' he say. Well, I'm family . . . ain't I?" (1.12). Brianna, though, effectively reverses D'Angelo's opinion by reinforcing precisely the sentiments that Avon expresses:

> You like for him to step up, take all the weight, and let you walk? Because he will. . . . But if he gotta go away, that mean you gotta step up and fill his shoes. . . . Now if you wanna get even with him, you can. But if you hurt him, you hurt this whole family. . . . This right here is part of the game, D. And without the game, this whole family would be down in the fuckin' Terrace living off scraps. Shit, we prob'ly wouldn't even be a family. (1.12)

For Brianna, as for Avon, family and business are intricately interwoven, but neither will sacrifice family purely for financial gain. While D'Angelo and Avon subsequently share time in prison, Avon continues to look after D'Angelo, and D'Angelo's repeated rejections and rebuffs cause Avon visible distress, culminating in his lament, following D'Angelo's apparent suicide, that D'Angelo "did that shit to hurt [him]" (2.07). Despite D'Angelo's protests to the contrary—he tells his girlfriend Donette, "When they got no more use for you, that family shit disappears. It's just about business" (2.05)—Avon remains sincerely committed to family and community. In Season Five, he agrees to help Marlo Stanfield (another West-sider) circumvent (East-sider) "Prop Joe" Stewart's control of heroin importation, only on the condition that Marlo first gives Brianna $100,000 (5.02).

Stringer, however, is seldom depicted except as businessman. Indeed, the only depictions of his domestic life occur when he has usurped

D'Angelo's position with Donette, and when, after his death, Detectives Jimmy McNulty and Bunk Moreland search his lavish condominium, an inversion of the bleak and empty rowhouse in which Wallace dies. Unlike Avon, Stringer's characterization relies, first, upon the settings in which he conducts his business: the towers and terrace, Orlando's club, the copy shop, the funeral home, meetings with lieutenants and the New-Day Co-Op, meetings with lawyers and politicians (in Baltimore and beyond), meetings with contractors at B&B Enterprises' properties, and even his visits to Avon in prison. Within these spaces, Stringer's discourse is thoroughly economic, often disinterestedly corporate. In what amounts to a concentrated parable of the ways finance capital and information technologies—two driving forces behind globalization— have reshaped economies, Stringer plays "Wall Street" from his car, selling off stock in Nokia and Motorola via his mobile phone and explaining to his drivers theories of "market saturation" that apply as easily to the drug trade as they do to Wall Street (2.02). Throughout Seasons Two and Three, Stringer attempts to distance himself and his organization from the "territory" and "real estate" over which Avon obsesses: he wants his lieutenants to avoid conflicts over "corners" and to "handle this shit like businessmen. Sell the shit, make the profit, and later for that gangster bullshit" (3.01).

Stringer's efforts eventually fracture his relationship with Avon. While Avon continues to think of himself as "gangster" and strives to maintain control of his corners, he mocks Stringer's efforts to become a "suit-wearing businessman" and player in the "money game" (3.06). Avon correctly sees Stringer's efforts to distance himself from the street as threats to their local control of drug traffic. Unlike Avon, Stringer willingly cedes control of real estate to Prop Joe in exchange for access to Joe's heroin "connect" and membership in the New-Day Co-Op. He demonstrates this corporatist mentality further when trying to convince Avon not to war with Marlo: "The fact is we got every mob in town, East Side, West Side, ready to pull together, share territory on that good shit that Prop Joe puttin' out there. . . . I mean, we past that run-and-gun shit, man. Like, we find us a package and we ain't got to see nothing but bank. Nothing but cash. No corners, no territory. Nothing" (3.06). Stringer's "nothing but cash" mantra emerges logically from the culture of monetarism—of cash without territory or industry—that has eviscerated West Baltimore neighborhoods formerly reliant on employ-ment in the manufacturing sector. His focus on the "package" and "bank" without regard for the community itself replicates the very sources of economic and political violence against undeserving urban terrains, even if it does temporarily reduce physical violence between rival territorial organizations.

This utter disregard for family and community also leads to Stringer's demise. For Stringer, capital comes before all else and must be pro-tected at all costs. As he explains to Avon regarding D'Angelo's apparent inability to do his time, "He flip, man, they got you and me and fuckin' Brianna! . . . Now, I know you're family. You loved that nigga. But you wanna talk that 'blood is thicker than water' bullshit, take that shit somewhere else, nigga. That motherfucker would've taken down the whole fuckin' show!" (3.08). More even than this stark explanation, Stringer's plot to kill D'Angelo reflects his corporatist ethos. To orchestrate the hit, Stringer must reach not only outside of the West Side but outside of Baltimore entirely to an associate from Washington, DC, whose cousin performs the hit. Together with his interactions with the Co-Op, Stringer's efforts to move beyond the circumscribed borders of Baltimore's West Side enrage and disillusion Avon enough that he sacrifices Stringer to vengeful hit-men Omar Little and Brother Mouzone. In another brutal irony, Stringer's many attempts to deterritorialize the Barksdale family's operation end in a scene of execution mirroring Wallace's death (3.11). Like Wallace, Stringer is executed in an empty, depopulated domestic space, the building that B&B Construction is converting to loft condos. And like the empty row house where Wallace dies, the empty lofts represent another outgrowth of the shifting economy, away from a production-based and toward a consumer-based economy. In the background of the window before which Stringer is shot lurks a sign reading, "Com-ing Soon, Residential/Retail Opportunities from B&B Enterprises" (3.11), an overt symbol of the very reasons Avon willingly gave Stringer up. Despite Stringer's valiant efforts to transcend the territorial vio-lence of drug trafficking, the writers and producers never let us forget the calamitous socio-economic effects of Stringer's paradoxical route of escape. Framing the scene of Stringer's death with the B&B Enter-prises sign in the background signals their condemnation of the economic principles that defined his efforts to reform and transcend the game.

Because of his efforts to reform the violence of the game, Stringer does remain a redemptive character and his death a tragedy of sorts. The same cannot be said, though, for the arch-capitalist known as "The Greek" whose operation the Major Crimes Unit investigates in Season Two. Indeed, Simon refers to The Greek as representative of "capitalism in its purest form," which, for Simon, means an utter lack of affective "allegiance" to anyone or anything but profit (O'Rourke). The entirety of Season Two explores, more overtly than the Barksdale-Bell narrative, the stakes in allowing for expansion of the economic principles The Greek comes to represent. The season is framed by two very different reflections on the ramifications of corporate globalization for Baltimoreans. When the season opens, Jimmy McNulty is aboard a police boat in Baltimore Harbor, surveying the now-closed factories that line the once-active industrial center. McNulty and his partner, Claude Diggins, discuss what the retraction of industry has meant to their families:

McNulty: My father used to work there.
Diggins: Beth Steel?
McNulty: In the shipyards there, yeah.
Diggins: I had an uncle who was a supervisor there. Got laid off in '78, though.
McNulty: '73 for my dad. (2.01)

For those who have remained in Baltimore, including the many dock-workers depicted in Season Two, the globalizing economy has meant a series of layoffs and plant-closings, and the families dependent on this industrial work continually endure hardship and poverty. In contrast to this, The Greek and his associate Spiros "Vondas" Vondopolous, who claim no allegiance to the city, use Baltimore only as a market for their traffic in heroin and in women. And when they depart in Season Two's finale, The Greek tells the airline attendant their reason for travel is "Business. Always business" (2.12).

Between these moments, much of Season Two's narrative focuses on the economic and familial tragedy of the Sobotka family, a family deci-mated by the failing Baltimore economy and the hard choices they must make to survive. The hardest of these is Frank Sobotka's decision to continue working with The Greek's network after the discovery of fourteen murdered women, part of the global sex trafficking industry, in an unloaded shipping container. This choice is a complicated one for a number of reasons, not least of which is Sobotka's evident devotion both to family and to community. Like Avon and Stringer, Sobotka's characterization relies heavily on the spaces in which he operates. Sobotka's first scene occurs in the union hall, where he discusses with his union brothers their desperate need to get more ships and more work (2.01). Though defined, like Stringer, by the space of his labor, Sobotka's characterization also runs counter to Stringer's corporatism. In his next scene, Sobotka makes a large cash donation to his Polish Catholic parish. Sobotka rapidly emerges as a character who maintains strong allegiance to the local community, even if such allegiance comes at the cost of affiliation with The Greek's global crime syndicate.

Through his combined local-familial concern and his willingness to participate (blindly) in The Greek's crime network, Sobotka actually comes to resemble Avon. Like Avon, Sobotka is often depicted as part of a broader familial network working the Baltimore docks, as well as an integral part of a traditional, fraternal organization that structures not only his working life but his social life as well. Sobotka also fears the dramatic shifts that are redefining his place in the Baltimore economy, often blending familial and economic discourse much in the way that Avon has. During a conversation with lobbyist Bruce DiBiago, Sobotka brilliantly encapsulates the reshaping of the U.S. economy since the 1970s: "You know what the trouble is, Brucie? We used to make shit in this country. Build shit. Now we just put our hand in the next guy's pocket" (2.11). This sentiment reprises a series of similar statements. After he attends a presentation on the use of "modern robotics" in Rotterdam to fuel "an exploding global economy"—a haunting depiction of globalization's effects on the shipping industry, and on stevedores specifically—Sobotka tells DiBiago, "after the horror movie I seen today . . . Robots! Piers full of robots! My kid'll be lucky if he's even punchin' numbers five years from now" (2.07). For Sobotka, antiglobalism goes hand in hand with both a localist pro-union and pro-family stance. When his nephew, Nick, complains of not getting enough days and of needing more money, Sobotka asks why Nick didn't come to him.

Referring to the cash Sobotka has dispensed recently, Nick mocks what he assumes is his uncle's feigned altruism: "Ah, yeah. Frankie Sobotka is Father fuckin' Christmas on the docks lately. No doubt, his pockets are full." An irate Sobotka responds, "You think it's for me? . . . It ain't about me, Nick!" (2.04). And, as Nick well knows, Sobotka's actions throughout Season Two bear this out: he continually sinks money into failed political schemes to bring in more ships by rebuilding the granary pier and dredging the harbor; when "New Charles" loses his leg working the pier, Sobotka provides the family cash assistance; when another union member considers changing unions, Frank sends him to the local bar where a stack of bills awaits him.

None of this is to suggest, though, that Sobotka's behavior is beyond reproach. Indeed, the extended Sobotka family and the International Brotherhood of Stevedores union of which they are a part dissolve as a result of both Sobotka's desperate affiliation with The Greek and the younger Sobotkas' misapprehension of their elder's example. The utter differences between The Greek's and Sobotka's networks and commitments make Sobotka's decisions particularly troubling. Because of economic shifts that devastated his union and community, Sobotka must affiliate himself with the very type of organization responsible for that devastation. If Sobotka's focus rests on industrial prospects and a production-based economy where people "build shit," The Greek's focus is, first, on inspiring consumption. As he tells Sobotka in one of their meetings, "It's a new world, Frank. You should go out and spend some of the money on something you can touch" (2.08). Extending this notion of a "new world" represented through globalized capital, Nick tries to explain to Sobotka the extent of The Greek's network and its political reach. Framed pointedly by the closed factories lining the harbor in the background, Nick explains, "These guys, they got a big operation to protect. They're global-like" (2.11). From the importation of heroin and of Eastern European women to the transatlantic exportation of stolen cars, The Greek's operation spans far beyond the local economy and culture it helps destroy, and it maintains a stance largely inimical to the maintenance of familial ties. As Vondas explains to Nick, presaging a similar comment from The Greek, "It's just business with us. Everything is just business with us" (2.05). When Vondas and The Greek discuss their troubles with the Sobotka family and Vondas intimates a paternal affection for Nick, The Greek mockingly retorts, "You are fond of him, Spiros. You should've had a son." Vondas knowingly replies, "But then I would've had a wife" (2.11). Though they laugh at this, the joke reveals a dark underside of global capitalism. As was the case with Stringer, both men are defined entirely through their relation to capital, and neither exhibits anything but a purely transactional relationship with others. Vondas and The Greek are presented as actually incapable of familial affection and their motivations lie solely in desire for and security of capital. Thus, when they return in Season Five, they readily accept Marlo's "insurance" plan against the possible demise of Prop Joe, effectively green-lighting Joe's execution despite the amiability and established business relationship developed between Joe and Vondas.

Mirroring much of the dominant American discourse of globalization, Season Two seems to present the progress of globalization as an inevitable force against which localities and families have little or no hope of surviving. Before his death, for instance, Sobotka laments the cost of enmeshing his family and union with The Greek's global syndicate: "I flushed my fuckin' family, for what?" (2.11). Despite Sobotka and Nick's eventual cooperation with Major Crimes in dismantling the organization, the season ends with ominous scenes of continued global exchange: a new group of (Eastern European) women offload from the back of a truck, and new shipments of heroin roll in. Business as usual seems to have resumed, despite a slight hiccup on the docks. In contrast to the final montage and the laments of Officer Beadie Russell that "the port is still screwed" (2.12), there is a guardedly optimistic image of resistance to the entrenchment of global capitalism. Major Stan Valchek, the "company man" who spitefully initiated the investigation of Sobotka's union, opens a piece of mail containing a photo of a stolen surveillance van, loaded aboard an outbound ship by union members. Throughout Season Two, Valchek has received a series of similar photos from ports increasingly distant from Baltimore, and the final photo depicts smiling Australian longshoreman mocking Valchek from half a world away. Though admittedly a very minor element of the season's intricate plotting, this strand of the narrative counterbalances the tragic narrative of Sobotka's entrance into the global corporate economy. The photos of I.B.S. laborers reclaim a sense of the "international" from global capitalism and do so through a traditional expression simultaneously of fraternal affection and sincere economic resistance.

The docks, of course, are not the only site in *The Wire* where commitments to community and family prevail over corporatism. This same dynamic returns in the series finale, the closing montage of which mirrors the combined cynicism and guarded optimism that marks the juxtaposition of commercial and familial narratives. Within that montage, Vondas reemerges in the diner, meeting now with new dealers Fat Face Rick and Slim Charles. Initially, the inclusion of Rick, a long-time Co-Op member who uses the bureaucratic city-development machine like Stringer to siphon millions for worthless property, suggests the maintenance of Stringer's corporatist ideal in the Baltimore drug trade, echoing the ominous continuation of the global trade at the close of Season Two. The inclusion of Slim, however, suggests a continued resistance to this corporatism. Though originally a mercenary enforcer, Slim has evolved into a traditionalist like Avon, Prop Joe, and even Omar in his adherence to the rules of Baltimore's game. It was Slim who disciplined two unruly soldiers at Avon's homecoming bash; who chastised those same soldiers for violating the Sunday morning truce by attacking Omar and endangering his grandmother, a "bona-fide colored lady" (3.09); who, with Avon's assistance, resisted Stringer's desire to assassinate the corrupt State Senator, Clayton Davis; who looked out for Bodie after the fall of the Barksdale-Bell network; and who correctly advised Prop Joe to tread carefully with Marlo. Most significantly, it was Slim who was derisively accused of being a "sentimental motherfucker" when he cost the Co-Op $900,000 by precipitously killing Melvin "Cheese" Wagstaff (5.10), the opportunistic dealer who killed his own uncle, Prop Joe, to curry favor with Marlo.

Slim's sentimental opposition to Marlo and Cheese replicates precisely the oppositions structuring conflicts between Avon and Stringer, and between Sobotka and The Greek: obligations to local and communal tradition counter the push toward purely transactional relations to others. Like Avon and Sobotka before him, Slim has tried throughout to balance the demands of a shifting Baltimore economy and its heightened production of human worth-less-ness against the opposing demands of upholding local and familial traditions. Importantly, Slim is required to negotiate these competing demands with the two networks—represented by Stringer's Co-Op and Vondas's global syndicate—most responsible for the corporatization of Baltimore's drug trade. Through this final repetition of the inherent conflicts between corporate economies and the maintenance of traditional modes of social organization, which structure much of the five-season arc of *The Wire*, the show's creators emphasize the significance of the familial and communal traditions that Avon, Sobotka, and now Slim represent as sources of potential resistance to the divisive practices of contemporary capitalism.

10

Barksdale Women: Crime, Empire, and the Production of Gender

Courtney D. Marshall

In *Ain't I A Woman?*, bell hooks writes, "One has only to look at American television twenty-four hours a day for an entire week to learn the way in which black women are perceived in American society—the predominant image is that of the 'fallen' woman, the whore, the slut, the prostitute" (52). She argues that the sexual logic which buttressed chattel slavery lives on in popular culture images and public policy. HBO's *The Wire* challenges hooks's cataloging of black female stereotypes on two grounds; it allows for women's participation in crimes other than prostitution, and it invites us to see "fallen" women as complicated characters. On *The Wire*, black women are murderers, thieves, and drug dealers; they are also mothers, sisters, and girlfriends. By setting up black women vis-à-vis black men, the show examines gender variability within criminal networks. However, where hooks would see these depictions as detrimental to black women, I contend that these characters have a lot to teach us about black women's economic and organizational lives. *The Wire* demonstrates the central importance of the practices and discourses of crime, law, order, and policing to the formation of black female power and identity.

This chapter argues that rather than depicting mothers as failures because they are unable to keep their male relatives from committing crimes, *The Wire* challenges the very language on which we deem mothers successful. By looking at three women in the Barksdale empire, Donette, Brianna Barksdale, and De'Londa Brice, I will argue that the show invests mothers with the job of teaching civic values, even if those values are criminalized.[1] As a result, crime produces gender within the Barksdale empire.[2] Capitalism imposes a sexual division of labor, and women are obliged to fulfill the mother role in order to ensure the system a steady supply of labor. The show sets up a striking distinction between the close-knit Barksdale organization with the new generation of drug sellers in Marlo's crew.[3]

Insights into the gendered workings of *The Wire* are encouraged by new insights in black feminist criminology. These innovations lead to a more nuanced way of engaging representations of black female criminals. Jody Miller, for example, looks at the ways poverty, crime, and sexual violence are mutually constitutive in the lives of young black girls living in St. Louis. She conducts extensive interviews with young black boys and girls in order to "investigate how the structural inequalities that create extreme—and racialized—urban poverty facilitate . . . social contexts that heighten and shape the tremendous gender-based violence faced by urban African-American girls" (3). She situates her project within a tradition of feminist criminology which has significantly shaped the ways we theorize women's participation in the criminal justice system, both as victims and offenders. She examines victimization as a precursor to offending, and emphasizes the "contemporaneous nature of victimization and offending by examining the impact of gender inequality on street and offender networks" (3). Miller implores us to expand our scope when it comes to female offending, looking at the ways that a society stripped of social services for women then criminalizes these very women when they participate in underground economies and criminal activity in order to care for themselves and their families. At the same time, we must work toward a more textured analysis of how patriarchy structures the economies in which they seek alternatives.

This new vision of female crime must come along with a more critical consumption of popular culture images of black female criminals.

In depicting black female criminals, *The Wire* walks a fine line between making them stereotypical and making them victims, and as viewers we also walk a line between glorifying and rejecting representations of criminal behavior. Patricia Hill Collins identifies four overarching stereotypes of black women: the mammy, the matriarch, the welfare mother, and the whore. She writes that "each image transmits clear messages about the proper links among female sexuality, fertility, and black women's roles in the political economy" (78). While the mammy is asexual and devoted to upholding white societal values, the other three stereotypes are built upon hypersexuality, and to varying degrees, disordered gender roles. Collins writes that "the matriarch represents the sexually aggressive woman, one who emasculates black men because she will not permit them to assume roles as black patriarchs. She refuses to be passive and thus is stigmatized" (78). This particular stereotype of black womanhood serves a racist social order by implying that black communities, in their unwillingness to promote ostensibly proper gender and family relations, are thereby unfit for inclusion in the larger body politic. Margaret M. Russell argues that "Hollywood movies and television have served as the primary medium for the replication and reinforcement of stereotypes" drawing a critical genealogy which stretches from Sapphire of *Amos 'n' Andy* (adapted for television 1951–53) to contemporary television shows. As a result, black motherhood is a highly contested term in black cultural studies. Russell goes on to suggest that the black female viewer is caught in an ethical bond with a number of responses open to her: "stoic detachment, awkward ambivalence, derisive laughter, deep embarrassment, stunning rage" all buttressed by a need to distance oneself from the "detestable image on the screen" (137). This range of responses is interesting for what it shows about the limited ways we are asked to evaluate these images. Like Collins and hooks, Russell can find no oppositional space within depictions of female criminals and no virtue in the depiction of female vice. I'm not interested in vilifying or recuperating these characters, but critical reluctance to engage them is a problem, particularly given our voracious consumption of these images. While we can condemn these images of complicit mothers, a more useful approach would be to take their choices seriously and analyze why these fictional women seek refuge in crime for their families and what the criminal network offers them.

Donette, Brianna, and the Barksdale Code

While the first seasons center on the relationship between Avon Barksdale and Russell "Stringer" Bell, the two male heads of the Barksdale enterprise, the women of the Barksdale family play significant roles in its complicated sex-gender system. Donette is the girlfriend of D'Angelo Barksdale, a drug dealer and Avon's nephew. We first see her when D'Angelo brings her and their son to a neighborhood party organized by Avon. Stringer asks her to "C'mon, give us a twirl, let's take a look," and it is clear she finds this inappropriate (1.02). Avon asks Stringer to get some food for her and remarks on her skinniness. D'Angelo replies that she has a big appetite. The scene's awkwardness is based on her body's appetites being fodder for the men's conversation. Though neither Stringer nor Avon know her very well (when she and D'Angelo first walk in, Avon asks if this is their baby), they do not ask her any questions that would demonstrate that she has a life beyond D'Angelo. To them she is a body whose function at that moment is to be scrutinized and discussed, the result of her reproductive capacities evaluated and admired. When Avon and D'Angelo begin to talk, Avon hands the baby to a woman and tells her to be careful with his "little soldier, his little man" (1.02). While it can be argued that "soldier" is a term of endearment, in this context it also suggests that her son will be brought up to work for and defend the family business just like his father. While he will be loved and cared for, like all soldiers in Barksdale's army, eventually he will be a disposable pawn.[4]

D'Angelo is imprisoned for 20 years at the end of Season One, and Donette's role within the organization shifts. When she fails to visit him on a regular basis, Avon and Stringer decide to school her on jailhouse protocol. They first appeal to her loneliness and present themselves as viable social and economic alternatives to D'Angelo. When Stringer comes to visit her, she offers him one of D'Angelo's shirts, and when she bends over to place the shirt across his chest, she says, "You know it's a shame to let things go to waste" (2.03). While we can interpret the line to refer to her body, the line also connotes a sense that while she loves D'Angelo, anyone can wear his clothes. Stringer can replace D'Angelo both in his clothing and in his relationship. The show doesn't go so far as to imply that Donette is sexually indiscriminate. Rather, the exchange suggests that her version of domesticity is constituted by the public side of Barksdale criminal dealings.

Stringer quickly lets Donette know that as D'Angelo's girlfriend she has a part to play in the Barksdale organization, namely giving comfort to her imprisoned boyfriend. He tells her that prison is very stressful on men and it is imperative that the women in their lives keep them tethered to the outside world. "Only one thing he needs to be secure about, and if not then he might start thinking he can't do that time and then we all got problems" (2.03). D'Angelo's personal relationship problems risk becoming a catastrophe for the entire organization. Donette is responsible for fulfilling a very different familial need than the men who work for Avon. In the scene, her feminine role within the organization is emphasized by her pink clothes and the ring on her wedding-band finger. Though she is not legally D'Angelo's wife, she is expected to fulfill the duties as if she were; she must be his sweet thing.[5] This becomes even more interesting in light of the message *The Wire* sends about the affective bonds of law. The state structures family ties through the institutions of marriage; the modern family is constituted by the law. Stringer, Donette, and the other members of the Barksdale organization do not allow their economic gain to be bound by the law, just as they don't let the law determine who their family is. They sell illegal substances, use illegal weapons, and do not allow the law to dictate their affective ties. Though she and D'Angelo are not together anymore, Donette continues to fill a necessary function in the Barksdale organization through her domesticity.

In case Donette isn't moved by emotion, Stringer makes an economic appeal and shifts from treating her like a family member to treating her like the spouse of an injured employee. D'Angelo's hard work as a drug lieutenant has allowed her to have an apartment, car and money, and even though D'Angelo is in prison, Avon continues to support her as D'Angelo would. Stringer tells her, "We all got a job to do, and your job is to let D'Angelo know we still family" (2.03). Gender is central to the ways in which social relations are negotiated, built, and secured. Donette challenges these relations when she refuses to go to the prison, and Stringer must put her back in her place. The show highlights the interdependence of male and female gender roles as D'Angelo's continued cooperation relies upon Donette's feminized dependence on the masculine strength of the crew. D'Angelo is constantly reminded of the good job that his family has done for his girlfriend and son. Donette is being paid for her important domestic functions.

This arrangement is not egalitarian, however. Certainly, if Donette wanted to leave D'Angelo and make a new life with another man, she would become a target for the organization. The danger of girlfriends on the show is that there is no telling how much their men have told them about the inner workings of the organizations. To remedy that problem, Stringer has sex with her. This is important because throughout the scene she flirts with him, but rather than call her actions inappropriate and admonish her for wanting to have sex, he gives in to her advances and acts as a sexual substitute. Stringer recognizes that if Donette is not satisfied sexually, there will be a greater likelihood that she will go outside of the organization to find another man, potentially passing on sensitive information. As the shot ends, the camera pans across the couch to the end table where we see a number of pictures of Donette and D'Angelo. If the show implies that she wants to move on from that relationship, her sexuality is made safe by having her be with Stringer. Stringer does not allow her to explore what split affinities could arise if she were to have a relationship with anyone outside of the Barksdale crew. Recognizing the danger of her sexuality, they want her to use her femininity on their terms, and they want to keep it contained within the organization.

Though Stringer sends her on a mission to keep D'Angelo feeling like he is a part of the organization, D'Angelo clearly wants out of the crew and disputes her claim that Avon and Stringer support their relationship and their desire to raise their son. By the end of her tenure on the show, Donette has mourned the deaths of both D'Angelo and Stringer, and in her last scene she cries alone on the couch while her son plays nearby (3.12). In a short time, she has had to bury two men that she loved, and with the fall of the Barksdale empire, it is unclear what her future holds. She is never depicted with other family members. She is not even given a last name; she is literally not a Barksdale. In her situation, black female sexual desire was used to crystallize the hierarchy of black masculinity and to maintain ties between them. Like a chess piece, she is moved from one man to another, and in the end she is abandoned.

While Donette represents the ways romantic ties are used to manipulate people within the organization, Brianna Barksdale represents a more successful negotiation of maternal ties. Brianna is Avon's sister, D'Angelo's mother, and a key player in the organization. We first see her when she brings a special lunch to D'Angelo while he is working in the Terrace. She gets the food from Sterling's, a local restaurant, and while D'Angelo is familiar with the restaurant, Wallace, one of the young men he supervises, is not. The show juxtaposes Wallace's limited exposure to the world outside of the Terrace with Brianna's easy movement in and out of the Terrace. Though the car she drives is a direct result of the work that boys like Wallace do, their labor allows her to not be bound to poverty like they are. Bringing food to D'Angelo places her squarely within traditional representations of motherhood.

When D'Angelo is arrested in the rental car with drugs, Brianna's maternal instincts cause her to challenge her brother. Like Donette, she is reminded that all of the material comforts she enjoys are dependent upon D'Angelo's cooperating with Avon and not sharing information with the police. Their reliance on D'Angelo puts them all in precarious relationships, but again, the men of the organization pretend that it is only the women who benefit and do not work. However, because Brianna is also Avon's sister and has been around the work all her life, she calls him on his lax supervision and is very angry that he would jeopardize her son's freedom so carelessly. Avon tells her that she needs to use her position as D'Angelo's mother to remind him of his commitment. Avon is able to manipulate D'Angelo's close ties to his mother in order to keep his empire strong. Brianna tells him, "You ain't gotta worry about my child. I raised that boy, and I raised him right" (1.12). While she knows that D'Angelo is being used as a pawn, she still demands that he be treated with respect. Her dual role provides an important context for understanding her cooperation and complicity with crime. Unlike Donette, whose influence remains limited to the domestic, Brianna can articulate motherhood and deploy it to sanction her own participation in the business. She successfully mobilizes the construction of motherhood to stake her claim in Barksdale politics.

Brianna is also regarded as a trusted leader within the organization, a role that is unusual in televisual depictions of female criminals. When Avon is released from jail, she tells him that she and Stringer will rebuild their earnings while he sits back. Until the police stop watching him so closely, she will handle the money and Stringer will handle the drugs. Though Brianna is conventionally feminine in many ways (marked most obviously in her makeup and clothing), in this scene she is also marked as being much like the men. While Avon and Stringer wear plain beige shirts, she stands out in a low-cut red outfit. She smokes a cigarette in a nonchalant way, making it clear that she is not nervous when talking about the drug game. She stands with her arms folded, in an exact physical echo of Stringer's body language. The scene makes the three of them look like a united front. They respect her opinion and follow her advice; she is given the same number of lines in the scene as they are. When they get to the subject of D'Angelo, she is both mother and employer, telling Avon that she will visit after she situates the new drug buy. She speaks to Avon as both a sister and a partner, telling him that he will definitely pay for D'Angelo's service. The action of the scene literally revolves around the efficiency and maternity of her body, and during this time of crisis, she is burdened with a wide range of Barksdale policies and practices.

When D'Angelo wants to leave his family behind and "breathe like regular folk," his mother's visit becomes even more important (2.06). She tells him he has two choices: do the time or step into Avon's place and let him do it. Either way, he must fulfill his place in the family. Brianna warns him that if he talks to the police he will bring down the entire family: "All of us. Me and Trina and the cousins" (2.06). The job of women here is to remind men of their masculine duties. Though she is a trusted advisor in the organization and certainly not incarcerated, Brianna manipulatively constructs herself, Donette, Trina, and the children as all being dependent upon D'Angelo, Avon, and the rest of the men. It then becomes D'Angelo's job to keep his mouth shut and save them all from living "down in the fucking Terrace . . . on scraps" (2.06) She even goes so far as to say that without the game they might not be a family. Their familial ties are strengthened by their participation in illegal activities, and this is the logic on which gender roles are constructed. When the organization needs the women to look pretty and be helpless, they do it. When it needs them to be fierce leaders, they do that too. Donette and Brianna are required to perform a flexibility that is integral to the workings of the group. They represent the complex negotiations that occur between and among different constituencies in the imperial context.

Like Father, Like Son

If Donette represents the mother in limbo whose son might carry on the legacy of his dead father, and Brianna sacrifices her son for the sake of family, De'Londa Brice's entire life is built upon the ambitious dream of running the empire even after her ties to it are severed. The drama of De'Londa and her son Namond plays out like a younger version of Brianna and D'Angelo, and, like Donette, she was also romantically involved with one of Avon's employees. However, unlike Brianna, she has no qualms about exposing her son to the harshness of street life. Brianna uses her closeness to Avon to negotiate for more safety and better working conditions for D'Angelo while De'Londa uses her tenuous ties to the Barksdale organization for her own self-interest. When we meet De'Londa, Wee-Bey has already been imprisoned for life, and she is being supported by a pension from the Barksdale organization. Like the other women, she is accustomed to certain material comforts, but unlike the other women, she depends upon her boyfriend's good name and on her son in order to maintain them.

De'Londa is introduced in the show's fourth season, a season which revolves around the home and life of four boys, Namond Brice, Randy Wagstaff, Michael Lee, and Duquan Weems. Out of all these boys, Namond is the only one who has a biological mother who cares for him. Duquan's family consists of drug addicts who steal his clothes and abandon him; Michael's mother sells groceries for drugs; and Randy lives with a foster mother. If we follow the conventional cultural logic, De'Londa is the most successful mother of the bunch. Unlike the other boys, Namond wears nice clothes and has all the latest video games and stereo equipment because his mother wants the best for him. With this comes the expectation that he should continue to live the life of a soldier's son. This is in stark contrast to Michael's mother who, when detectives come by to look for him, only knows the he and his brother have found their own place to live. She tells them, "I popped him and Bug out my ass, and they forgot where they came from" (5.06). We can never forget where Namond comes from because De'Londa never has a scene without him or his father, and we rarely see her outside of a domestic setting.

Being the son of De'Londa Brice is not without its hardships. In a move that mirrors the first two seasons, Namond decides that he does not want to be in the family business. This is when the show deploys another conventional female role: keeper of traditions. It is De'Londa's job to remind Namond of all the sacrifices she and his father have made for him; she does not appear fragile or dependent. Though Wee-Bey is in jail for life without parole, she uncritically holds him up as an example to follow. Their confrontation reaches new heights when she yells at him for not beating up Kenard, a younger boy who stole drugs Namond was to sell. Namond wants to use diplomacy to solve the problem, while his mother wants Kenard to "feel some pain for what he did":

De'Londa: This how you pay me back for all the love I showed? Shit, I been kept you in Nikes since you were in diapers.

Namond: What he done got him locked up.

De'Londa: That's right. Wee-Bey walked in Jessup a man, and he gonna walk out one. But you out here, wearing his name, acting a bitch! Aw, look at you, crying now. (4.12)

De'Londa transforms familial love into contractual obligation; Namond owes her loyalty and financial comfort because she has provided nice material things for him. However, Namond points out the inherent contradiction of the contract. Familial love is acted out by participating in illegal activities, but the punishment for those activities, in this case prison, breaks families apart. Wee-Bey was a good provider, but now he is in jail and is unable to do anything for them. The only way for Namond to show that he loves his mother is to take care of her in a way that will lead to his own imprisonment or death; he must sacrifice himself for her happiness. In pointing out that his tears are inappropriate, De'Londa polices the boundaries between the feminine and the masculine.[6] She has an obsessive fixation on teaching Namond how to be a man by forcing him to be like a man he rarely sees. It is only in her stories about him that Wee-Bey attains model status. Later, when the police call her after Namond runs away, she says, "Put that bitch in baby booking where he belongs. Let him learn something" (4.10). In a season that revolves around education and the Baltimore public school system, we see a mother who believes that the penitentiary would serve as the best academy for her son. She does not talk to her son after this pronouncement, suggesting that prison will be the final shaper of his male identity. Eventually the show offers alternative caregivers for Namond as it attempts to separate familial ties from economic ones. Howard "Bunny" Colvin offers to take Namond into his home and show him a different way to live under a different type of masculine authority. Colvin's home represents a chance for Namond to have a present father figure, but more importantly for the show's argument, for him to have an appropriate mother figure.

De'Londa uses her son in order to stay connected to the Barksdale crew after it crumbles. She feels that she is teaching Namond to be an upstanding citizen in a criminal community. While they are not law-abiding citizens, she teaches him that to participate in the underground economy of drug selling, certain characteristics are desirable. There is intense sadness in her voice when she realizes that the change in her son's prospects also necessitates a separation from her. When Colvin visits Wee-Bey, he says, "Your boy is smart and funny and open-hearted . . . He could go a lot of places and do a lot of things with his life. Be out there in the world in a way that, you know, didn't happen for you and me" (4.13). Colvin portrays the life he can give Namond as being vastly more expansive than the one De'Londa can offer. Namond is being given the chance for a legal life, a life where social class and material possessions are not jeopardized by police and incarceration. Colvin appeals to Wee-Bey using shared memories of the West Side and tells him that the game he ran is not the same one in which his son will participate. He differentiates the two of them from a new generation by saying that the new crews have "no code, no family." This generational shift is emphasized in the lack of female characters in Marlo Stanfield's crew. His crew is not bound by blood, and Felicia "Snoop" Pearson, its only woman, is consistently masculinized. The show no longer portrays female counterparts to the male criminals fulfilling feminine roles. The new women are killing machines.

Though the show portrays strong women who break the law, we are always reminded that their strength is a result of how well they perform their assigned roles. Black mothers do not hold all the cards. Colvin tells Wee-Bey that Namond's future is up to him, and does so without involving De'Londa. The later exchange between Namond's parents is fascinating for the way it maps gender and parental roles. Wee-Bey is depicted as wanting Namond to have a life full of opportunities, while De'Londa's only concern seems to be how Namond ties her to Wee-Bey, and by extension, to the now fallen Barksdale organization:

Wee-Bey: You put him out, huh?
De'Londa: He need to get hard.
Wee-Bey: If he out, then he out.
De'Londa: Oh no you not. You ain't gonna take my son away from me, not for this—
Wee-Bey: Remember who the fuck you talking to right here. Remember who I am. My word is still my word. In here, in Baltimore, and in any place you can think of calling home, it'll be my word. They'll find you.
De'Londa: So, did you cutting me off too?
Wee-Bey: You still got me. We'll get by. But you gonna let go of that boy. Bet that. (4.13)

Lest we believe that De'Londa is in control, Wee-Bey makes it known that even from jail he has the ability to send people out to hurt her if she does not do as he wishes. Like the other Barksdale women, De'Londa's freedom is tempered by the tremendous burden she carries and by an implicit threat of violence. Having a boyfriend and a son whose lives are shaped by their participation in crime shapes her understanding of womanhood. She is desperate after having been cut off by the Barksdale organization, and she has to rely on her son to fill the economic need that Wee-Bey cannot and the Barksdales will not.

Representations of crime in black popular culture have focused primarily on men and masculinity. When women are discussed, they often exist solely as wives or mothers who support the men in their lives. *The Wire* disrupts this narrative and suggests that womanhood, like all roles within capitalism, is not without a desire for self-preservation. The organization of crime depends upon the inherent gendered nature of domesticity, and women are just as invested in their own survival as men are. As a result, the show's black mothers symbolize both assets and liabilities in their attempts to assert themselves within the organization. These women are neither Madonna-like "angels of the hearth" nor the neglectful fallen women Collins and hooks describe. By using crime as a lens through which to understand more fully the nexus of women's work in depictions of familial networks, *The Wire* accepts and even embraces some stereotypical roles ascribed to black mothers and uses them to transform the horizons of the audience's expectations.

Notes

1. There is, of course, much to say about other forms of motherhood in the show, notably in Kima Greggs and Cheryl's lesbian motherhood and Anna Jeffries's foster mothering of Randy. I do not want to imply that these other forms of motherhood are unimportant to my discussion. In fact, in opening up forms of male parenting, *The Wire* makes significant interventions in discussions of black parenting on television. See, for example, Michael and Duquan's caring for Bug, Howard Colvin's fostering of Namond, and Bubbles's caring for Sherrod. *The Wire* declines to make caretaking strictly the role of women.

2. I use the word empire deliberately both to suggest the control that Avon Barksdale has over broad areas of Baltimore and the ways that he uses family ties to sustain his operations.

3. Without overromanticizing the brutality of the Barksdale organization, they are depicted as family-oriented. By the end of Season Five, though, family structures break down. Michael Lee asks Chris Partlow to kill his stepfather, and Calvin "Cheese" Wagstaff conspires with Chris Partlow and Felicia "Snoop" Pearson to have his uncle, Proposition Joe Stewart, killed.

4. In Season One, D'Angelo teaches chess to two other drug dealers, Wallace and Preston "Bodie" Broadus. They speak in metaphors which relate the chess game to drug game. In both settings, pawns "get capped quick" while "the king stay[s] the king" (1.03).

5. Mary J. Blige's "Sweet Thing" (1993) plays in the background during this scene.

6. Wee-Bey also tells Namond to cut off his long hair, but because it makes him an easier target for the police.

11

After the Towers Fell: Bodie Broadus and the Space of Memory

Elizabeth Bonjean

Our interest in lieux de mémoire *where memory crystallizes and secretes itself has occurred at a particular historical moment, a turning point where consciousness of a break with the past is bound up with the sense that memory has been torn—but torn in such a way as to pose the problem of the embodiment of memory in certain sites where a sense of historical continuity persists. There are* lieux de mémoire, *sites of memory, because there are no longer* milieux de mémoire, *real environments of memory.*

—*Pierre Nora, "Between Memory and History:* Les Lieux de Mémoire*"*

The day is bright in West Baltimore as three young African American men walk through the center of an alley framed by debris that lines the perimeter—castaway garbage cans, a tire, an old chair, a broken refrigerator. These soldiers from Avon Barksdale's crew trace familiar pathways to their destination—the Franklin Terrace Towers—their purposeful steps punctuated by the insistent orations of Mayor Clarence Royce and the cheering approval of a crowd. Navigating the public streets, Preston "Bodie" Broadus, Malik "Poot" Carr, and Herbert De'Rodd "Puddin" Hearns banter about their personal and collective histories lived on this spot, a long-held Barksdale drug trafficking territory (3.01). The soldiers' journey to the Towers is interspersed with Mayor Royce's pronouncements of the promising future that will thrive on this ground. Distracted by the pageantry of the occasion and their desire for a safer environment, the community overlooks the economic realities of what redevelopment might mean for them in terms of affordable housing and the remaking of what Liam Kennedy has termed the "space as a social product" for the City of Baltimore (8). Instead they are blinded by the ingratiating smile of the mayor standing on a platform with a patriotic red, white, and blue banner as his backdrop. Attempting to intertwine Royce's identity with the site of transformation, the signage reads: "Building for the Future. New Beginnings for West Baltimore," with credit given to "Mayor Clarence V. Royce" in disproportionately larger letters than the "citizens of Baltimore." Royce lays further claim to the space by calling for a forgetting of all the ills that came to be associated with the Towers in order to make way for a new community.

As Bodie, Poot, and Puddin arrive at the Towers, they are ironically separated from their history and memories by a police street barricade; the soldiers stand watch as the assembly of onlookers takes part in a collective countdown to the demolition. Despite Bodie's bravado that the Towers are a housing project that should have been "blown up a long time ago," he is transfixed by the violent spectacle as explosives are detonated and the first of the two Towers crumbles. An intense surge of smoke blankets the blue sky, billowing out onto the street where a green traffic light seems to signify its unexpected arrival. We continue to connect with Bodie's experience of the event as the sound of his voice is heard exclaiming, "Oh shit" as clouds of dust overwhelm the crowd. Bodie's words lead us to an image of the second tower collapsing and an environment suddenly overcome by elements it had sought to eradicate: even in its death, the essence of the Towers cannot be easily contained. As at-home viewers, we are voyeurs of this fictional event, yet instantly are transported back in time to 11 September 2001 when Americans— and the world—witnessed the collapsing World Trade Center Towers in New York City replayed over and over on television. This reimagining of 9/11 excludes the terrorist element that perpetuated the attack, but remains fixated on the locus of capitalistic enterprise and the aftershocks that ripple through a community when it is destroyed by a powerful, outside force (DVD commentary 3.01). When this episode first aired on

19 September 2004, the governors of New York and New Jersey, along-side New York Mayor Michael Bloomberg, had only days before ceremoniously laid the cornerstone for the new Freedom Tower to be built at Ground Zero, with an accompanying memorial to "honor and remember those who lost their lives" (RenewNYC.org). Conversely, Mayor Royce avows that the footprints of West Baltimore's towers are meant to be built over and forgotten; the people who subsisted there are deemed unworthy of remembering.

This chapter explores the powerful presence of the Towers as focal point in the surrounding community of family, home, school, and mar-ketplace. Focusing on Bodie, I look at the Towers as representative of the Barksdale organization and their role in defining cultural space and in shaping the identity of the young black men who grow up within their social sphere. Amidst this environment and the eventual downfall of the Barksdale gang, Bodie's growing need to locate himself in relationship to the iconic Towers moves him through stages of grief for people, codes, loyalty, respect, and territory. The illegal, violent terrain Bodie navigates complicates our comprehension of his losses. Therefore it can be reveal-ing to engage with a question philosopher Judith Butler asks in her post-9/11 work *Precarious Life*: "What counts as a livable life and a grievable death?" (xv). Questions such as this may lead to connections about what loss and grief in the world of *The Wire* can teach us about our own humanity before and after the Towers fell. We might wonder, as Butler does, about the transformative possibilities for individuals and for society as a whole, when given freedom to openly grieve a painful loss (21–23). We might reconsider a question of what constitutes valu-able life by searching for the possibilities of hopefulness in a warring humanity.

Before the Towers Fell

The Franklin Towers are established as cultural markers in the initial episode of *The Wire* as D'Angelo Barksdale arrives at his place of busi-ness only to be demoted from this prime territory until he can prove himself (1.01). The Towers' looming significance is later shown in relationship to the neighboring low-rises, another Barksdale territory referred to as "the Pit." In this space, crew members are educated in the rules of the drug game as they dream of someday working their way up to a position in the Towers. The first glimpse of Bodie is in the center courtyard of the Pit, seated alone atop an orange couch. Bodie is 16 years old, but his eyes look older than his years as he watches over the area. His time in the game has made him smart about people and procedures, while his strong dedication to the Barksdale gang as family sets him apart from his friends and co-workers, Poot and Wallace.

Though a Barksdale by blood, D'Angelo does not have the edge that his relatives and other members of the Barksdale crew possess; his uncle Avon reprimands him for his "emotional" responses to situations, while Avon's business partner, Russell "Stringer" Bell lectures D'Angelo about the importance of never "show[ing] weakness" to others. Ever watchful, Bodie observes D'Angelo's softness with his employees and customers, and he is at times frustrated by D'Angelo's nonviolent choices in dealing with the shortcomings of others. Bodie's own response to such situations is to react quickly and sharply, as when Bubbles's friend Johnny attempts a con with fake money. Caught and detained by the Pit crew, Johnny is beaten by a furious Bodie, who declares that Johnny should be "thrown onto the expressway" as just punishment (1.01). Witnessing Johnny's fear, D'Angelo's approach is to talk quietly to him and take the real money Johnny possesses. An incredulous Bodie waits for a directive to right the wrong committed against them, but D'Angelo simply walks away. Yet Bodie will not let the issue go without sending a message about respect, leading an attack that lands Johnny in hospital. What Stringer has classified as weakness in D'Angelo, is depicted here for the viewer as strength of character, a desire on D'Angelo's part to retain a "sense of human vulnerability" in his encounters with others as he endeavors to connect to a "collective responsibility" (Butler 44–45).

The steps that Bodie is prepared to take in order to assert the hierarchical power of the Barksdale gang in the West Baltimore drug-trafficking community, and his identity within it, are extreme and persistent, reflecting the rigid systems gang cultures employ in order to create and maintain their place in the social order. Elijah Anderson details the rules at work in African American street subculture and how understanding and operating within the established code system is necessary not only for survival on the streets, but to affirm and reaffirm one's identity through actions that show a demand for respect:

> Street culture has evolved what may be called a code of the streets, which amounts to a set of informal rules governing interpersonal public behavior, including violence. The rules prescribe both a proper comportment and a proper way to respond if challenged. They regulate the use of violence and so allow those who are inclined to aggression to precipitate violent encounters in an approved way . . . At the heart of the code is the issue of respect—loosely defined as being treated "right," or granted the deference one deserves. (82)

Anderson's study of violence, poverty, and gang culture emphasizes how codes of behavior are instilled in children at a young age—through modeling adult interactions or hands-on mentoring from an older family member who teaches them how to negotiate their way through the complexities of their social environment. Early indoctrination into the code leads to a lifetime of learning to read the nuances of people and conditions, and an active wrestling with one's self-identity in relationship to issues of respect. Such learned behaviors reinforce the code we see at work in the fictional streets of *The Wire*.

As Anderson documents, "The code revolves around the presentation of self. Its basic requirement is the display of a certain predisposition to violence" (86, 88), making Bodie's keen sensitivity to interpreting the code all the more essential to the development of his character. A small but significant negotiation of identity and respect surfaces when D'Angelo interrupts Wallace and Bodie's game of checkers, laughingly telling them they are playing the wrong game on a chess board (1.03). Adhering to the principle that one must never look weak, Bodie resists the interference and guards himself against D'Angelo's laughter, perceiving it as a move to embarrass Wallace and himself because they do not know how to do something the right way. Bodie eases into D'Angelo's tutelage when he grasps that D'Angelo is not ridiculing their intellect, but simply wants to teach them the rules of the game. As Bodie and

Wallace engage with the rules of chess, they relearn the constructed nature of their parallel universe on the street. Here, Bodie enters into a moment of rare reciprocity with D'Angelo when he pushes for tactics necessary to win the game. The pawns are "like the soldiers. They move like this, one space forward only," D'Angelo cautions.

Bodie: All right so . . . If I make it to the other end, I win?
D'Angelo: If you catch the other dude's king and trap it, then you win.
Bodie: But if I make it to the other end . . . I'm top dog.
D'Angelo: No. It ain't like that, look. The pawns in the game, they get capped quick. They be out of the game early.
Bodie: Unless they some smart-ass pawns. (1.03)

This momentary negotiation of power and identity demonstrates Pierre Nora's concept of a *milieu de mémoire*—the social space of memory-making within a community. Nora describes an environment of memory as a social memory that is active, always engaged in a process that requires an endless give-and-take between creating, instilling, forgetting, remembering, and re-creating as part of a living, breathing collective identity:

Memory is blind to all but the group it binds—which is to say, as Maurice Halbwachs has said, that there are as many memories as there are groups, that memory is by nature multiple and yet specific; collective, plural, and yet individual . . . Memory takes root in the concrete, in spaces, gestures, images, and objects. (9)

The everyday gestures within the Barksdale community are representative of social memory at work shaping a group identity. Like pieces on a chessboard that can be moved in a series of patterns, the Barksdale leadership defines and redefines its social space for its members. A whistle, a hand gesture, a rotating stash house, a pager, a cell phone—these are all external, concrete locations of memory in operation, inscribing a system of order, hierarchy, and respect. The *milieu de mémoire* of the

Pit functions within the larger context of the Barksdale environment as a whole. Yet this subgroup is charged with the influence of D'Angelo in the remembering, forgetting, and rethinking of their social practices. From handling the altercation with Johnny, to teaching the rules of the game to Bodie and Wallace, D'Angelo negotiates the social space with compassion, humor, and the free sharing of knowledge. Such alterations to the defining of the social space of the Pit make room for the reimagining of self-identity in the social world of the Barksdale gang and in the social life of West Baltimore. For Bodie, the discovery that there is a remote chance that he can move beyond the role of a soldier means he can aspire to a longer, more successful life. In time, the influential experiences of working under the Barksdale organization and under D'Angelo as an individual will cause Bodie to integrate memories of the Pit into the Barksdale group code, ultimately infusing the rules of the game with not only nuances of professional possibility for himself, but a ·fuller appreciation of individual and collective responsibilities.

If, as Nora reminds us, "memory is by nature multiple and yet specific; collective, plural, and yet individual" (9), then Bodie's memories are not only shaped by the Barksdale culture, but by his personal memories living life in the socially-devalued territory of West Baltimore. In this environment, a common family element is the vital role of grandmothers in child-rearing due to absent or economically challenged parents (Rosenblatt and Wallace xvi–xviii; Shelden, Tracy, Brown 83–87). Yet as widespread as these conditions are, the lived experience of their realities is uniquely individual. In first encountering Bodie we can readily identify him with the customary associations of youth in gang subculture: he is angry and violent, he adheres to the street code, and he is involved in illegal activity. The introduction of Bodie's grandmother is a point of departure for understanding the personal environment of memory that has helped mold Bodie's self-identity. In search of Bodie after he has assaulted a police officer and subsequently escaped from a juvenile detention center, police officers Thomas "Herc" Hauk and Ellis Carver aggressively enter Bodie's grandmother's house, hunting unsuccessfully for her grandson. As he is about to leave, Herc takes a moment to look at the home he has just stormed through and sees the human dignity in the face of the woman who quietly folds laundry in her front room. Herc speaks to her and apologizes for his brash behavior and silently receives her unexpected reply:

> Is it the drugs again?
> *Herc nods.*
> Would you like to sit down?
> *He sits.*
> Preston came to me when my daughter died. He was four years old. But even then, I knew he was angry. His mother lived out there, caught up in it. After a while, you couldn't make her see nothin' else. So how you think you gonna carry it? (1.04)

Bodie's grandmother disrupts the dehumanizing strategies that often brand marginalized members of society. In her minimalistic narrative, Bodie's grandmother contextualizes the harsh entity of West Baltimore as a place of lived histories and memories that have meaning to individuals and families. In restating how her daughter lived and died, the grandmother simultaneously reinscribes her daughter's memory into the landscape of her home environment as a mother and daughter, and into the space of the community as a participant in a culture that cultivates drug addiction and drug trafficking, marking the community as complicit in her daughter's death. Bodie's place as an innocent child in this story elicits compassion from Herc and provides a new lens with which to view Bodie: no longer another essentialized young black gang member from the streets, he is an individual with a face and borne of circumstances.

In the private social space of his grandmother's home, the memory of Bodie's mother lives, for "memory is life . . . [i]t remains in permanent evolution, open to the dialectic of remembering and forgetting, unconscious of its successive deformations, vulnerable to manipulation and appropriation, susceptible to being long dormant and periodically revived" (Nora 8). Bodie's memory-making of his mother did not stop at the age of four with her physical death, but moves in multiple directions from that point, recapturing recollections from the first few years of his life and the memories formed in her absence. Bodie's personal memories are in dialogue with those sheltered by his grandmother—photographs of family adorn the walls of her home and look out from shelves and tables as if arrested in time. Together, they constitute resistance to the hierarchies of "grievable life" that Butler exposes, which allow some people to remain undeserving of any gesture of mourning because of race, creed, class, nationality, or politics. Hierarchies of grief are possible, Butler explains, when hierarchies of life exist. A system like this orders individuals in terms of societal worth, and categorizes people into group entities—things—devoid of all personal background and all qualities that make us uniquely human (32). The particularized memories Bodie and his grandmother retain, combined with the physical objects of their shared family history and memories which remain alive in their home, rupture the narrative myth of the dominant culture which excludes African American gang subculture from human conditions of family, love, and felt loss.

Such hierarchies overlook the pressures of individual survival in African American subcultures where life in racialized and violent communities often means that very young children lose their parents, making "the support of a close family member . . . extraordinarily important": the need to have someone in that role feeds feelings of abandonment by the parent who has died (Rosenblatt and Wallace 64). In this way, the death of Bodie's mother can be interpreted as an abandonment that stimulates an unresolved grief Bodie carries with him. As he searches for a solidity to her presence in the past and in his present, Bodie must continually reposition himself, reminded when he bumps up against absence that memory is fluid.

Like memory, grief is a process—it flows, changes directions, gets buried, resurfaces, adapts. As part of the warring Barksdale organization, Bodie's personal losses mount, as do the strains of memory. The first of Bodie's fresh losses will haunt him for the remainder of his life due to the unique circumstances: it is Bodie himself who brings about the death, and the victim is not a member of a rival gang, but his childhood friend, Wallace (1.12). Trapped in a downward spiral after the brutal murder of Omar's lover, Brandon, an overwrought Wallace feels complicit and assuages his guilt with drugs. As the Barksdales grow suspicious of Wallace's loyalty to the organization and his strength of character, Stringer charges Bodie to carry out Wallace's murder. Bodie and Poot accept this turning point in the game, realizing that as soldiers they must maintain the front line. Yet Poot is reluctant to eliminate his friend, while Bodie steels himself to the personal side of their assignment. The coldness Bodie harnesses in order to rationalize and carry out the impending murder is increasingly intensified at the murder scene as Bodie is confronted with the living, breathing human being of his friend. Bodie fights his vulnerability, verbally denouncing Wallace as a "weak-ass nigger," a "boy" who needs to "stand up straight" and "be a man." Listening to the barrage of insults, an emotionally distressed Poot can no longer bear Wallace's trauma and implores Bodie to shoot him. In a defining moment of what Elisabeth Kübler-Ross and David Kessler describe as "anticipatory grief" (1), Bodie hesitates. Standing fixed in place, the only movement seen is the shaking of his hands in apprehension of pulling the trigger and completing the act; Bodie enters into a momentary "state of limbo" with his grief where "fear of the unknown" and the reality of the coming loss of Wallace co-mingle (1, 4). In *On Grief and Grieving*, Kübler-Ross and Kessler emphasize that to be stuck for any length of time in an emotional abyss, terrified of the unknowable and of the future pain we will experience in respect to loss, is a foundational element of anticipatory grief. Their outline of the grieving process and its five stages of grief—denial, anger, bargaining, depression, and acceptance—is modeled on Kübler-Ross's renowned examination of how human beings come to terms with the final stages of life in *On Death and Dying*, and is useful here in exploring Bodie's personal journey in relationship to loss.

Because gang subculture operates in relation to power and violence, it is rife with the tenuous nature of life and death. Such conditions can breed a perpetual, if unacknowledged, fear of loss and pain among gang members. When an anticipatory or realized grief presents itself, the bargaining stage may take effect. Characterized by a sense of being "lost in a maze" of self-deception, bargainers enter into the language of "what if" and "if only" statements as they try to alter the inevitable or actualized outcome of their loss (17). Though grief studies counsels that one must eventually endure sorrowful feelings in order to make progress in the grieving process, bargainers like Bodie are not yet ready and "will do anything not to feel the pain of this loss," including inflicting or wallowing in guilt (17). With this in mind, the scene of Wallace's murder can be further explored.

Bodie's bargaining begins as soon as he has the courage to point his gun at Wallace. Branding his friend with the accusation that he is "weak," Bodie belittles Wallace to manage his own guilt for the treacherous act he is about to commit (1.12). If another tactic of bargaining is to reverse the guilt, placing the blame on the other, then Bodie's admonishment of Wallace as weak puts the responsibility for this deadly course of events on Wallace for not being stronger. Bodie's further allegations aim to infantilize Wallace, targeting him as behaving like a "boy," and demanding that he must "stand up straight" and be a man. In the bargaining language of "what ifs" and "if onlys," Bodie seems to indicate, "If only you could have grown up and behaved like a man, things would be different." With Anderson's code of the streets enmeshed in Bodie's grief process, Bodie wears a tough mask. He will, as Kübler-Ross and Kessler describe, "do anything not to feel this pain" (17), and so tries to force onto Wallace's shoulders the weight of his own death through guilt and blame. Yet grief and memory-making are messy processes. In the space between the verbal prologue and pulling the trigger, Bodie's hesitation betrays his harsh exterior. In the intimacy of this moment, Bodie wants and needs to erase his memories of Wallace, to render him faceless in front of the barrel of the gun. But Bodie cannot effectively dehumanize his friend. Thus when he does finally shoot the gun, Bodie leaves Wallace critically wounded, and Poot must finish the job. This violent act now complete, the intimate social environment of these three friends has forever altered: it has "taken root in the concrete space" (Nora 9) of Wallace's room in the low-rises, and now binds their individual and collective memories to it.

After the Fall

In the aftermath of D'Angelo's murder (2.06), the demolition of the Franklin Towers (3.01), and the disintegration of the Barksdale gang (3.12), Bodie finds himself to be one of the last former Barksdale crew members on the street. The game has changed, as has his place in it. Pushed away from a prime corner by new king Marlo Stanfield, Bodie runs a corner in territory that has no locus to replace the absent Towers and their symbolic resonance of productivity and a shared code for the community. Bodie is at sea. Slim Charles, another Barksdale survivor, reminds Bodie, "Ain't like the old days, dog. Mayor Barksdale left. You out here on your own, dog" (4.01). What persists is a small nucleus of associates Bodie surrounds himself with as family—including Poot and Little Kevin—reminiscent of the close-knit inner workings of the Pit under D'Angelo's management. When Little Kevin suddenly disappears from this world, it is a loss that destabilizes Bodie's social environment even on this new corner, hindering the cohesiveness of a group identity shaped by their reciprocal network of memory-making. Though Bodie suspects Kevin's absence means something is amiss, he remains in a state of denial, his grief suspended until he receives word from Slim Charles that Kevin's vanishing is permanent: he has been killed by Marlo's crew. Reeling from the news, Bodie stands alone on his corner—stunned by the reality of the loss and the effective erasure of Kevin from the social system (4.10).

Does the post-Towers world of Marlo Stanfield give way to a codeless community? Is it a space, as Judith Butler suggests of our post-9/11 world, in which "certain lives are not considered lives at all" (34)? If so, Butler contends, human beings can be rendered faceless, nameless, deemed as unworthy of a "narrative, so that there never was a life, and there never was a death" (146). Marlo's blatant disregard for humanity illustrates this point as his denial of human dignity is extended not just to the living, but the dead whom his crew entombs in vacant houses where he believes the faceless will be forgotten. One of the faceless, Little Kevin, begs Marlo's crew before his death to be left where his family and friends can find him, so that they can give him a proper "home go," but even that small amount of dignity in death is not allowed to him (4.10).

If dehumanization is at work in the world of *The Wire*, then the reawakening of old wounds in Bodie following the loss of Kevin has purpose. The loss sets in motion a spiral of grief that demands Bodie's full attention in order that he might reach personal acceptance of his pain, and along the way he might fully bear witness to who and what has been lost. One of the steps on Bodie's journey is his opportunity to bear witness to D'Angelo publically with the Barksdale family. Bodie's choice of a material tribute reiterates the significance of the Towers in the real-world shaping of identity—the bonds between space and identity fused in a floral arrangement shaped like the Towers with the numbers "221" representing the Tower D'Angelo took great pride in having once managed (2.07). The other memorial he makes to D'Angelo is in the living form of a group system on the new corner modeled on D'Angelo's training and tactics. Bodie's interactions with D'Angelo in the Pit showed him the possibility of people being treated with decency and seen in all their humanity.

Bearing witness to loss within the social environment means the privacy of pain must be made public. In making meaning out of one's inner life, what "one has learned and the person's values, beliefs, and psychology" (Rosenblatt and Wallace 71–72) are often shared in narratives, as Bodie's grandmother demonstrates in her account to Herc. Sitting alone in a park with Officer Jimmy McNulty, Bodie struggles with another stage of grief—the burden of depression—as he evaluates the conditions of his life and the frustrations that inform his narrative:

> I feel old. I've been at this since I was thirteen. I ain't never fucked up a count, never stole off a package, never did some shit I wasn't told to do. I've been straight up. But what's come back? . . . They want us to stand up with them, right? But where the fuck they at, when they supposed to be standing by us? . . . This game is rigged, man. We like them little bitches on a chessboard. (4.13)

It is a dark December night in West Baltimore as Bodie, Poot, and Spider work Bodie's corner. Pawns or soldiers, these three men know the game and that they are under attack. The Towers are gone, yet Bodie stands tall on his corner in memory of those he has lost and grieved; the others flee. In full acceptance of his fate, Bodie shouts, "I'm right here!" calling attention to his territory and to his humanity—resisting in vain what Butler calls the "violence of derealization" (33), the exclusion from a hierarchal society that leaves him dead with no one from his community by his side. Social environments of memory are collapsing. In their place, remembrances are being encased in sites of memory until we are ready to look at the footprint of our humanity and face our pain.

III

Twenty-first-Century Television

12

"The Dickensian Aspect": Melodrama, Viewer Engagement, and the Socially Conscious Text

Amanda Ann Klein

One of the most frequently noted features of *The Wire* is its realism or authenticity. The show is compelling television, many critics claim, because it is so "real" (Bowden), because of its "obsessive verisimilitude" (Weisburg) and because it is rooted in "primary sources" (Stanley). This focus on the so-called realism of *The Wire*, however, marginalizes the series' reliance on the codes of melodrama—a mode that is frequently read in opposition to realism—in order to enlist viewer identification. Linda Williams points out that "the word melodrama seems to name an archaic form—what vulgar, naïve audiences of yesteryear thrilled to, not what we sophisticated realists and moderns (and postmoderns) enjoy today" (*Playing* 11–12). Indeed, melodrama, "a broad aesthetic mode existing across many media," is frequently characterized as excessive, old-fashioned, indulgent and in bad taste (Williams, *Playing* 12). In spite of these claims, melodrama has historically been deployed as a means for grappling with moral questions during times of moral uncertainty (Brooks 15). Most great melodramas, like Charles Dickens' *Oliver Twist* (1838), Harriet Beecher Stowe's *Uncle Tom's Cabin* (1852), or Douglas Sirk's *Imitation of Life* (1959), have been produced during periods of social crisis when the balance of power was firmly on the side of those who were determined to abuse it, when the powerless were routinely exploited or manipulated by the powerful, and when arcane laws of social decorum were driving individuals to despair. The sprawling story of *The Wire* was also conceived in a time of interlinked social crises: when the nation's War on Drugs has failed (Season One); its unions are fraudulent, ineffective and dying (Season Two); its political system is irredeemably corrupt (Season Three); its schools are glorified daycare centers (Season Four); and the media is more concerned with selling stories than reporting the news (Season Five). And, like Dickens, Stowe, and Sirk, the creators of *The Wire* rely on melodramatic codes as a method for generating viewer empathy and engagement. Standard conventions of melodrama include a focus on powerless victims, an emphasis on corruption and injustice as the primary source of conflict, and the characters' frustrating inability to effect change around them. These qualities encourage the viewer to experience outrage or indignation over the plight of the victim. These tactics also function to place the weak on a higher moral plane than the powerful (Gaines 169).

Despite their reputation for being emotionally manipulative, escapist and/or improbable, most melodramas seek to uncover some ostensible truth about a social ill and to explain its existence and consequences to the audience. The revelation of that truth is often marked through a visual tableau: a moment in which it is either "in the nick of time" or "too late" for a character with whom the audience has been encouraged to identify (Williams, "Melodrama" 69). For example, throughout Season One, Wallace, a young hopper in the Barksdale organization, has been characterized both as an innocent in need of protection and as a selfless custodian of numerous young orphans, two character traits that encourage the audience to identify with him. When he can no longer tolerate the profitable sadism of the drug trade, Wallace provides testimony to the Baltimore Police Department and then abandons the dangers of city for the relatively safe space of his grandmother's house in "the country." Wallace eventually tires of this quiet life and returns to Baltimore in the season's penultimate episode, a choice that will result in a conventionally melodramatic death scene (1.12). Wallace is killed by his old friends, Preston "Bodie" Broadus and Malik "Poot" Carr, and the two men must look their powerless victim in the eyes before pulling the trigger. Furthermore, Wallace is murdered in the same room where his young charges sleep at night, thus converting this space of innocence and safety into a terrifying and bloody crime scene. This violent tableau serves as a reminder of Wallace's suffering and offers a wordless condemnation of the Baltimore system in which the innocent are passively slaughtered.

The Wire relies on such melodramatic conventions (the powerless victim, the vivid scene of suffering) in order to generate sympathy for characters that may not otherwise deserve it (drug dealers, murderers, corrupt politicians), but it diverges from other socially engaged, melodramatic texts by constantly undercutting its ability to generate viewer affect. Affect—that deeply felt, visceral emotional response on the part of the viewer—is a key feature of the melodrama. It has been argued that this "excessive" viewer engagement with the melodramatic text (usually manifested in the form of tears) acts as a displacement or diversion away from the very real problems addressed by the text. Tears are "always a kind of false consciousness" since they take place when it is no longer possible for the viewer to intervene (Williams, *Playing* 31). In fact, crying may even take the place of action, since it provides the viewer with the satisfaction of having done something on the behalf of the victim. For this reason "melodrama" is frequently deployed as a pejorative term—as a dishonest or "politically constrained" method for engaging audience empathy (Gaines 178).[1]

However, the audience's relationship with the melodramatic text functions somewhat differently in *The Wire*. In this chapter I examine key melodramatic moments in all five season finales—those moments in the narrative when many of the show's key storylines are expected to yield satisfying, emotionally-charged conclusions—as a way to understand how the series engages and then denies or subverts several key melodramatic pleasures. These pleasures include the catharsis of tears, narrative closure, moral legibility, individualistic solutions to social problems, and nostalgia. In this way the series does not engage in the sleight of hand whereby generalized injustices are resolved through the salvation of the individual, or in which moral certainty is offered as a viable solution to the otherwise complex realities of contemporary social problems. Furthermore, because the series constantly challenges its own affect, the audience is left feeling dissatisfied and agitated; anger, sadness and outrage are not purged in a moment of intense emotional release. This uneasy viewing position is a central part of the specific audience engagement that is created by the series.

The Denial of Narrative Closure

In the melodramatic mode, a last-minute rescue or an untimely death (or both) is always a possibility until the final or penultimate scene. Audiences remain riveted to the narrative, waiting to be carried, emotionally and bodily, from moment to moment. This visceral aspect of the melodramatic mode, what James C. Whiting, editor of *The Baltimore Sun* in Season Five, once called "the Dickensian aspect," is particularly useful for engaging audiences in real life issues (5.06). Historically, this reliance on empathy has been central to the melodrama's moral and social project of creating awareness of injustices (Williams, "Melodrama" 42). If empathy is not generated—if the audience is not made to feel—then the melodrama has failed. The Season One finale of *The Wire* generates a powerful inducement to cry throughout the episode, and then undercuts this impulse in its final moments. Although D'Angelo Barksdale was a crew leader for his uncle Avon Barksdale (and thus a murderer), the series' creators made him a possible point of identification by characterizing him as more conflicted than his peers and by revealing more of his life outside of the drug trade. For example, D'Angelo is tortured by the murder of Wallace and bemoans his death in a typically melodramatic fashion, through self-blame and the futile desire to turn back time. "I needed to do more . . . I shoulda done more . . . That's on me," he laments as he sits in an interrogation room, contemplating the loss of time that is so crucial to melodrama (1.13). D'Angelo's guilt over Wallace, combined with his desire to escape his untenable position by becoming "regular folk" has convinced him to turn state's evidence in exchange for his freedom. D'Angelo's decision could potentially shut down the Barksdale crew for good, but by the end of the finale he changes his mind. Significantly, the moment in which he makes this climactic decision is revealed to the viewer through secondary sources and employs several distancing strategies to weaken the scene's potential affect.

The scene begins when Assistant State's Attorney Rhonda Pearlman gets a call from the New Jersey prison where D'Angelo is being held.

Until this point the viewer, like Pearlman, is unaware that her "career fucking case" is in jeopardy. The camera then cuts to the New Jersey jail, and Maurice Levy, the corrupt Barksdale family lawyer, grabs the phone. Rather than remaining to listen as Levy gives Pearlman the bad news that D'Angelo will not be their key witness (thereby destroying their case), the camera continues to pan to the left, past Levy, to reveal D'Angelo seated in a holding room in the background of the frame. Our view of D'Angelo is partially obscured by jail bars and a smudged window and he appears small within the frame. His head hangs low and his mother, Brianna Barksdale, massages his shoulders. When she looks up, as if to meet the camera's gaze, the image immediately cuts to a new scene. This scene adheres to the conventions of the melodrama in that this wordless display offers a "bodily expression of what words could not fully say" (Williams, *Playing* 30) and yet the distance of these bodies from the camera, the iron bars and grimy window that obscure the characters, and their brief time on the screen fails to indulge the viewer's desire for emotional catharsis. Throughout Season One, the viewer watches as a large corkboard charting the inner workings of the Barksdale clan is meticulously filled with photographs of key players. At the end of the season finale the board is empty again, not because the case has been solved, but because it has been closed. The empty board is a visual rendering of loss, for the police department, the District Attorney's office, and presumably for justice. Furthermore, while the episode has led us to believe that Wallace's death was not in vain—that it has encouraged D'Angelo to do the right thing—in the final moments of the episode our desire for justice is thwarted. We want to rail at D'Angelo, to weep in frustration and anger, but the image and tone shift abruptly before these emotions can be properly vented. The end result is that viewer remains dissatisfied.

Moral Ambiguity and the Denial of Nostalgia

In Season Three, impending elections force the police department to doctor its crime statistics in order to salvage funding and to avoid further meddling from the Mayor's office. In response to this pressure and to the near loss of one of his officers in a routine drug bust, Major Howard "Bunny" Colvin hatches his plan for a "Free Zone" (which becomes known as "Hamsterdam"), a defined area where junkies and drug dealers can conduct their business without intervention. The officers under Colvin's command, as well as the drug dealers and junkies, are initially confused and even angry about this radical plan that essentially rewrites the rules of the American War on Drugs. One dealer even asks, "Why you got to go and fuck with the program?" (3.04). The arrangement is illegal and, more problematically, its success depends on the police being able to cultivate the trust of drug dealers and junkies. Indeed, the odds are stacked against Colvin and his project, but Hamsterdam continues to triumph over setback after setback, from the elderly resident who refuses to abandon her home in the Free Zone to the BPD's premature discovery of the arrangement. Hamsterdam succeeds in generating a precipitate drop in crime statistics, offers an opportunity for aid workers to administer clean syringes and other medical care to drug addicts and sex workers, and leaves Baltimore's residential corners free of shootings, drugs, and fear.

Viewers follow the highs and lows of Hamsterdam all season long, becoming increasingly invested in the experiment's success. We have become frustrated with the failures of the police department and, like Colvin, see Hamsterdam as a potential, though radical, solution. But by the season finale, Hamsterdam is crawling with indignant reporters and politicians looking to capitalize on the self-destructive choices of others. We see Deputy Commissioner William Rawls joyfully give the order "Over the top gentlemen!" as he blares "Flight of the Valkyries" from his squad car—a nod to the famous scene in Francis Ford Coppola's *Apocalypse Now* (1979) in which American soldiers appear to enjoy firebombing a village of Vietnamese women and children. In the version of this scene in *The Wire*, hoppers and junkies are tackled mid-run, squad cars corner their prey, and one addict is even pulled out of a vacant building with his pants down. The viewer witnesses an orgy of supposed justice both at the street level and from above, since local news stations have deployed helicopters to capture the story. Had the season ended with this chaotic scene, the viewer could unambiguously mourn the end of Hamsterdam and its pathetic, seemingly unjust destruction.

Instead, the finale concludes with a plain-clothes Colvin surveying the ruins of his idea. Reginald "Bubbles" Cousins, who is there collecting scrap metal, approaches and gestures toward the wreckage surrounding them: "That's somethin', huh . . . Before a dope fiend come down here, cop a little somethin'. Ain't nary a soul hassle 'em. Hoppers and police. They just let 'em be." Colvin smiles and nods, "It was a good thing, huh?" Here is the standard place where melodrama would generate its strongest emotional response from its engaged viewers. All season long we have empathized with Colvin's radical idea, and therefore this shot of an empty, quiet block dotted with piles of bulldozed refuse—a sign announcing "HIV Testing" here, a bed post there—would typically encourage the viewer to mourn the end of Hamsterdam. However, Bubbles does not indulge Colvin's (and by extension, the viewer's) nostalgia. He shrugs and lowers his eyes, remarking, "I'm just saying," as he walks away. The melodramatic mode conventionally allows the viewer to weep with relief over the triumph of justice or anguish over the destruction of it by clearly identifying innocence and villainy. Indeed, Williams argues that the "quest for a democratic, plain-speaking recognition of innocence and guilt, a guilt or innocence that can be spoken out loud and seen by all, is inherently melodramatic" ("Melodrama" 81). *The Wire* subverts the conventional, black-and-white melodramatic morality by refusing to tell the audience whether the loss of Hamsterdam is something to be mourned or celebrated. Even Bubbles, who presumably had the most to gain from the Free Zone that granted him safe access to drugs as well as medical care, is ambivalent. The scene concludes with a long shot that cranes backwards, revealing ever more of the ravaged urban landscape. It is silent except for the rattling of Bubbles's grocery cart over the broken road. Then the shot fades to black without a clear demarcation of right and wrong. This finale lacks an explicit articulation of moral compass, leaving the viewer lost in a thicket of values that they must parse on their own.

The Failure of the Good Benefactor

The introduction of a benefactor (an individual who intervenes in the affairs of a destitute youth) places the burden of the victim's survival on the shoulders of a kind-hearted stranger willing to do good. This plot device is melodramatic since it relieves society of the burden of widespread reform.[2] Society does not need to change as long as a few wealthy individuals intervene in the nick of time. Therefore, it is not surprising that Season Four of *The Wire*, which focuses on how the city of Baltimore continues to fail its children, introduces the melodramatic device of the benefactor or advocate. In this season, the viewer is offered four Dickensian characters for viewer identification: Randy Wagstaff is an orphan; Duquan "Dukie" Weems and Michael Lee are parented by drug addicts; and Namond Brice suffers a lazy mother obsessed with money. The season encompasses many storylines (Professor David Parenti's alternative education experiment, the rise of Marlo Stanfield's empire, the Mayoral elections) but these stories continually return focus to the boys and their fates. It is particularly useful to contrast the storylines of Randy and Namond since their fates are directly tied to the successful or unsuccessful interventions of their adult advocates.

After his foster home is torched as retribution for "snitching," Randy finds himself homeless and once again ensnarled in the system, a victim of fate. Sergeant Ellis Carver, who feels responsible for Randy since the boy only agreed to testify at his urging, spends most of the episode trying to keep Randy out of a group home, but ultimately fails to overcome the bureaucratic child services system. As they approach the group home, Randy tells the dejected Carver, "It's okay. You tried. You don't need to feel bad. Thanks" (4.13). Carver is clearly startled by this exchange, by a 13-year-old attempting to calm the fears of an adult, but Randy's words are not soothing. Instead this conversation highlights Randy's grim acceptance of the status quo; he knows that things do not work out for boys like him. Indeed, soon after his arrival in the home, Randy's bed is vandalized with the words "Snitch Bitch," and his money is stolen. The last shot we are offered is of a group of boys administering him a brutal beating. Carver, however, does not stick around long enough to see Randy's fate as the audience does. Instead he quickly exits the boys' home, climbs into his car and slams the door. The camera captures his movements in a long take and then remains outside the door, observing Carver through the window as he repeatedly pounds the steering wheel with his fists. This scene is a reversal of the melodramatic convention of the benefactor because despite all of Carver's hard work and his genuine concern for Randy, his individualistic solution to the flawed child welfare system fails. It is too late for Randy, and this leaves the audience wondering if it is too late for all the other children Carver has encountered in his job.

Season Four does not conclude with the failure of the benefactor, however, but on the bright, sunny sidewalks of Bunny Colvin's neighborhood. The camera slowly pans from the quiet streets, where the sounds of chirping birds can be heard, to Namond, who eats his breakfast and completes his homework before heading inside his new middle-class home. When he briefly returns to the porch to retrieve his breakfast plate, the sound of rap music can be heard offscreen. Namond looks up to see a black SUV slowly driving past the house. Immediately the viewer is anxious: will Namond be killed, just like Wallace, D'Angelo, Bodie, and all the other young hoppers who expressed a desire to get out of the life? We are relieved when the next shot reveals that the driver is Donut, a 13-year-old car thief and one of Namond's old friends. He waves at Namond, and speeds through a stop sign, nearly hitting another car, before disappearing over the horizon. Donut's presence in this final scene serves as a reminder of Namond's old life as a hustler, of what he has given up, and what he has gained by moving in with the Colvins. Namond smiles and turns to go inside. The closing shot of the finale reveals the same street: in the distance a man and a child cross the street, friends greet each other, and leaves rustle. Namond has been rescued "in the nick of time" and the feeling this intervention provides the viewer is undeniably pleasurable. And yet, this ending is as unsettling as any other season finale: being happy for Namond does not erase the images of Michael losing his soul, Dukie selling heroin on the corner, and Randy being beaten by a group of bullies. Melodrama ideally offers "the hope that it may not be too late . . . that virtue and truth can be achieved in . . . individual heroic acts rather than . . . in revolution and change" (Williams, "Melodrama" 74). Here, we cannot pin our hopes on the success of the individual when so many others are failing.

The Denial of Catharsis

The dialectic between "in the nick of time" and "too late," which causes the viewer to recognize and feel empathy for the plight of the virtuous, is frequently established through the time-honored technique of parallel editing. Audiences are shown two or more events, such as a victim in peril and the victim's would-be savior racing to the scene, which are taking place simultaneously in separate spaces. Parallel editing heightens suspense by expanding screen time and delaying the ultimate resolution of the narrative. Linda Williams adds that the use of parallel editing in the melodrama offers audiences hope that "that there may be still be an original locus of virtue, and this virtue and truth can be achieved in private individuals and individual heroic acts" (*Playing* 35). The closing montages that serve as capstones for each season finale of *The Wire* appear to function in a similar fashion. By stringing together a series of images of major characters, the viewer is given the impression that although it might be "too late" for one character (thus provoking viewer indignation over class- and race-based inequalities), problems are solved "in the nick of time" for others (providing a measure of relief).

The closing montage of the Season Two finale opens with Nick Sobotka walking beside a chain link fence that overlooks Baltimore Harbor (2.12), which had been the source of his family's livelihood and is now the final resting place of his uncle Frank, who was murdered in the previous episode by the Greek's henchmen (2.11). Nick should be hiding out in a witness protection program, and so when the camera pans left to reveal a car driving slowly along the harbor, his death feels imminent. Rather than glimpse Nick's demise, the audience is offered a montage of "too lates": the waterfront is now patrolled by U.S. Marshals and Frank's office sits empty; Ziggy Sobotka, framed in a long shot, looks small and frightened in his orange prison jumpsuit; and Lester Freamon symbolically places a lid on a box of surveillance photographs entitled "Port Investigation 2003," the case that Cedric Daniels and his team had attempted to solve all season long. The most disturbing image of this montage, however, is the last: several pretty young women clumsily exit the back of a cargo container in their high heels and tight jeans, along with boxes of other illegally imported goods. The camera moves in for a close up of their faces, but the women squint and shield their eyes from the glare of car headlights. They are anonymous victims, walking offscreen to a life of indentured prostitution in a Baltimore brothel. The montage then returns to a medium shot of Nick, who wipes away his tears and turns his back to the camera. As he lumbers along the harbor we wait for the gunshot that will end his life, but it never sounds. The camera pans left again to reveal that, for now at least, the road is empty and Nick is safe. But after so many "too lates," Nick's "nick of time" salvation does little to restore the viewer's hope for the future.

The series finale in Season Five also establishes dialectic between "in the nick of time" and "too late." Dukie's final scene is set at night, in the dirty alley by the Arabber's horse stables. The boy and his new mentor are framed in a long shot with both characters in the background of the image, making it difficult to read their facial expressions. The placement of a chair and a horse cart in the mid-ground of the frame further add to this distancing effect. But as the camera slowly tracks to the left, as if it is trying to slink away undetected from this disturbing sight, Dukie tightens a tourniquet and raises a syringe to his arm. We can contrast Dukie's fate with that of another drug addict, Bubbles. His final scene opens with an extreme low angle shot of the basement door that had always been closed to him and has now been opened by his distrustful sister. After enduring the loss of two young protégés, frequent beatings at the hands of street thieves, and a five-season-long battle with heroin, he has suffered enough to purge himself of his sins and to be worthy of this "nick of time" salvation (5.10). The last image of Bubbles shows him seated at the dinner table with his sister and nephew, the light of the setting afternoon sun suffusing the room with a warm glow. This conclusion induces viewers to cry because despite overwhelming odds, Bubbles has achieved sobriety and become a functioning member of society (a fact confirmed by a news story in the *Baltimore Sun*). The improbable has become probable and hope has become reality.

Steve Neale argues that "the longer there is delay [between the introduction of the problem and its resolution], the more we are likely to cry, because the powerlessness of our position will be intensified, whatever the outcome of events, 'happy' or 'sad', too late or just in time" (12). However, as with the Season Two finale, this closing montage does not privilege success over failure, or failure over success. We cannot locate victory in Bubbles's sobriety, Rhonda Pearlman's appointment to a judgeship, or Lester Freamon's blissful retirement because these instances of individuals overcoming the system are placed on the same plane as all of the failures we have just witnessed. This concept is underscored by the use of the opening credit song, "Down in the Hole," as a nondiegetic, acoustic counterpoint to these images. The song is neither celebratory nor mournful, and the viewer's familiarity with it after five seasons emphasizes that there is nothing exceptional about what we are seeing. These snippets of life, the good and the bad, are all equally important and all equally constitutive of the state of Baltimore.

Conclusions: A Different Kind of Viewer Engagement

The Wire employs these various melodramatic tactics in order to enlist viewer empathy and to engage us in its otherwise daunting, sprawling narrative, and yet, as Cheese Wagstaff announces, moments before he is shot in the head in the series finale, "There ain't no back in the day, nigger. Ain't no nostalgia to this shit here" (5.10). And so, after five seasons, we are left to wonder—why enlist our empathy only to push it away? Some television critics have argued that the ultimate message of *The Wire* is that injustice, corruption and suffering are inevitable in urban America and that change is not possible (Sternbergh). Others argue that "individuals are capable of change, but institutions are not" (Ryan, "Full Circle"). But why devote five seasons of television to a show with a message that boils down to "nothing can be done"? Certainly, HBO has built its reputation on television series that subvert classical genre expectations, with the controversial black screen finale of *The Sopranos* (2007) being only one particularly famous example. However, *The Wire* plays with convention neither in order to demonstrate its sophistication or difference from common network fare, nor as a reflection of postmodern storytelling practices. Rather, play with melodramatic conventions is employed in *The Wire* to subvert the passive, satisfied viewing position typically established by the primetime social melodrama. In its place the series constructs an active, socially engaged viewer. As David Simon admits, "My stuff is a hard sell even if a network is doing all it can, particularly since so many Americans regard their television sets as a means of relaxation rather than a means of provocation" ("1st Exclusive").

Writing on Italian Neorealism and its function, theorist and screenwriter Cesare Zavattini has said, "It is not the concern of an artist to propound solutions. It is enough, and quite a lot, I should say, to make an audience feel the need, the urgency, for them" (56). Simon has

Mike Fletcher, the sympathetic young *Sun* reporter, echo these very sentiments in the series finale of *The Wire*. When Fletcher explains to Bubbles what will appear in the article he is writing about him, Bubbles asks, "What good is a story like that?" Fletcher explains, "People will read about it, think about it, maybe see things differently." Fletcher's words are simple and idealistic but they usefully describe the primary achievement of *The Wire* as a series. By watching these stories and characters, and thinking about them, engaged fans, like Fletcher's ideal reader, will begin to see things "differently" (Klein). In *The Wire* the melodrama's passive viewing position is replaced with a more pragmatic one that demands engagement with the social conflicts described in the series, not merely the fictional characters that are animated by them. Viewers may feel sad at the end of a season, and possibly cry, but they will also likely remember their outrage long after the credits have rolled and their tears have dried. It is the urgency that lingers.

Notes

1. Williams disagrees with the idea that emotional climaxes discourage social action: "if tears are an acknowledgement of a hope that desire will be fulfilled then they are also a source of future power; indeed, they are almost an investment in that power" (*Playing* 32).

2. This is also a convention of the social problem film: "The characters and the social conflicts were polarized, the treatment of the social issues subordinated to the emotional conflicts experienced by the protagonists, and the conflicts often resolved through a populist benefactor or through the efforts of an exceptional individual who overcame economic and social constraints in the interests of the community" (Landy 433).

13

It's All Connected:
Televisual Narrative Complexity

Ted Nannicelli

"*The Wire* deserves a Nobel Prize for Literature," remarks *Time* magazine writer Joe Klein in *The Wire Odyssey*, a documentary bonus feature included as part of the program's Season Five DVD set. Much of the critical praise for *The Wire* has not only been equally effusive, but has also invoked literature as a means of praising the show, as well as describing what it does and what sort of an artwork it is.[1] Klein's assertion is particularly interesting because it seems that the highest commendation he can give *The Wire* is to suggest that the show somehow transcends its art form—that it should be considered a work of literature rather than a television program.[2] As rhetoric, Klein's implication is benign puffery. But it belies a demeaning attitude toward television that is insidious when couched in panegyrics upon television for its putatively un-televisual properties.

When critics like Tim Goodman write about the supposed "novelistic approach to storytelling" in *The Wire*, they usually have in mind the show's narrative complexity, its depth of character development, and its astute sociological insight. But these things do not belong solely to the province of literature. According to Wendell Pierce, who plays William "Bunk" Moreland, David Simon "told [the cast] from day one, 'It's a novel.'" But Pierce put it more accurately when he told a journalist that *The Wire* "showed the possibility of television used as an art" (quoted in Wiltz).

Indeed, while the shallow analogies between *The Wire* and literature may garner the show some well-deserved attention, they will not do very much analytic work; they will not help us to understand with any depth or nuance how the show does what so many critics and fans find utterly compelling and innovative. In this chapter, I offer some preliminary analysis of *The Wire*'s innovation as a television program in three important areas— narrative complexity, character development, and social commentary.

A number of television scholars have identified a relatively recent development in television programming—a hybridization of the older, established forms of the series and the serial. Sarah Kozloff summarizes the distinctions between series and serial: "*Series* refers to those shows whose characters and setting are recycled, but the story concludes in each individual episode. By contrast, in a *serial* the story and the discourse do not come to a conclusion during an episode, and the threads are picked up again after a given hiatus" (91). However, most contemporary television scholars recognize that the series and the serial are not binary opposites, but rather opposite ends of a continuum (Allrath *et al.*; Ndalianis). Furthermore, many agree with Robin Nelson's claim that "the dominant form of TV drama today is a hybrid of the series and the serial" (quoted in Allrath *et al.* 6). The language and theories with which these scholars describe the hybridization phenomenon sometimes differ, but for the most part they are talking about the same thing. Following Jason Mittell, I see contemporary television's increasing hybridization and tendency towards serialization as one element of a broader move towards what he calls "narrative complexity."

For Mittell, narrative complexity is "a distinct narrational mode" and "is predicated on specific facets of storytelling that seem uniquely suited to the series structure that sets television apart from film [and, of course, literature] and distinguish it from conventional modes of episode and serial forms" (29). More specifically,

> at its most basic level, narrative complexity is a redefinition of episodic forms under the influence of serial narration—not necessarily a complete merger of episodic and serial forms but a shifting balance. Rejecting the need for plot closure within every episode that typifies conventional episodic form, narrative complexity foregrounds ongoing stories across a range of genres. (32)

To this description, Mittell adds some other common characteristics of narratively complex shows. Most relevant to a discussion of *The Wire* is a lack of explicit storytelling "signposts" or elements of narrative redundancy. Collectively, these features require more active engagement on the part of the viewer (34–38). Mittell suggests that shows like *Dallas* (CBS, 1978–91) and *Hill St. Blues* (NBC, 1981–87) were early incarnations of this narrational mode, which has since evolved and moved towards greater seriality in shows such as *Buffy the Vampire Slayer* (WB, 1997–2001; UPN, 2001–03), and *The Sopranos* (HBO, 1999–2007).

Mittell's conception of narratively complex television offers a good starting point from which to analyze *The Wire*—a show that is, according to skeptical Emmy voters, "so multilayered, so dense" that it is "practically impenetrable to new viewers" (quoted in Levine). Indeed, it is crucial to emphasize the extent to which *The Wire* represents the more radical end of what Mittell has in mind. In the first place, *The Wire* sits far to the serial side of the series-serial continuum. The first episode of the third season, "Time After Time" (3.01), demonstrates this. The episode ends with the following scenes: to Major Howard "Bunny" Colvin's dismay, Officer Thomas "Herc" Hauk and Sergeant Ellis Carver bring in yet another possession and loitering case; Detective Jimmy McNulty reopens the previous year's files, whereupon we see photos of D'Angelo Barksdale and Wallace; Fruit tells Dennis "Cutty" Wise that he is not going to get his drug money back; Colvin rides through his district and is shocked by the depth of its problems when a young teenager tries to sell him drugs.

These final minutes of the episode demonstrate quite a bit about *The Wire*'s overall narrative strategies—particularly with regard to seriality. Clearly the end of this episode raises questions that will not be answered until a future episode; this is typical of narratively complex shows. But in contrast to most other narratively complex shows, this episode offers no narrative resolution whatsoever. This lack of closure should not be overstated, for as television scholar Michael Newman notes about series-serial hybrids (or, as he calls them, "contemporary scripted prime-time serials"), "most typically, certain questions go unanswered episode after episode, but they are not the kind of questions that obstruct narrative clarity" (20). Yet as we see in this example that *The Wire* regularly refuses to offer viewers any sort of episodic narrative closure or even the promise that dangling questions will be answered in the next episode.

In place of narrative closure within an episode, *The Wire* frequently offers another sort of closure identified by Newman: "the unification of themes and motifs into an orderly, integrated whole" (20). The closing scenes of "Time After Time" (3.01) constitute a thematic coda. Herc and Carver's inability to improve upon their inveterate and ineffective methods of policing the corners, McNulty's comment, Cutty's return to the street, and Colvin's patrol tie together and recall the episode's other allusions to the possibility (or impossibility) of reform. Yet rather than contributing to narrative closure, this thematic coda opens up more questions—questions about the possibilities for Councilman Tommy Carcetti to achieve his ambition of reforming the city, for Cutty to adjust to life outside of prison, for Herc and Carver to change the way they do police work, for Colvin to salvage his neighborhoods, and for McNulty not to "do the same shit all over again." More importantly, it opens up a question for which there will be no simple answer: Are our society's largest institutions even capable of reform?[3]

One final observation about the end of "Time After Time" that underscores the seriality and narrative complexity of *The Wire* is that despite the fact that this is the first episode of a new season, the audience is challenged to recall details from the previous season (including the death of D'Angelo) in order to make sense of current developments. In this expectation that viewers follow narrative threads not only across multiple episodes but across multiple seasons, *The Wire* reveals a particularly strong affinity with the narrative strategies of the serial. Furthermore, the number of different narrative threads—from past seasons as well as Season Three—explored in these final minutes of the episode is another indication of narrative complexity. "Multi-threading," a term I borrow from Steven Johnson to describe the multiple layering of narrative threads within and across episodes and series, is another important development in contemporary series-serial hybrids.[4] As Newman notes, series-serial hybrids "are typically ensemble dramas, and each episode has multiple, intertwined plots" (18). He summarizes the standard structure of the series-serial hybrid as follows: "Major plots ('A plots' in teleplay jargon) involving a main character have at least six beats [i.e. scenes], often more. An episode usually has two or more A plots and several B or C plots with a number of small beats each" (18). So, the series-serial hybrid threads together these multiple story lines, and more narratively complex shows will typically contain more threads.

Here again, *The Wire* exhibits more narrative complexity than most other series-serial hybrids. Because the program embraces seriality to such a great degree, it demands that its audience not simply track more narrative threads, but—as the reference to D'Angelo Barksdale in "Time After Time" (3.01) makes clear—that its audience track more narrative threads that reemerge sporadically and circuitously over greater periods of time. This is to say that the measure of narrative complexity cannot simply be how many storylines are threaded through a single episode. Consider "Middle Ground" (3.11). By my count, there are 13 different narrative threads in this episode—some of which overlap within the episode. Although 13 different (sometimes overlapping) narrative threads may seem like a lot for a single episode, this number does not really indicate the depth of narrative complexity the episode contains.

Brother Mouzone's attempt to find Omar Little, and Omar's quest for vengeance against the Barksdale organization are two narrative threads that intersect in this episode. But only the viewer of Season Two understands the complexity of their relationship and the ways in which their narrative threads not only intersect with those of Avon Barksdale and Russell "Stringer" Bell, but relate directly to Avon and Stringer's efforts to double-cross one another. In Season Two, Avon hires Brother Mouzone to help retain territory from Proposition Joe Stewart's drug dealers, unaware that Stringer has an undisclosed agreement with Prop Joe. In order to rid himself of Mouzone, Stringer convinces Omar that his boyfriend, Brandon, was tortured and murdered by Mouzone when in fact Stringer and Avon are themselves responsible. After shooting (but not killing) Mouzone, Omar realizes that Stringer has lied to him, whereupon he embarks on his quest for vengeance against the Barksdale organization. Understanding that Omar was set up, Brother Mouzone tells Stringer that his deal with the Barksdale organization is nullified. At this meeting, Stringer accidentally tips his hand and Mouzone realizes that it was in fact Stringer who crossed him. In short, only viewers who have tracked all of *The Wire*'s narrative threads since the beginning of the show will be attuned to the depth of narrative complexity that underlies many scenes like opening of "Middle Ground" (3.11), in which Brother Mouzone solicits Omar's help to kill Stringer Bell.

David Bordwell has written about such "network narratives" in the cinema and suggested that an increase in the narrative complexity of a film oftentimes requires increased reliance upon the conventions of classical Hollywood storytelling. He concludes that "whatever new shapes degrees-of-separation plots [or muti-threaded narratives] take, most remain coherent and comprehensible, thanks to the principles of causality, temporal sequence and duration, character wants and needs, and motivic harmony that have characterized mainstream storytelling (not just in cinema) for at least a century" (*Hollywood* 100). Kristen Thompson has made similar arguments. She contends that "the increase in the number of plotlines that interrupt each other has made such dramas concomitantly even more dependant on redundancy, dialogue hooks, appointments, deadlines, and, especially emphatically marked dangling causes that can carry over several scenes involving other plotlines" (58).

Although the breadth of empirical data and the depth of their analyses put Bordwell and Thompson on firm ground, *The Wire* indicates that it is possible for increasingly narratively complex television to depend less upon the sort of devices that engender narrative redundancy they hypothesize. Here again, the innovations of *The Wire* need to be framed as developments in the context of television rather than somehow outside of it. To begin with, the amount of recapping the show does is insufficient to bring the casual viewer up to speed. Typically, shows recap—or reiterate pertinent narrative information—in two ways: through lead-in "previously on" segments or in expository dialogue. According to Newman, "in serialized narratives recapping is especially important because of the large quantity of data about the story world that forms the background of any new developments" (18). However, *The Wire* differs drastically from more conventional serialized shows in its use of these two common recapping devices.

Some of the "Previously on *The Wire*" segments seem to attempt to distort past events rather than clarify them. Many of these segments rearrange the temporal order of narrative events from multiple episodes prior to the one that was "previously on." The segments are also striking in what narrative threads they choose to foreground. Consider, for example, the "Previously on *The Wire*" lead-in to "Mission Accomplished" (3.12). The segment starts by recapping Roland "Prez" Pryzbylewski's accidental shooting of a fellow officer. The segment then cuts to Mayor Clarence Royce, Commissioner Ervin Burrell, Deputy Commissioner for Operations William Rawls, and Councilman Carcetti cryptically discussing the idea of "keeping this thing going without calling it what it really is." Here, the viewer unfamiliar with earlier episodes in the season will have no way to know that the "thing" in question is Bunny Colvin's legalization of drugs in Hamsterdam. Instead, the editing of the segment suggests that the "thing" is some sort of conspiracy around the shooting.

The second way shows usually recap narrative information is through expository dialogue. Thompson uses the term "dispersed exposition" to denote "a type of redundancy that seems specific to television" (65). She goes on to analyze the way that recaps of narrative details are embedded in the dialogue of episodes of *Murphy Brown* (CBS, 1988–98), *Bad Girls* (ITV, 1999–2006), and *Fawlty Towers* (BBC2, 1975–79) in order to bring viewers up to speed or ensure their understanding. Dialogue in *The Wire* rarely recaps narrative details for viewers in this way. On the contrary, David Simon and other creators are forthright in their DVD commentary sessions about the pleasure they take in making episodes so dense that viewers may not absorb all of the pertinent information in a single viewing. Throughout Season Three, for example, Baltimore City Councilwoman Euneta Perkins's name is mentioned by a variety of characters—Mayor Royce, State Delegate Odell Watkins, Carcetti, and prospective City Councilwoman Marla Daniels—in discussions of how her increased detachment from the political scene may be a help or a hindrance to their own political agendas. But even the most dedicated viewer will be unable to recall what Perkins looks like or how exactly she fits into the narrative. This is because Perkins does not appear in the flesh until the final episode of the season!

Characters on *The Wire* may refer fleetingly to events that viewers have seen in previous episodes, but this is rarely cause for detailed recapping. Imagine a viewer who begins watching *The Wire* with the first episode of Season Four, "Boys of Summer" (4.01). One of the major narrative threads of this season involves Prez beginning to teach at a West Baltimore middle school. Through exposition, the viewer learns that Prez used to be a Baltimore Police officer, but does not find out that he has left the force because of his fatal shooting of another officer (although this information is revealed in "Previously on *The Wire*" segments). Even more significantly for dedicated viewers, the memory of Prez pistol-whipping and blinding a young teenager in Season One hangs over the whole of Season Four. This crucial narrative detail—which colors the viewer's understanding of Prez's entire teaching experience—is never once recapped either dialogically or in a Season Four "Previously on *The Wire*" segment.

Dialogue in *The Wire* is more likely to hold subtext than it is to overtly recap narrative details or provide what Johnson calls "flashing arrows" pointing towards the show's themes. Consider for example, the dialogue in the final part of the balcony scene with Stringer and Avon after each has crossed the other in "Middle Ground":

Stringer: You know I don't take my work too seriously.
Avon: That's right. It's just business.
              Stringer gives Avon an extended look.
Avon: Us, motherfucker.
              They embrace.
Stringer: To us, man. (3.12)

Only the viewer who recalls that Stringer's justification of selling out Avon to Colvin in a prior scene was "it's just business" will understand Stringer's look at this moment. The tight framing of Stringer's face and the extended duration of the shot may cue viewers to think that Avon has said something important or that for some other reason this is a weighty moment. But the viewer also needs to recognize the parallelism of the lines of dialogue to understand Stringer's emotional arc fully. Moreover, only the viewer who recalls that in previous episodes in which Avon was imprisoned, the two men put their hands up against either side of the prison glass and said "us," will have a sense of how hollow these words are now.

Some readers may justifiably wonder what room all of this narrative complexity leaves for character development. I would argue that the narrative complexity of *The Wire* actually promotes development of character. Layering multiple, intersecting narrative threads as a narrative strategy gives the creators leeway to branch off from an "A plot" and follow a less prominent character or narrative thread without giving viewers the sense that the major storyline has been interrupted. In the context of a single-protagonist, three-act structure narrative, most viewers would not accept these interruptions of major plotlines for the sake of character development. But, ironically, what may strike some viewers as the more plot heavy complex narrative structure of *The Wire* gives the show the freedom to explore character in more depth because it forces viewers to change their narrative expectations as they realize that the show creates a vast and complex social network.

The show's serial format allows it to track these less prominent narrative threads for extended periods of time across multiple episodes and even seasons. In Season Three, for example, we follow Detective Kima Greggs outside of the Major Crimes Unit and see tensions rise between her and her partner, Cheryl, over Kima's anxieties about parenthood and commitment. We track this narrative thread in very brief and occasional scenes, and it has little bearing on more prominent storylines, but it allows for an exceptional amount of character development. It helps us to understand Kima's increased hostility towards authority, as well as the various parallels that are made between her and McNulty over the course of Season Three. Perhaps most significantly, the serial form of *The Wire* permits Kima's character arc to unfold slowly across the duration of the series until, in Season Five, she comes to embrace motherhood and she takes a stand against the wayward police tactics of McNulty and Detective Lester Freamon.

Earlier I suggested that, in *The Wire*, dialogue is rarely used as a tool for narrative exposition. In many cases, this is because the creators refuse to sacrifice character development for the sake of narrative redundancy (or, for that matter, clarity). Recall the pre-credits opening scene (in industry jargon, the "cold-open") of "Boys of Summer" (4.01). Because this is the first episode of a new season, one might expect this scene to feature a prominent character—say McNulty—offering some sense of what has happened leading up to where Season Four begins or, perhaps, where it might be going. Instead, we have a scene in which Felicia "Snoop" Pearson buys a nail gun in a hardware store.

Clerk: I see you got the DeWalt cordless . . .
         He pauses to assess her.
         Your nail gun—DeWalt 410.
Snoop: Yeah . . . Trouble is if you leave it in a truck for a while, need to step up and use the bitch, the battery don't hold up, you know?

The clerk describes the finer points of a few of the powder-activated models he sells, and then:

Clerk: The DX 460 is fully automatic with a .27 caliber charge. Wood, concrete, steel to steel—she'll throw a fastner into anything. And for my money, she handles recoil better than the Simpson or the P3500. Now, do you understand what I mean by recoil?
Snoop: Yeah, the kickback. I'm with you.
Clerk: That's right.
Snoop: .27 caliber, huh?
Clerk: Yeah. Not large ballistically, but for driving nails it's enough. Any more than that, you'd add to the recoil.
Snoop: Man, shit. I seen a tiny-ass .22 round-nose drop a nigga plenty of days, man. Motherfuckers get up in you like a pinball, rip your ass up. Big joints, though? Big joints, man, just break your bones, you say, "Fuck it." I'm gonna go with this right here, man. How much I owe you?

Rather than elucidating anything about the prominent storylines of the show, the dialogue in this scene obfuscates. The creators have suddenly dropped the viewer into the middle of a hardware store in Baltimore to listen to an authentic conversation about nail guns without any narrative signposts whatsoever. Remember, too, that on an initial viewing, much of what Snoop says may go unrecognized or misunderstood by viewers unfamiliar with her cadence and diction. Now, the nail gun is not immaterial to one of Season Four's "A plots," for it turns out that

Snoop and her partner, Chris Partlow, use it to board up vacant houses where they dump the bodies of their murder victims. But the scene in which Snoop actually buys the tool is hardly essential to this narrative thread. Rather, the scene functions to reveal Snoop as a character within a social context. We get a glimpse of Snoop's world in this scene, but, more importantly, we also get a sense of the extreme disconnect between her world and the world of the white, middle-class store clerk, who is baffled by the end of their conversation.

In this example, we have what is perhaps the most deservedly acclaimed result of the narrative complexity of *The Wire*—examinations from a variety of perspectives of the way societal contexts shape characters and their arcs. As Martha Nochimson puts it in her discussion of the importance of seriality to *The Sopranos*:

> seriality in television incorporates into mass culture the experimental modern narrative techniques that bring relativity to bear on a subject . . . American mass culture has been profoundly hostile to ambiguity and nuanced ethical perspectives, but these are the essence of televisuality by virtue of what serial television does to narrative structure. Television, when permitted to operate along the grain of its narrative tendencies, builds the nuances and ambiguity of relativity into the narrative.

While *The Wire* offers the hope of redemption for some of its characters (notably Bubbles and Cutty), it simultaneously shows us that societal and institutional forces make the classical Hollywood arc of the goal-oriented protagonist something that is not possible for everyone. In Season Five, we see that only a year or so after his first appearance in "Boys of Summer" (4.01), Randy Wagstaff has been—in Prez's words— "chewed up by the system" and transformed from a bright, motivated, and warm child into a hardened thug (5.06). Character arcs in *The Wire* are also abruptly halted by so-called "random violence." But when Kenard murders Omar (5.08), the fastidious viewer recognizes that the violence is not random but cyclical. In Season Three, we have seen Kenard and his friends "playing Omar" after witnessing a shoot-out between Omar's crew and Barksdale soldiers (3.03).

The immobility of society's largest institutions, *The Wire* posits, not only ensures that some characters will not be able to progress within society, but affirms that they are part of much larger cycles, whereby the individual personalities or characters may change but the roles available remain the same. By the end of Season Five, Bubbles is able to find his way off the street, but the social conditions that let him fall so far in the first place still exist for people in his socio-economic group. Thus, when another formerly bright and motivated student, Duquan "Dukie" Weems, hustles Prez for drug money (5.10), the viewer understands that Dukie will be the next iteration of Bubbles. But whereas there is now some glimmer of hope for Bubbles, the final shot we get of Dukie—in which he is shooting up in an alley—conveys only despair. Having followed Dukie's narrative thread across two years, we recognize that this is not the result of a classical Hollywood protagonist making poor decisions, but rather of social forces that will create a Bubbles or a Dukie over and over again.

In *The Wire*, narrative structure, character development, and social commentary are not disparate elements, but rather deeply intertwined—indeed, the show's ability to create rich characters and offer astute social commentary stems from its narrative complexity. Furthermore, I have argued that *The Wire*'s narrative complexity is not "borrowed" from other arts, but arises from the show's innovative use of serial narrative techniques in a televisual format. *The Wire* has not, of course, invented serial narratives and it bears similarities to serials in other types of narrative art (literature, in particular). But serial narratives, are not inherently linked to a particular medium, so it makes little sense to talk about *The Wire* as being novelistic when in fact the show creatively appropriates and adapts a well-worn narrative device for a new use in a different art form.

Notes

1. For example, Tim Goodman of *The San Francisco Chronicle* writes, "Over the course of its first three seasons, *The Wire* on HBO has been one of the great achievements in television artistry, a novelistic approach to storytelling in a medium that rewards quick, decisive, and clear storytelling."

2. The irony—of which Klein and the critics such as Jason Weisberg, who are fond of comparing *The Wire* to a nineteenth-century (more specifically, Dickensian) novel, seem unaware—is that, as David Bordwell points out, it was common through the nineteenth century for critics and artists to describe the novel in terms of older (and more esteemed) art forms—notably painting and theatre. Even for Charles Dickens himself, "every writer of fiction . . . writes, in effect, for the stage" (quoted in Bordwell, *Narration* 7).

3. The show does offer an unequivocal answer to this question by the end of the season, which is apparent as Colvin surveys the wreckage of his bulldozed social experiment in "Mission Accomplished" (3.12).

4. For discussions of muti-threading in Hollywood, see Evan Smith, as well as Bordwell's *Poetics of Cinema*.

14

Dislocating America: Agnieszka Holland Directs "Moral Midgetry"

Kevin McNeilly

Renowned Polish expatriate filmmaker Agnieszka Holland has directed three episodes of *The Wire*: "Moral Midgetry" (3.08), "Corner Boys" (4.09) and "React Quotes" (5.05). As a non-American helming a television program that is, as its creator David Simon puts it, "rooted in the logic and ethos of a second-tier city, of a forgotten rust-belt America" (Alvarez 10), Holland is admittedly out of place, a foreigner. But this sense of unresolved displacement closely informs her directorial approach to the fraught American content of *The Wire*. The Baltimore depicted in the series consists of characters and places shaped by a fundamental estrangement. Holland's visual tactics, particularly in "Moral Midgetry," intensify the challenges of representing those forgotten persons. I want to present a close reading, a close watching, of that episode in order to draw out the ethical imperative: the demand that we regard and treat each other humanely, that underlies Holland's unflinching, fricative television.

A distinctive sense of dislocation, with its attendant textures of alienation and discomfort, imprints itself on her work both for film and for television. The lost, stifled, and misidentified children of *Olivier Olivier* (1992), *The Secret Garden* (1993), *A Girl Like Me* (2007), or even *Washington Square* (1997, based on the Henry James novel) find counterparts in the corner boys and drug runners of *The Wire*; D'Angelo Barksdale's doomed struggle for self-worth, within and against his family and friends, is not far removed from Jewish teenager Solly Perel's compromised humanity in *Europa Europa* (1990), as Solly conceals himself among the Nazi Youth he ardently admires and reviles. Complicity, for Holland, is not a moral exception. Solly, like Brianna Barksdale or Stringer Bell, isn't ever subject to Holland's unqualified judgment. Instead, her cinema traces a character's compromises and inconsistencies, focusing on difficult moments of their tenacious humanity, when the necessity to live outweighs programmatic absolutism, fixed ideology, or authoritarian dictate. As Holland's viewers, we are implicated in tangles of disavowal, allegiance, and betrayal; we are invited to see mirrored in their self-scrutiny something of our own troubled connections to our world, as both onlookers and living participants.

Holland says that she prefers a "disorienting" cinema—not packed with dizzying or shocking visuals but "demanding," Maria Stalnaker argues, "a re-examination of traditional representations" of the ways Holland's audiences and her characters take their world for granted (316). If *The Wire* is "rooted" in "the forgotten," as Simon suggests, then it can be understood as an intervention in the self-contradictory claims to place and citizenship (or even personhood) made by the lost and forgotten people whom the civil order cannot begin to recognize or serve. All Americans in *The Wire*, no matter how entrenched in the civil order, appear as essentially displaced persons. Barksdale or McNulty, whatever side of the Baltimore drug war you are on, *The Wire* sees you and hears you partially and brokenly as a stranger to yourself. (We could recall the many misfired forms of surveillance and mistaken interpretations throughout the show's five seasons, our broken and incomplete view epitomized by the image in the title credits of the cracked lens of a video camera.) This estrangement is exactly Holland's turf. She is the quintessential nonresident cinéaste; she lives, films, and writes, as Stalnaker puts it, "in translation" (314), consistently troubling cultural and national boundaries that define the ways human beings craft their sense of place. Holland's work unsettles.

Before directing *The Wire*, Holland worked a bit in American television, helming several episodes of *Cold Case* (CBS, 2003–present), but more notably directing the made-for-TV movie *Shot in the Heart: I Was Gary Gilmore's Brother* (2001) for HBO. The producer of *Shot in the Heart*, Nina Kostroff Noble, drew Holland to the attention of David Simon. Holland was keen to be a part of *The Wire*, which she has described as "far more stylistically and thematically courageous than most Hollywood movies" and has compared to a "great American novel" (quoted in Baker, "New Frontier"). After shooting *The Secret Garden*, Holland describes herself as having "an allergic reaction to the working methods of the American studio," unable and unwilling to accommodate the commercial pressures of that "system" (Jenkins). If her work studies situations of moral or existential compromise, Holland rarely compromises her own hard-eyed vision, and never turns her lens away from those troubling moments of selling oneself short; it is toward such moments, in fact, that Holland's interest as a filmmaker is most forcefully directed. Her approach, she says, is to "try to capture an original, sensual, visual truth that works for each story." Because her subject matter often intensifies the loss of various cultural, social, or moral bases upon which any claims to truth can be made by her characters, the nature of that "visual truth" needs to be carefully understood as predominantly a kind of critical scrutiny: an objectification of the crumbling of various objective grounds of knowing.

The best way to understand this approach is to think of Holland not so much as a writer, but as an engaged reader. She made *The Secret Garden*, a sweet-tempered children's film that initially appeared out of keeping with her typical post-Holocaust subject matter, because Frances Hodgson Burnett's novel "was my favorite book as a child, so when I was asked to make my first film for an American studio I decided to go back to this story I loved, and it gave me strength to impose my vision while working in this whole new way, in America" (Jenkins). Films, for Holland, emerge from text, and in particular from the act of reading. Discussing her Henry James adaptation in a Polish interview, Holland claims, "I am a reader and certainly know him better and have a deeper connection to him than many other American directors" (quoted in Stalnaker 327). What she means by claiming this connection, however, isn't some pretense to authority, but an identification with the sort of reading of America in which James himself engages. As a critical, visual reader, she scrutinizes aspects of a broken America, and finds the means both to destabilize and to rework her viewer's presumptive perspectives.

The opening scene of "Corner Boys" (4.09), the second episode Holland directed, gestures toward alternative ways of seeing, a reorientation of perspective based on the debunking of institutionally sanctioned structures of representation. In the first three seasons, these structures were depicted principally as the buildings and other compromised urban spaces that came to represent, for the smugly moral mayor's office, the dissolution of a viable life, but in Season Four this intersection of social authority with cultural reality happens in a pedagogical context. Roland "Prez" Pryzbylewski has made a career shift from police work to teaching in a public school. When Prez presents the narrative for a math problem on the chalkboard to his students, he has his idiom corrected—his highfalutin' term "distributed" gets changed to the more direct "gives out" that his students can understand.

Holland's adoption of a busy, mobile, embedded point-of-view in this scene emphasizes the distractedness and unruliness of the classroom, as Prez fails to hold his students' attention. When he asks for a solution to the problem, one of the students, Calvin, gives him the right answer, not because he has worked out the math, but because he has in fact paid closer attention to the material realities of the room and his teacher's physical habits. Calvin knows the right answer because he sees the "dinks" around it on the board—the places where, in the previous class, Prez has touched the board with his chalk or his finger, next to the right answer. This is still a form of reading: not of texts or images (representational schemas like math word-problems), but of people, of the ways in which human beings interact bodily with their surroundings. Importantly, Holland cuts to a close-up of a student's notebook in which the "dinks" are reproduced in pen around the right answer; what we see, effectively, is a new way of writing, closer to graffiti than to note-taking, in which the inarticulate jots and scribbles, the waste scrawls around the proper language of the "correct" answer, begin to assume meaning. We see, in miniature, a brief return of the hand-made, unkempt, abject mess of "people" to the pristine representational surface of the blank page. If Holland understands her vision primarily as that of a proactive reader, then here we see her start to unfold the visual tactics of her reading style, of how to see differently.

Holland's way of seeing is primarily micrological, focused on small, momentary details that unfold into her larger project, to alter how we watch each other. This practice of close looking seems appropriate to television as a medium, given for example that *The Wire* is made for the small screen, even to the extent of retaining standard television's 4:3 aspect ratio, rather than opting for 16:9 "widescreen" which at the very least would imply an attempt to imitate the big screen spectacle of theatrical films. *The Wire* operates in the small, and Holland's direction of "Moral Midgetry" (3.08) exploits this micrological mode of visual attention fully. Opening in "Hamsterdam," the drug-dealing enclave created by Major "Bunny" Colvin's experiment in harm-reduction policing, the first scene depicts two uniformed police officers in long shot sitting on the hood of their car, one reading a newspaper, the other being talked at by a young girl and clearly not listening; the focus pulls in close, and we see a packet of drugs change hands across the foreground. This brief hand-off concentrates Holland's own focus on miniatures: she focuses in close, drawing a line of sight toward the camera. It is important to acknowledge the significance in this episode of the work of the director of photography, Eagle Egilsson; Holland plays aggressively with how we look and what we see, and her camera needs to be mobile, shifting, attentive—an unflinching directness Egilsson's careful cinematography delivers.

This opening scene also lays out a local human geography, a tangle of fleeting, fluid interactions among a plurality of people and perspectives, moving like molecules within a contained chaos. Dealers, junkies, and others go through doorways, like inset versions of the television screen's rectangular frame, like actors entering and exiting a dramatic stage. As embedded observers, courtesy of the fluid ground-level camera, we remain on the street exterior for a minute or so, looking on as black-market commerce swirls around us. In one passing moment we witness two youths carry a third outdoors as a landlord, or a dealer, complains "I saw his nuts!" There are some things, apparently, that shouldn't be seen, codes of conduct organic to the new, tolerated form of community emerging from the Western District precinct's permissiveness.

Those codes are at once articulated and suppressed in Colvin's subsequent reports to the deputy commissioner—texts that provide a narrative arc in facts and figures, to overlay on the city's politically motivated demand that the murder-rate be radically reduced in the district. His reports are not "cooked" or fictionalized, he says, but represent an accurate account of an implausibly steep decline in violent crime in the West, a decline that seems to be a direct and immediate result of the surreptitious creation of Hamsterdam following the major's unsanctioned initiative.

The scene of his latest report, about half way through the episode, begins with the camera panning up across a pair of computer screens with a "Baltimore COMSTAT" screensaver that immediately shifts to a multicolored city map. The same image appears behind Colvin (who is presenting statistics to the deputy commissioner), linking foreground and background, reversing the focal movement that we followed in the episode's opening sequence back along a centrifugal sightline, now shifting from working hands (in this case, indicated metonymically by the sound of finger-taps on the keyboard just out of frame) to uniformed cop. Colvin isn't looking down reading his paper but looking up from his lectern, explaining the written notes to us. We are still in the same eye-level embedded position, this time looking over his audience's shoulders, but our relationship to police surveillance and intervention has changed. Now, instead of presenting itself as an unregulated pocket of disregarded humanity, created to keep the rest of Baltimore (statistically) safer, Hamsterdam becomes an unmentionable site of ethical intervention. This is what Colvin, with a veneer of astute political correctness, describes as "an intensive reach-out to the community," an unmapped and unnamable urban space that essentially makes policing work better.

When the deputy commissioner wants to have his people audit the Major's figures, Colvin tells him to "pull everything," and affirms that his numbers "will stand" any scrutiny. Colvin has, of course, pulled something of a fast one, since his tactics are hardly regulation, but the numbers themselves, what the commissioner's office understands as "facts," are irrefutable. This scene offers us a moment of collision between absolute clear-sightedness, in the guise of clean-lined computerized representations of tendencies and percentages, and absolute blindness, in the complete erasure and silencing of the human hubbub in which we were first immersed.

Those perspectives collide, however, only for us; within the narrative framework of the episode, they miss each other entirely. And missed connections are exactly what Holland's direction aims to emphasize. In both scenes, reading produces disengagement: the officer reads his paper so he doesn't have to look around him or do his job, while Colvin reads out his figures to keep the administration from finding out about Hamsterdam. How exactly does Holland's visual style here invite us to watch as readers, to interpret what we see in front of us? This incommensurability of perspectives is established not only with the officers willfully ignoring the need for them to intervene in the human mess before them, but also in the various relationships we glimpse, fleetingly, among the dealers and junkies roaming the street before our eyes. A dealer leans into a customer's car-window, crossing a visual threshold, to ask "How y'all doin' today?" while his runner fetches the drugs. When the female buyer counters, "No offence, but can we just get the 8-ball?" the dealer nods and draws back out, apologizing "A'ight, a'ight, just being social." Passing cars and pedestrians cross the image foreground, interrupting our visual access to the exchange. We are repeatedly reminded of the impediments between people. The "social" character of the Hamsterdam experiment (which appears to be working as a harm-reduction strategy) also remains fraught with alienated human relationships.

When this same dealer is tricked by the fake prospect of making easy money, he passes out of the visual ken of the apathetic police through a dark doorway, where he has his money stolen and his mouth, hands, and feet duct-taped. We subsequently see an image of the closed door, cut into a scene of the two officers who describe the ODs and other business-as-usual of the drug trade, but who have not noticed anything. When the dealer crawls like a worm back out onto the step, an image that suggests abject dehumanization, Sergeant Ellis Carver rushes up and pulls the tape from his mouth, only to be cursed: "God damn, can't you get a fucking police when you need one?" The irony is thick and obvious, but it bears remembering that this isn't merely a case of "moral midgetry" as the episode title states, but it also enacts a deeply embedded contradiction in the project of serving and protecting itself, in the work of surveillance as social rehabilitation that is the city police mandate. What we are and are not capable of seeing invites us to reconsider, via the television screen, the visual tactics of police-work, of the gaze of the law as both the imperative and the impediment to positive change.

This reconsideration is carried forward in the subsequent scene, in which Hamsterdam's robbery victims—all dealers—come into a police station to make complaints and to identify the perpetrators who stole their drug money. This action switches them ironically from their normal roles as criminals. The dealers play around with the computer's facial drawing software, the Make-a-Face. Apparently, they are better at using it than the police: "How do you know how to do this?" Officer "Herc" Hauk asks them. "How do you don't know how to do this?" they reply, tossing his incredulity back at him by inverting his smug question. The unreliability of witnessing quickly comes into play, as they stop attempting to be accurate and, at Herc's bemused insistence, begin cartooning, trying to "Chinese up them eyes like Beyoncé" and to turn the procedural aid of the Make-a-Face into a fantasy.

This duplicity plays against a later scene, where Prez uses FBI computer software to blow up a video image brought in by McNulty and Detective Kima Greggs. Like the dealers playing at being upright citizens, Prez toys with his buddies, pretending not to know what he is doing with the upscale technology, then quickly turns his obvious facility with the equipment into a comedy by parodying the voiceover from an imaginary superhero action film. He punctuates each sentence with a keystroke, blowing up the image of a car license plate further as his voice builds in mock intensity:

Uh oh, nothing there. It's so tiny. No mere mortal can . . . Ohhh. You see what he just did? What? He did it again! . . .Who is this man? Where does he come from? Can anybody stop him? Please don't hurt us. My eyes, my eyes, it's so big and clear and bright!

Like the dealers with the Make-a-Face, Prez draws on the language of celebrity and movie glamour, exaggerating playfully while apparently distilling pertinent, incriminating fact from the surveillance tape—a version of a wire that, for once, does not appear to have failed or been misconstrued. But the fictionalizing in which this technological clarity is couched suggests that it is more about showing off, about what feats of visual acuity Prez can perform, than about the ethical demands of police work. Prez becomes a surrogate for the director here, given that Holland's approach depends on tactics of refocusing and reframing, of looking closely in order to disorient. However, Prez's attention is drawn not to people but to signs and markers: identifications rather than identities; numbers, names and representations that are legible to the system and that can be used to close out an investigation.

In the background of the scene with the mock-visionary Prez, we glimpse McNulty on the phone to "Mama Barksdale," Brianna, as he pursues the officially closed case of the apparent suicide of her son D'Angelo. This leads directly to an intimate scene at the center of the episode that concentrates its visual and thematic elements, suggesting— partially, uncertainly, as is the way with *The Wire*—a contingent answer to the question of what we watch for. McNulty's interview with Brianna offers a decisive moment of catharsis and disclosure. Holland's stagings often work through instances of quiet intensity, points that say much more, with more subtlety, than they might seem. Her visual practice concentrates on small points of revelation, when we have our way of seeing incrementally reoriented. In this scene, Holland focuses not only on visual forms, or on reframing other images within her camera's field of view (here, photographs from D'Angelo's autopsy), but also redirects our attention to the reactive face of the dead teen's mother, asking us to read her looks, to watch her expression for signs of feeling as she realizes her complicity in her son's death. More importantly she realizes that McNulty sees her for who she is, a mother who has betrayed her own child, a role she never wants to admit she has played. ·

The scene opens outside the door of the interview room, as we watch McNulty cross the threshold into the enclosed space, entering a windowed cubicle that mimics the box casing of an analogue television set. Instead of following McNulty in, the camera tracks left along the partition, outside the room, trailing McNulty's obscured shape in the corrugated glass. Our vision is impaired and slashed rather than enabled by these windows, a directorial tactic that, by interfering with our line of sight, draws attention to the visual processes of how we are engaged as viewers. The blockage is instantaneously cleared, however, as the scene abruptly cuts to inside the room. Brianna and McNulty talk about

D'Angelo, but Holland reworks the over-the-shoulder, shot/reverse-shot juxtaposition of points-of-view we might expect from filmed dialogue. We start over Brianna's left side, laying the basis for this visual set-piece. When McNulty first enters the room, we watch him from just behind Brianna's shoulder, looking slightly up; the focus immediately moves from her raised arm and hand—which will now remain blurred, in shots from this perspective, for the rest of the scene—to McNulty's face. Behind McNulty, the horizontal striations on the window mimic bars and graphs; there is a paper map of Baltimore pinned up behind Brianna, overlaying a grid pattern on urban geography, while the metal blinds on the outer window across the room also echo this rational, rectilinear form. Those neat geometries are disrupted by the presence of human bodies, as the actors move through the frame. When McNulty and Brianna begin to talk, for example, we don't change to McNulty's point-of-view to look back at Brianna. Instead, the camera is positioned as if viewing the exchange from another chair at the table; our eye-line is in fact slightly lower than the seated Brianna's. The viewer is located as a secondary, diminished onlooker, but is also indicated as a participant, present at the table.

This bodily closeness becomes increasingly relevant to what Holland wants to suggest by reorienting our attention. When the camera cuts away from Brianna's face to regard McNulty again as he begins to disclose the details of D'Angelo's file, the perspective shifts back to the first over-the-shoulder shot; instead of offering us a clean, well-crafted image, Holland has Brianna's out-of-focus and slightly moving left hand continue to block the lower part of the frame and obscure McNulty's torso, as a distraction. This visual interference could easily be taken as sloppy film-making, or perhaps to suggest the deliberately rough-hewn textures of documentary realism, appropriate to the gritty visual style of *The Wire*. But this tactic does much more here than merely support a general theme of dissolution or urban decay. This moment of blurring and disruption offers a careful visual echo of the opening scene, in which the image of a police officer leaning back with reading-matter near to hand—McNulty holds a mug of tea, with the case-file folder on the desk beside him—is interrupted by a blurred, African American hand. In the opening scene, the focus pulls back to the dealers on the street, and we lose the image of the police in a haze; in the interview scene, a reversal of that refocusing happens only when McNulty enters, but we never refocus on that hand. Blurred images of Brianna's body repeatedly thwart any attempt to picture McNulty neatly in the frame: when he walks in front of Brianna to drop a teabag in the wastebasket, the camera passes behind her head as it follows his movement, briefly blocking him out entirely. D'Angelo, McNulty recounts, purportedly hanged himself with a belt on a doorknob; images of doors as both impediments and thresholds, as barriers and frames, have permeated this episode. McNulty explains that this scenario isn't possible: D'Angelo was in fact strangled—by human hands—and has been badly framed for his own killing. The brutal physicality of his death, and the realization that his narrative isn't as neatly closed as the police department wants, is corroborated visually in this scene by the refusal of human bodies, particularly Brianna's, ever to leave the frame cleanly.

The need to arrive at an explanation of D'Angelo's death pushes Brianna to question meaning and plausibility, cause and effect in D'Angelo's story: "What are you saying?" she asks, and McNulty, like the dealers in the Make-a-Face scene, merely throws the question back at her: "What am I saying?" D'Angelo's murder was sanctioned by the Barksdale leadership, but this admission, the only possible explanation, is both unspeakable and untenable in the illusory scheme of family bonds to which Brianna clings. (Brianna: "Avon and D was family." McNulty: "Family. Right.") Her love for her son, McNulty implies, as well as her brother's beneficent leadership, can only be a fiction.

"This is just you talking, right?" Brianna asks, reducing the apparent factuality of McNulty's account to mere words. As she stands up to leave, McNulty opens the file on the table, and our point-of-view is momentarily doubled. At first, we look around the blurred left half of her body, at approximately waist-height, mimicking the seated perspective of the earlier shot, but then the perspective quickly identifies with hers, as we look down at the photos of D'Angelo's bruised neck and body. The camera cuts briefly back to our initial position, and we see her eyes move down, directed to the photos. We see the contents of the file itself only briefly, with the autopsy Polaroids laid out in a quadrilateral grid, but the grid itself tilted and skewed obliquely across the right angles of the screen.

We look for a trace of something in Brianna's face, something McNulty discloses more fully, when Brianna asks him why he didn't come to her with this information before. McNulty's response is cold: "Honestly? I was looking for somebody who cared about the kid. I mean, like I said, you were the one who made him take the years, right?" Richard Price's dialogue, in the guise of the colloquial, provides the cue for Holland's direction here. Holland is also honestly looking for somebody who cares, and wants to enact a particular way of looking as a form of care, of ethical engagement. The angled and disruptive visuals of the scene, while certainly subtle and brief, invite a form of seeing as reading, as a mode of disclosure that doesn't lay claim to truth in appearances or ideologies but rather in the tactical debunking of those false fronts, those put-ons. McNulty, compromised though he may be, asserts—by having Brianna reread herself and what she has told her son to do—the possibility that care may not be merely a rhetorical ploy, a ruse to bring down the Barksdales.

The presence of those unruly, living bodies in those grids and boxes, bodies that won't be contained except violently by institutional structures and unjust moral codes, suggests that care remains as a kind of abject residue, an embodied connection that can't ever be overwhelmed or enclosed. As the camera moves in closer on Brianna's face, we see her nostrils flare, her mouth tremble, a tear run from her left eye. While it would be easy to overplay this reaction, Holland and actress Michael Hyatt focus, literally, on the cracks in appearances, the momentary upwellings of feeling that play across the tightly guarded surface of the face. What the close perspective wants us to do, really, is to read Brianna's visage, to look for some sign that she is not the horrifyingly unfeeling mother that McNulty suggests she had to be. We read, in Holland's view, not necessarily for sense, but for its opposite, for what exceeds the symbolic strategies of containment. What Holland's micrological reading tactics emphasize isn't arriving at an understanding of what can be said. Rather, it is opening up language and sight to the unsaid and the unsayable.

The final scene of this episode, a duet between Stringer and Avon, extends and adapts this closely attentive visual process. "We gotta talk," Stringer tells Avon, who has been holding court in an old armchair and telling his cohorts about the need to get back to old times to fight Marlo Stanfield. Stringer is still in his suit, while Avon, who has just had a wound stitched up with rawhide, is in a white undershirt and jeans.

The camera moves around the two, taking up a variety of perspectives, observing them from the positions that the members of Avon's inner circle have just vacated. At one point early in the exchange, there is a shot of Stringer, at a medium distance, over Avon's left shoulder. In the background, behind Stringer's right shoulder, we see Avon's image, slightly out of focus, reflected in a small rectangular mirror over a sink, creating a sort of embedded screen, in which we see the conventional reverse shot for the dialogue, miniaturized. They argue over what Stringer claims is Avon's proclivity for indiscriminate murder, at the end of an episode that has emphasized the decline of the murder rate in the Western District. Avon derides Stringer's masculinity, suggesting that he hasn't got the hardness to "snatch a life," which leads Stringer to confess his complicity in D'Angelo's murder. "You want to talk that blood-is-thicker-than-water bullshit. . . . That motherfucker would have taken down the whole fucking show, starting with you, killer." For Stringer Bell, lives are governed by theatre, by the "show" in which family plays its staged part. Dressed up in a suit like a city hall man, his striped tie echoing visually the bars on the windows, he holds Avon down, and our point of view remains tight in between them, compressing the shot/reverse-shot technique into as close and proximate a range as possible as they speak, losing sight of any of the mechanics of framing and representation we may have noticed around them and instead coming as near to their bodies as the camera can.

Our perspective is, as McNulty puts it earlier, "squeezed between the sides". It is a deadly position for D'Angelo, that implicates us directly as close watchers, as close as the television screen or camera lens can come to sweating, spitting, bleeding bodies, in the visceral, ethical negotiation—family versus business—unfolding before us. They part, and the perspective pulls back, circling behind Avon as he stalks the room and then sits on a bed in the back corner. There is no dialogue now, only the sound of their exhausted breathing. We have reached the limits of what is sayable. D'Angelo's murder, once admitted, disrupts the bond that hold the Barksdales together, a "social" bond that essentially enabled their attempts to legitimate or even to humanize themselves.

Through Holland's dislocated visuals, we witness the complicity of Avon and Stringer in their own undoing, and the dismantling of any vestiges of care. The camera pulls back slightly from Avon, now in the middle distance, and pans left, so that we now see Stringer's form in the left foreground, blurry and slightly shadowed. The aperture pulls and shifts, and his face comes into focus; once again, Holland uses a visual tactic of reorientation by refocusing, which we watched Prez enact within the episode as he enlarged the image of the license plate, but it is coupled here with a mobile, fluid perspective (rather than a fixed line-of-sight); this merger of fluid curvature with decisive linearity recalls the juxtaposition of living bodies in various scenes with rectilinear doors, frames, and boundaries. That counterpoint manifests itself in the final shot of the episode, which positions us on the outside of a dirty window, looking through the squared grid of the six-paned frame at Avon and Stringer, who are separated and segmented not only by space, but also by the vertical and horizontal grille-strips. The rectilinear graph into which the social order wants to organize the city is overlaid onto their alienated bodies. The episode finishes not with resolution, but in wounded separation. We leave the men apart, and the camera tracks right, off the window and onto the dark wall beside it, leaving watchers finally excluded and barred, even from light. Still, Holland doesn't close "Moral Midgetry" by rendering judgment on the untenable and compromised situation of Avon and Stringer. Instead, that undefined darkness helps to keep open and unsettled her visual interrogation of the fictions and of the necessities that dislocate her America.

15

"Gots to Get Got": Social Justice and Audience Response to Omar Little

Kathleen LeBesco

If you're pissed about Omar, be pissed about the game and how dead inside the people that kill each other without a thought truly are. Be pissed about the world that put them in that position. [...] Let the show teach you something. Make it a wakeup call.

Phuck that pole smokin queer...

—*fan postings, HBO.com*

Mere samples of viewer response to the character of Omar Devon Little—an honorable queer gangsta involved in storylines related to crime and justice—the epigraphs to this essay demonstrate Omar's function as a kind of *agent provocateur*. They also suggest the value of studying how fans make sense of *The Wire* rather than merely presuming that they internalize the intentions of its creators. Utilizing a theoretical framework and methodology based in cultural studies, this chapter explores audience dialogue about issues of social justice on the show. The study focuses on the show's fan forum on the HBO.com website, which was very active during the run of the series and continues to be accessible, though lightly trafficked. In particular, I am interested in how viewers negotiate attitudes toward crime and how these attitudes are integrated with other perspectives on a socially just vision of living with respect across difference. Omar serves as a lightning rod for the articulation of both ambivalent attitudes toward homosexuality and progressive beliefs about the need for social change in the overinstitutionalized U.S. today.

Beyond Media Effects

Historically, scholars interested in the relationship between mediated representations of crime and audience response have posited an overly simplistic model of media effects wherein media representations of crime are reductively imagined to have clear, direct, and measurable effects on the behavior or attitudes of viewers (e.g. Lefkowitz *et al.*, "Television Violence" and *Growing Up*). In contrast, Aaron Doyle exhorts researchers to attempt to determine the meaning of crime stories for audience members, as a supplement to research focused on the political and institutional effects of crime and the media ("How Not" 867). This chapter takes up Doyle's project by exploring how watchers of *The Wire* make sense of crime stories, particularly those centered on Omar.

By acknowledging and mining a complicated connection between *The Wire* and its fans, we stand to learn more about the capacity of media to spawn social and political change. By examining the meanings that fans hold for crime and violence in the show, we can avoid a quantitative preoccupation on the amount of crime and violence depicted, making it harder for simple media-blaming to mask the real social, political, and economic causes of crime and violence (Gauntlett 54).

This project is essential for gauging the extent to which *The Wire* serves as a corrective—not only to formulaic cops-and-robbers shows but also to ideologically regressive attitudes about justice and crime—in the minds of its viewers. Series creators David Simon and Ed Burns see the problems with "the system" (Rose 84–85), and their desires for social justice and social reconstruction are palpable in the series (and in media interviews; see Ryan). They seem to concede, with Stuart Hall *et al.*, that crime is merely a form of unproductive labor, illegal but thoroughly capitalistic and "adapted to the system on which it is parasitic" (364). Joel Best argues that our tendency to view crime "as a melodrama in which evil villains prey on innocent victims" frightens and confuses the public, and obfuscates attempts at designing and carrying out effective social policies (xii; see also Surette 209). Following this logic, one might presume that the complexity of *The Wire*—its general lack of melodrama, its subtlety and its avoidance of what Steven Johnson has termed "flashing arrows" (i.e. easily readable clues to a text's meaning, leaving the audience little cognitive work to do)—might push audiences in the opposite direction, emboldening them to put their hard-won comprehension of social justice issues to work in the streets and in the realm of policy change.

Audience Analysis

Rather than issuing from on high a proclamation about the cultural work that *The Wire* accomplishes or fails to accomplish (as does Suderman), we need to ask how audiences understand the show (Schiappa 5). How do audiences read the series in terms of a call for social reform? My answer is based on a careful study of thousands of posts by fans of the series on the HBO.com website in the fan forum for *The Wire*. The forum contains hundreds of thousands of posts by fans in response to threads— discussion prompts—generated both by the HBO staff and by other fans. Perhaps no thread was more active in the final weeks of the series than that devoted to the death of Omar Little, whose fictional death warranted an obituary on the pages of *Newsweek* where he was tagged "Robbin' Hood" (Alston 15).

Omar is a fascinating character for a number of reasons, not the least of which is his unexpected collision of identities. A man with a code who also robs and kills, sensitive and openly gay in a hypermasculine black urban subculture, and somehow off the radar while embedded in a surveillance-saturated culture that disproportionally and systematically targets young black men (Doyle, *Arresting Images* 72), Omar is a bundle of seeming contradictions. It is the very complexity of his character that makes Omar an excellent site for interpreting audience understandings of a number of issues related to social justice.

In "Clarifications" (5.08), Omar is shot and killed by Kenard, a boy from the neighborhood, while buying a pack of cigarettes at the corner store. Aware of his enormous popularity, the proprietors of HBO.com immediately created an official discussion entitled "Omar Little R.I.P.", which garnered over 1300 responses, most of them posted in the few days after the episode depicting his death aired.[1] A great number of the posts are inadequately detailed to provide any clues about their author, but many posts include biographical information that leads me to believe that the *Wire* boards at HBO.com are a magnet for a diversity of stances and opinions, from economically liberal would-be sociologists to, socially conservative survivors of the streets, and everyone in between.

According to Arthur Raney, a viewer's moral judgments about the behavior of characters onscreen shape his or her affective disposition toward the characters, and also influence the viewer's level of pleasure from the viewing experience (145). Raney's work compels me to consider the moral judgments, both positive and negative, associated with Omar's behavior as a key not only to the pleasure of the fans but also as a lens on moral perspectives on justice. Taking the wide range of fan backgrounds into consideration, a number of themes emerge from my analysis of their posts. The most prominent are that Omar is respectable and beloved by fans "despite" his homosexuality and because of his code; and that the characterization of Omar motivates reflections on and action in the realm of social justice.

Omar's Sexuality and His Code

Fan conversation on Omar's death centers around either the viewers' shock and frustration with the writers for ending Omar as they did, or on praise for writing a complex character. Azz24446, who elsewhere identifies as an older, politically conservative white male, writes,

> Omar Little is one that most all of us will remember for years to come because he combined such mutually-exculsive concepts as a sociopathic killer with someone who operated by internal moral code ("I never put no gun on a citizen."). He was NOT a cookie cutter personality.[2]

The vast majority of posters echo this sentiment, citing their admiration of Omar's code (no cursing, no thuggery on Sundays, no targeting law-abiding citizens, etc.) and his quirks (a love of Honey-Nut Cheerios, a wordsmith's talent for aphorisms, and a propensity for whistling while he works), as well as their shock at the manner in which his character "got got."[3]

As might be expected in a culture stained by homophobia, though, not all fans embrace Omar, despite his many charms. Blocchead writes,

> Damn shame when society comes to a point where someone like, Omar, can be considered a 'real nigga'. I mean, FUCK- he's a fuckin FAG! Does that make him any less of a man!? -HELL YES IT DOES! [...] Don't get it twisted- I'm not homophobic to the point of being an out-n-out bigot against gay folks, but, to be idolizing a character such as 'Omar' is just down right disgusting to me. He may have been portrayed as an ethics-bound killer (how oxymoronic), but the only thing 'G' about him was his sexuality. Fuck that.

This fan's anti-queer hostility is apparent, but his post is still noteworthy for its recognition of the ironies of being an "ethics-bound killer." Most fans on the boards write lovingly of Omar and his much vaunted code (which I discuss below), unable or unwilling to square his murderous activities with their affection for him.

In a similar vein, Jaemil writes, "Phuck that pole smokin queer......yea kenard my boy keep it real taking out faggot ass mother fuckers all day!!!!!" This provokes many other fans to respond by reinforcing Omar's credibility as "true G" despite his homosexuality. There are few defenses of queerness here—or even distancing "tolerance" moves;[4] instead, most fans seem to see queerness and hardness/gangsta status as not mutually exclusive, and they don't mind saying so. In a seething rebuke, Demonic1 replies, "what the man do behind closed doors with whom ever or what ever is the mans business.. all this anger Jaemil is showing down there with his post aint nothing but built up anger that he secrectly enjoys watching men." Not a single fan in the "Omar Little R.I.P." thread admits enjoying Omar's sexuality or discusses his/her desire to see Omar be affectionate with his lovers, but, at the very least, most fans here are not trafficking in the worst, most reductive stereotypes about gay people.

Whatever progressive views of justice may reign on the boards, there is also ambivalence about Omar's homosexuality. Most posters who mention it maintain a distance, saying things like "despite Omar being a fag, I liked him . . ." But even the issue of justice is vexed. For some fans, the preoccupation is with dramatic justice: they wanted Omar to go out gloriously, shotgun blazing, and whistling "The Farmer in the Dell," rather than see him taken out by a "li'l hopper". These fans do not, for the most part, talk about other conceptions of justice. In the parlance of dramatic justice, the vast majority of fans called for the head of Kenard, a young boy—not exactly a progressive perspective on juvenile crime. This sense of vigilanteism seems particularly odd for fans schooled by Season Four's sharp, poignant assessment of the complex relationship between young inner-city boys and the variety of institutions that continue to fail them—families, foster care, juvenile detention centers, police, and schools.

Apart from the posts eulogizing Omar, there were a few interesting conversations about his sexuality while the character was still alive. In January 2008, a poster to the HBO.com boards started a new thread. After showing a fondness for Omar and acknowledging his homosexuality, annflood asked, "How do you suppose Omar reconciles his homosexuality with his strict religious upbringing and aversion to profanity—I would think that a man such as Omar with such a strict moral code would, at the very least, find two men together a sin against God." Sixty responses, in aggregate, painted an interesting picture of fan attitudes toward Omar's queerness, and queerness in general.

Several posters use the term "homo" to refer to Omar, and not (apparently) as part of an insider's ironic project of linguistic reclamation. One poster, NoShameinGame, self-identifies as gay and uses the thread as an opportunity to declare his admiration for Omar: "Call him homosexual, a homo, thug homo, label it as you please, but Omar is still a man of certain 'principles', and that's why I like him." DoninCincy agrees, arguing "Omar's sexual preferences are not a big issue to the writers. [...] Omar is too complex to be so tightly defined. [...] The majority of people who see Omar as one sided in the series are the gangster figures who feel that they have to posture as rough and tough to feel secure in their manhood."

Lest we get too far ahead of ourselves in lauding the progressive politics of fans of *The Wire*, note NoShameinGame's agreeable response to DoninCincy:

> I'm sure all these *so called* rappers, gangster rappers, whatever, are in the closet, and have experienced homosexual relations before.

All these *feuding rappers* are just a bunch of *closet queens* catfighting like women would do. No disrespect to women, but we all know women have their catfights against each other.

Appreciation of sexual diversity as a progressive value seems undermined here, and elsewhere on the boards, by old-fashioned misogyny. Echoing the perspective of many other fans, Prophetessroxy writes, "I loved Omar because even though he was a homosexual, he wasn't a 'stereotypical 'flamer'....he liked his boys, but he was gangsta to the bone... ." Here, Omar's performance of gangsta masculinity mitigates against his sexuality to produce a performance deemed acceptable by this fan, wary of stereotypes. Omar's "hard" masculinity salvages his citizenship, demonstrating in this context, being female/feminine is a larger obstacle to positive regard than being queer.

Areas of social life including religious association, family life, and local politics are crucial sites for the enactment of good citizenship—and they are also sites at which the homosexual has historically failed in US culture (Herrell 273). Richard Herrell examines the remaking of queer social identities at these sites, remarking that "If the 'citizen' is defined as 'not alien' by membership in the nation, 'bad citizens' are contrasted with the 'good' by their alienation from the collective moral purpose" (Herrell 276). As a man with a code, Omar is no stranger to the collective moral purpose. Omar as churchgoer has a code that extends protection crown-wearing grannies everywhere (see 3.09, "Slapstick"), thus marking him as a good citizen both in the realm of religious association and in family life. Furthermore, his Robin Hood behavior on the street, while a stretch from the electoral kind of politics practiced by Councilman (later Mayor) Tommy Carcetti, finds him in good stead in the politics of the hood. Inasmuch as Omar remakes himself in all three arenas of concern for Herrell, his sexuality recedes into the background of fan imagination, it seems.

The widespread adoration of Omar might indicate that his audience—particularly the liberal would-be sociologists—are well trained to see "authenticity" in intersecting identities. But this reading makes little sense for the socially conservative fans who declare their love for Omar "despite" his queerness. In this case, an interpretation derived from Herrell's theoretical argument—that Omar's recuperated citizenship allows his sexuality to recede—prevails.

A Call to Action

In decrying the unjust demise of Omar, fans of the show reveal varied perspectives on the possibility of real justice. Howsiah, for instance, writes,

> Omar was true Justice and now Justice is dead. We mourne. Not only was his death a tragedy. But the fact that this young boy did him in so precise and cold-bloodedly. Speaks volumes about the world they live in.

This poster couldn't be clearer about his vision of social justice—an impossibility. Darknastycash concurs:

> The Wire is not a hollywood, weepy, happy ending type of show. People like Omar don't die in their sleep at the age of 85. […] Omar was the closest thing to a hero the show had. After Omar died though, there were a bunch of clues as to how insignificant he was to the city. The newspaper passed on the story about the "mid 30's Male who was killed in a convenience store" and ran a different story. To us as fans, that was a slap in the face but this show has never been about pleasing the fans, that was just a pleasant side effect. Even the Coroner (who undoubtedly dealt with more than one of Omar's victims over the years) placed the wrong name tag on his body. That just goes to show how little of an impact he had on the civilian lives in Baltimore. […] It sucks, but that's the cold, harsh reality.

This poster evidences frustration with the death of an anti-hero, but also embraces the Simonian impulse to critique the way that society precludes justice from being done. But does "that's the cold, harsh reality" imply that this can be changed, or is this merely the semantic equivalent of a shrug? Other posters point out that Omar's death seems fitting for a show trying to communicate that justice is rarely served. What I'm interested in is what happens after this realization; do fans want social change? Or are they content with the lesson that life is not fair?

An analysis of how fans respond to discourse about the "American Dream"—with its attendant myths of striving, social mobility, and meritocracy—relative to Omar helps to answer these questions. At one point, Omar wears a t-shirt that reads, "I am the American Dream" (2.10). In many ways, his character did function as a dream—a dream that justice could be served in the midst of a corrupt system, a dream to be the watcher rather than the watched in surveillance-saturated society. Ironman9695 writes,

> This unforgettable force of a character came to define the essence of this incomparably exceptional program's most resonant and resounding message: He who allows himself to be beholden to the institution is its reformer at his peril. He who parts company with the institution is his own man.

Omar appears inspirational in his ability to part company with institutions, but it is not just his life that inspires. Fan Jenny15 argues,

> The creators of this show are brilliant; through Omar's ridiculous death, they have channeled to the viewers the very anger, frustration, and disillusionment of the characters and the people they portray. and the best part is, that we cannot even feel self-righteous in our grief and anger, since its a murderous bandit were mourning, after all.

Jenny15 thus imagines Omar's death as a narrative clarion call—a consciousness raiser for audiences far and wide.

Many, many fans on the HBO boards express frustration and disappointment with the way Omar was killed off on the show. The most popular sentiment is that it was unjust to the viewer to craft such an aesthetically and narratively unsatisfying ending for one of the most engrossing characters and storylines in the series. Most viewers articulate profound sadness that Omar's arc ended in the manner that it did, claiming it was not only inconsistent with what we knew of this careful, watchful, intelligent character, but also that it was just plain unjust and wrong to do that to loyal viewers. Critics might use Omar's demise as a jumping off point to speculate on the intentions of the show's creators—perhaps to say that senseless things happen sometimes, or perhaps to create exactly the sense of anger and frustration that might motivate action for social change. But it seems like a long way from being annoyed with the death of a fictional character to real-world agitation.

Fan Neutralitybias offers a plan regarding social justice for the engaged viewer of *The Wire*:

> So that's my challenge for you fans. If you're pissed about Omar, be pissed about the game and how dead inside the people that kill each other without a thought truly are. Be pissed about the world that put them in that position. [...] let your love for the character teach you something. Let the show teach you something. Make it a wakeup call.

"Be pissed" is not exactly a sophisticated and concrete course of action, but it is more than is advocated by most television series in terms of real world change. Nor is it the only call to action to be found on the boards. Beenthardunthat (whose handle bespeaks the wisdom of experience) writes, "The writers this year have done a fantastic job of trying to show us more than blood and beatings. They have tried to make us realize that we do have choices, both in the streets, our homes and at the ballots." Eschewing the bullets of Malcolm X, this audience member directs other fans to a time-tested course of action, the ballot box, as a path for the change advocated by *The Wire*.

Still other fans make intriguing connections between Omar's demise and the disappearance of the kind of institution that does not suffocate or oppress the individual. Rather self-effacingly, Noahblake writes,

> Omar is like a lot of institutions that are dying out -organizations and systems that if not perfect, were at least consistent....and are being toppled by people and forces with no sense of morality or honor whatsoever. [...] as weird as it may seem that I should emulate a murdering ganster -me, a dorky white suburban guy.....I hope I can stand up for the justice and "right" that exist in my world the way Omar did in his.

While this fan seems to defend institutions more than Simon would, what is interesting is his aim of standing up for justice. Here, Omar is undoubtedly a catalyst for change.

One final fan exchange about the extent to which *The Wire* offers a call to action illustrates the difficulty of declaring the show an ideologically transparent text. Celeak71 writes, "This show should give us all the gumption to think of ways of playing active roles in being a beacon of light in our communities, so Omars don't have to be maufactured in our hoods. (see the second chance for Namond Brice thanks to Colvin)."[5] This ignites a firestorm of responses by fans who find Celeak71 too critical of Omar and of the streets from which he hails. DRLHB writes,

> Omar WAS the embodiment of the 'code' that 'a man must have a code' which he sticks to no matter what the personal cost. That's the definition of 'integrity' and 'courage' and is one of the reasons why he WAS The Wire to many of us. Who else is gonna keep the devil down in the hole, except men and women of integrity and courage, no matter what their socioeconomic status, race, sexual preference, or which brand of smokes they prefer.[6]

Here DRLHB articulates a vision of social justice that can be pursued regardless of one's context, whereas Celeak71 sees the show as a cautionary tale about certain kinds of (depraved) contexts. Celeak71 responds,

> The tragedy is that the characters make irrational decisions because they are constrained by their experiences and cannot make sound holistic judgement. It is a mirror of society and a challenge to us to find ways to become again, a beacon of light to those who don't have the guidance - whether they are in the streets, in politics, on the police force, or in the media.

DRLHB retorts,

> At this point, I'd much rather have some 'fake ass hollywood bullshit' than the current 'fuck a coherent compelling story, we're going to teach these bitches some community college level sociology' bullshit. Don't rest in peace yet, Omar.

The poster continues, referring to the show's creators:

> While I admire them [...], their decision to write Omar out of the show in the way they did was wrong on just about every level.

It was succumbing to hopelessness, pointlessness, despair and the idea that just because something 'is,' it is somehow right. Which are the very things they condemn [...] Now THAT'S ironic.

This fan articulates the power of the vision promulgated by Simon *et al.* and critiques the descent into apathy that the demise of Omar signals. What I glean from the full exchange is that *The Wire* does not read transparently as a manifesto for social justice. Just as one fan can see the show as a cautionary tale about the "manufacture of Omars"—that is, the creation of thugs, however honorable they may be—another fan reads the series's championing of anti-heroic values as the only sensible path of resistance to institutionalized life. Some see the show's provocative ideologies as its highest calling, while others demand the political lesson and an aesthetic masterpiece.

It is the rare fan who is ready to take to the streets in pursuit of social justice after watching *The Wire*. However, discussion among audience members on the HBO.com boards indicates that the series functions effectively as a consciousness-raiser about the social, political and economic plight of individuals constrained by corrupt, failing institutions. Whether or not the fans see this as something that can be railed against varies. Some fans, already wise to issues of social justice, resent the civics lesson and demand masterly storytelling that fights against "hopelessness, pointlessness, despair."

Conclusion

In an interview, David Simon explains the title of the series: "The title refers to an almost imaginary but inviolate boundary between the two Americas . . . *The Wire* really does refer to almost a boundary or fence or the idea of people walking on a high wire and falling to either side" (quoted in Ethridge 154). Simon sees the American Dream as a charade and wants to use the series to unmask this reality. In her study of HBO.com discussion boards for *Six Feet Under*, Rhiannon Bury notes that fans take great pains to distinguish their admired series from typical network fare: "Because the process of signification is intrinsically linked to the process of subject formation, such fans not only construct themselves as 'quality readers' but also police the boundary of such a readership" (191).

We have seen this is also the case in online discussions of *The Wire*. In articulating what constitutes quality viewership, fans are reinscribing, rather than subverting, that very sense of two Americas that Simon is working so hard to expose and change. When fans have a hard time escaping even discursive elitism—working toward classlessness solely through conversation—it is indeed difficult to applaud the true impact of the show's ideological underpinnings. The series as text is rich and politically knowing; as consciousness-raiser, it is successful and evocative; yet as itself an agent of sociopolitical transformation, *The Wire* provokes ambivalent responses, which press each viewer to engage with the themes of the series critically.

Broadcast on a channel with an elitist tagline ("It's not TV. It's HBO."), *The Wire* seems from the start to congratulate its viewers for their excellent taste. Critics like Maureen Reddy voice concern about texts that position their readers as "liberal and humane, even progressive and nonracist" (167), all the while congratulating them on upholding socially dominant values. Is *The Wire* guilty of ideologically progressive flattery of those fans already assumed to have great taste? Not exactly: for Simon and Burns, fans are liberal and humane when they critique socially dominant values, not when they embrace them. Critics have applauded David Simon for his determination to go beyond providing mere entertainment and reinforcing audience beliefs in a moral and just society. At the same time, they have noted that his actual challenge to institutional life "lacks a clear articulation of an affirmative social and political project" (Ethridge 152). Blake Ethridge believes that figuring out how to solve these complicated problems is beyond Simon's purview; instead, "What is important for Simon is the representation of the problem and the provocation of the audience" (155).

My study of fan response indicates that not all of the audience necessarily reads the series as a polemic on the American Dream, and they content themselves with commentary on the high quality of the acting, writing, and direction in the show, or its realism. Those fans who do read the show as a polemic respond neither by stigmatizing Simon or the show, nor by doing nothing, or by, kowtowing to the utilitarian logic of institutional structure. Where the battle emerges is between doing nothing (as seems to be the case in the "it's all in the game" refrain that frequently resurfaces) and actively rejecting institutions (in theory or in practice). Although fan response illustrates that the series has goaded some to work for social, political and economic change, it has also inoculated others who seem so immersed in its realism that they cannot imagine any other way, shrugging off their shared responsibility for social change.

Whether this bifurcation in audience response strikes one as sufficient depends on one's expectations of subscription television as a change agent. Ethridge contends that Simon need not both agitate for change and direct that agitation (163). Few, if any, members of the televisual cohort of *The Wire* ever prompt heightened sociopolitical and economic awareness among fans; thus, it seems like a rush to judgment to indict *The Wire* for failing to deliver a clear alternative path to the institutional frameworks it so stunningly critiques. Aaron Doyle notes that "TV does not have greater ability than other media to let viewers see the 'truth' of institutional life; TV instead has greater power to validate the ideological stories it tells about what happens in other institutions" (*Arresting Images* 137–138). If we assess *The Wire* for the quality with which it has validated an unusually critical set of ideological stories about institutional life, it is an unqualified success. The fan responses I have analyzed here represent dynamic and complex responses to this critical set of ideological stories, especially those concerning homosexuality, racializations of sexuality, street justice, and the myth of the American Dream, bearing witness to the series's true and profound impact on those who tuned in.[7]

Notes

1. Discussions of Omar in this chapter are primarily drawn from this official "Omar Little R.I.P" thread, although there were many posts about Omar from user-generated threads as well. There was no overt difference in the tone or content of posts in network-generated vs. user-generated threads.

2. This and all posts that follow were made to *The Wire*'s discussion board at HBO.com. See the list of "Posts Cited" at the end of this chapter for full citation information. The poster is here referring to Omar's statement to Detective William "Bunk" Moreland in 1.07: "I do some dirt, too, but I never put my gun on nobody who wasn't in the game." Posts are cited verbatim, errors and non-standard English included. The posts quoted in this chapter are not meant to be statistically representative of views expressed on the boards or among fans generally. In fact, posts that are discursively

"extreme" in some respect are the most suggestive about social justice and are thus well represented here.

3. Omar first articulates the main element of his code in 1.07: visiting his wrath only on those "in the game." Fans witness Omar's fury that the ghetto's traditional Sunday morning truce has been violated in 3.09, when he and his grandmother are shot at on their way to church. In later episodes, like 4.03 we learn of Omar's fondness for Honey Nut Cheerios when he blames his lover Renaldo for letting the box "go light."

4. An excellent example of such a "tolerance" move would be "Not that there's anything wrong with that," which became a tag line for Jerry and his friend George on *Seinfeld* when they wanted to correct the misunderstanding that they were gay and simultaneously to exhibit their open-mindedness. See *Seinfeld*, "The Outing" (4.17), original air date 11 February 1993.

5. This poster's last comment refers to the Namond Brice storyline in Season Four that resolves with his move to the home and care of Howard "Bunny" Colvin. See 4.13.

6. This poster's rhetorical query about "who else is gonna keep the devil down in the hole" is a clear reference to the lyrical refrain of *The Wire*'s Tom Waits-penned theme song, "Way Down in the Hole." The post itself functions as a nod to the ways in which the series defines the language fans use to discuss it.

7. The author wishes to thank the editors of this volume, as well as John Shields and Laura Tropp, for feedback on this chapter.

Posts Cited

Except where noted, all posts were accessed successfully on 18 December 2008.

Annflood: <http://boards.hbo.com/topic/Wire-Member-Created/Omars-Homosex uality/1900001954&start=60>, posted 25 January 2008, accessed 26 July 2008. Posts in user-generated threads have been taken down, but can be accessed at <http://web. archive.org/web/20080131184241/boards.hbo.com/topic/Wire-Member-Created/ Omars-Homosexuality/1900001954&start=60>.

Azz24446: <http://boards.hbo.com/topic/Wire-Hbo-Official/Omar-Little-Rip/ 1900003292&start=1275>, 25 February 2008.

Beenthardunthat: <http://boards.hbo.com/topic/Wire-Archives/Omar-Little-Rip/ 1900003292&start=990>, posted 25 February 2008.

Blocchead: <http://boards.hbo.com/topic/Wire-Archives/Omar-Little-Rip/1900003292& start=270>, posted 4 March 2008.

Celeak71: <http://boards.hbo.com/topic/Wire-Archives/Omar-Little-Rip/1900003292& start=780>, posted 27 February 2008.

Darknastycash: <http://boards.hbo.com/topic/Wire-Hbo-Official/Omar-Little-Rip/ 1900003292&start=1155>, posted 25 February 2008.

Demonic1: <http://boards.hbo.com/topic/Wire-Archives/Omar-Little-Rip/1900003292& start=315>, posted 3 March 3008.

DoninCincy: <http://boards.hbo.com/topic/Wire-Member-Created/Omars-Homos exuality/1900001954&start=45>, posted 26 January 2008, accessed 26 July 2008. Posts in user-generated threads have been taken down, but can be accessed at <http://web. archive.org/web/20080131184939/boards.hbo.com/topic/Wire-Member-Created/ Omars-Homosexuality/1900001954&start=45>.

DRLHB: <http://boards.hbo.com/topic/Wire-Archives/Omar-Little-Rip/1900003292& start=780>, posted 27 February 2008;

<http://boards.hbo.com/topic/Wire-Archives/Omar-Little-Rip/1900003292& start=285>, posted 3 March 2008;

<http://boards.hbo.com/topic/Wire-Archives/Omar-Little-Rip/1900003292& start=195>, posted 6 March 2008.

Howsiah: <http://boards.hbo.com/topic/Wire-Archives/Omar-Little-Rip/1900003292& start=1110>, posted 25 February 2008.

Ironman9695: <http://boards.hbo.com/topic/Wire-Archives/Omar-Little-Rip/ 1900003292&start=150>, posted 10 March 2008.

Jaemil: <http://boards.hbo.com/topic/Wire-Archives/Omar-Little-Rip/1900003292& start=330>, posted 3 March 2008.

Jenny15: <http://boards.hbo.com/topic/Wire-Archives/Omar-Little-Rip/1900003292& start=945>, posted 26 February 2008.

Neutralitybias: <http://boards.hbo.com/topic/Wire-Archives/Omar-Little-Rip/ 1900003292&start=1035>, posted 25 February 2008.

Noahblake: <http://boards.hbo.com/topic/Wire-Archives/Omar-Little-Rip/1900003292& start=900>, posted 26 February 2008.

NoShameinGame: <http://boards.hbo.com/topic/Wire-Member-Created/Omars-H omosexuality/1900001954&start=45>, posted 26 January 2008, accessed 26 July 2008. Posts in user-generated threads have been taken down, but this post can be accessed at <http://web.archive.org/web/20080131184939/boards.hbo.com/topic/Wire-Member-Created/Omars-Homosexuality/1900001954&start=45>.

Prophetessroxy: <http://boards.hbo.com/topic/Wire-Hbo-Official/Omar-Little-Rip/ 1900003292&start=975>, posted 26 February 2008.

Works Cited

Adams, James Truslow. *The Epic of America*. Boston: Little, Brown and Company, 1931.

Alex. Brown & Sons. Advertisement. *Baltimore Sun* 9 February 1904: 2.

Allrath, Gaby, Marion Gymnich, and Carola Surkamp. "Introduction: Towards a Narratology of TV Series." *Narrative Strategies in Television Series*. Ed. Gaby Allrath and Marion Gymnich. New York: Palgrave Macmillan, 2005. 1–43.

Alston, Joshua. "HBO's Killer With a Code." *Newsweek* 151.9 (3 March 2008): 15.

Alvarez, Rafael. *The Wire: Truth Be Told*. New York: Pocket Books, 2004.

American Bonding Company. Advertisement. *Baltimore Sun* 9 February 1904: 1.

Anderson, Elijah. "The Code of the Streets." *Atlantic Monthly* 273.5 (May 1994): 80–94.

———. *Code of the Street: Decency, Violence, and the Moral Life of the Inner City*. New York: W.W. Norton Co., 2000.

Appadurai, Arjun. *Modernity At Large: Cultural Dimensions of Globalization*. Minneapolis: University of Minnesota Press, 1996.

The Architect. Dir. Matt Tauber. Magnolia Pictures, 2006.

Aristotle. "Poetics." Ed. and trans. Stephen Halliwell. *Aristotle, Poetics. Longinus, On the Sublime, Demetrius, On Style*. Ed. Stephen Halliwell et al. Cambridge, MA: Harvard University Press, 1995; corr., 1999. 1–141.

Baker, Houston. *Blues Ideology and Afro-American Literature: A Vernacular Theory*. Chicago: University of Chicago Press, 1987.

Baker, Peter C. "A New Frontier." *The National Newspaper* (United Arab Emirates) 14 May 2008. <http://www.thenational.ae/article/20080514/ART/260765471/1007>.

"Baltimore Housing Complex Demolished." *Washington Post* 28 July 1996. Final edn.: B4.

Belfoure, Charles. "In Baltimore, Public Housing Comes Full Circle." *New York Times* 19 March 2000. <http://www.nytimes.com/2000/03/19/realestate/in-baltimore-public-housing-comes-full-circle.html>.

Bennett, Michael. "Manufacturing the Ghetto: Anti-Urbanism and the Spatialization of Race." *The Nature of Cities: Ecocriticism and Urban Environments*. Ed. Michael Bennett and David W. Teague. Tucson: University of Arizona Press, 1999. 169–188.

Best, Joel. *Random Violence: How We Talk about New Crimes and New Victims*. Berkeley: University of California Press, 1999.

Biddle, Jeff E. and Daniel Hamermesh. "Beauty, Productivity and Discrimination: Lawyers' Looks and Lucre." *Journal of Labor Economics* 16 (1998): 172–201.

Bordwell, David. *Narration in the Fiction Film*. Madison: University of Wisconsin Press, 1985.

———. *Poetics of Cinema*. New York: Routledge, 2008.

———. *The Way Hollywood Tells It: Story and Style in Modern Movies*. Berkeley: University of California Press, 2006.

Bowden, Mark. "The Angriest Man in Television." *The Atlantic* (January/February 2008): 50–57.

Brooks, Peter. *The Melodramatic Imagination*. New Haven, Connecticut: Yale University Press, 1976.

Burns, Edward. "Gang- and Drug-Related Homicide: Baltimore's Successful Enforcement Strategy." *BJA (Bureau of Justice Assistance) Bulletin* July 2003. <http://www.ncjrs.gov/html/bja/gang/pfv.html>.

Bury, Rhiannon. "Praise You Like I Should: Cyberfans and *Six Feet Under*." *It's Not TV: Watching HBO in the Post-Television Era*. Ed. Marc Leverette, Brian L. Ott and Cara Louise Buckley. New York: Routledge, 2008. 190–208.

Butler, Judith. *Precarious Life: The Powers of Mourning and Violence*. London and New York: Verso, 2004.

Chaddha, Anmol, William Julius Wilson, and Sudhir A. Venkatesh. "In Defense of *The Wire*." *Dissent* (Summer 2008). 26 August 2008. <http://www.dissentmagazine.org/article/?article=1237>.

Clawson, James and Gerry Yemen. "Edward Norris and the Baltimore Police Department. (A and B)." 2003. Social Science Research Network. <http://papers.ssrn.com/sol3/papers.cfm?abstract_id=508762>.

Cohen, Charles. "Destroying a Housing Project, to Save It." *New York Times* 21 August 1995. <http://www.nytimes.com/1995/08/21/us/destroying-a-housing-project-to-save-it.html>.

Collins, Patricia Hill. *Black Feminist Thought: Knowledge, Consciousness, and the Politics of Empowerment*. London: Routledge, 1990.

Common. *BE*. "The Corner." Geffen Records. 24 May 2005.

Coronil, Fernando. "Towards a Critique of Globalcentrism: Speculations on Capitalism's Nature." *Public Culture* 12.2 (2000): 351–374.

Craig, Tim. "Baltimore's Troubles May Slow O'Malley—Rivals for Governor Would Focus on City." *Washington Post* 22 February 2004, Final edn.: C1.

Davis, James E. "Research at the Margins: Dropping out of High School and Mobility among African American Males." *International Journal of Qualitative Studies in Education* 19 (2006): 289–304.

Delaney, Sam. "Omar Little is the Gay Stick-up Man Who Robs Drug Dealers for a Living in The Wire." *The Guardian* 19 July 2008. <http://www.guardian.co.uk/culture/2008/jul/19/television.wire>.

Demarest, Michael. "He Digs Downtowns." *Time Magazine* 24 August 1981. <http://www.time.com/time/magazine/article/0,9171,949385-1,00.html>.

Doyle, Aaron. *Arresting Images: Crime and Policing in Front of the Television Camera.* Toronto: University of Toronto Press, 2003.

———. "How Not to Think About Crime in the Media." *Canadian Journal of Criminology & Criminal Justice* 48.6 (2006): 867–885.

Dyson, Michael Eric. *Race Rules: Navigating the Color Line.* New York: Vintage, 1997.

Ethridge, Blake D. "Baltimore on *The Wire*: The Tragic Moralism of David Simon." *It's Not TV: Watching HBO in the Post-Television Era.* Ed. Marc Leverette, Brian L. Ott and Cara Louise Buckley. New York: Routledge, 2008. 152–164.

"1st Exclusive David Simon Q & A." *The Wire on HBO: Play or Get Played in David Simon's Baltimore.* 16 August 2006. <http://www.borderline-productions.com/ TheWireHBO/ exclusive-1.html>.

First National Bank. Advertisement. *Baltimore Sun* 9 February 1904: 1.

Foucault, Michel. *Discipline and Punish: The Birth of the Prison.* Trans. Alan Sheridan. 1977. 2nd edn. New York: Vintage, 1995.

———. *Society Must be Defended: Lectures at the Collège de France, 1975–76.* Trans. David Macey. New York: Picador, 2003.

Freire, Paulo. *Pedagogy of the Oppressed.* Trans. Myra Bergman Ramos. New York: Continuum, 2002.

Freire, Paulo and Donaldo Macedo. *Literacy: Reading the Word and the World.* New York: Bergin & Garvey, 1987.

"Full Moon." *Homicide: Life on the Street.* Dir. Leslie Libman and Larry Williams. NBC. 5 April 1996.

Gaines, Jane M. *Fire & Desire: Mixed-Race Movies in the Silent Era.* Chicago: University of Chicago Press, 2001.

Gauntlett, David. "The Worrying Influence of Media Effects Studies." *Ill Effects: The Media/Violence Debate.* 2nd edn. Ed. Martin Barker and Julian Petley. London: Routledge, 2001. 47–62.

Geo. A. Fuller Company. Advertisement. *Baltimore Sun* 9 February 1904: 1.

Gibson, Campbell. "Populations of the 100 Largest Cities and Other Urban Places in the United States: 1790 to 1990." U.S. Census Bureau. June 1998. <http://www. census.gov/population/www/documentation/twps0027/twps0027.html>.

Giddens, Anthony. *Runaway World: How Globalization is Reshaping Our Lives.* 1999. London: Routledge, 2003.

Goodman, Tim. "Yes, HBO's 'Wire' is challenging. It's also a masterpiece." *San Franciso Chronicle.* 6 September 2006. <http://www.sfgate.com/cgibin/articlecgi?f=/c/a/2006/ 09/06/DDG7BKV7HK26.DTL>.

Gore, Jennifer. "What We Can Do For You! What Can 'We' Do For 'You'?: Struggling over Empowerment in Critical and Feminist Pedagogy." *Feminisms and Critical Pedagogy.* Ed. Carmen Luke and Jennifer Gore. New York: Routledge, 1992. 54–73.

Greig, David. *The Architect.* 1996. *Plays: 1.* London: Methuen, 2002. 91–201.

Hall, Stuart, Chas Critcher, Tony Jefferson, John Clarke, and Brian Roberts. *Policing the Crisis: Mugging, the State, and Law and Order.* London: Macmillan, 1978.

Harbison, Sarah F., and Warren C. Robinson. "Globalization, Family Structure, and Declining Fertility in the Developing World." *Review of Radical Political Economics* 35.1 (2003): 44–55.

Harvey, David. *Justice, Nature and the Geography of Difference*. Malden, MA: Blackwell, 1996.

———. *Spaces of Capital*. New York: Routledge, 2001.

———. *Spaces of Hope*. Berkeley: University of California Press, 2000.

———. *The Urban Experience*. Baltimore: Johns Hopkins University Press, 1989.

Havrilesky, Heather. "David Simon on Cutting 'The Wire.'" *Salon.com* 10 March 2007. <http://www.salon.com/ent/tv/feature/2008/03/10/simon/>.

Herbert, Steve. "Policing the Contemporary City: Fixing Up Broken Windows or Shoring Up Neo-Liberalism?" *Theoretical Criminology* 5.4 (2001): 445–466.

Herrell, Richard K. "Sin, Sickness, Crime: Queer Desire and the American State." *Identities: Global Studies in Culture and Power* 2.3 (1996): 273–300.

"Historical List of Governors of Maryland 1634–" Archives of Maryland. 26 July 2008. <http://www.msa.md.gov/msa/speccol/sc2600/sc2685/html/govintro.html>.

Hoffer, Peter Charles. *Seven Fires: The Urban Infernos that Reshaped America*. New York: Public Affairs, 2006.

Hoffman, Tod. *Homicide: Life on the Screen*. Toronto: ECW Press, 1998.

hooks, bell. *Ain't I A Woman?: Black Women and Feminism*. Boston: South End Press, 1981.

Hornby, Nick. Interview with David Simon. *The Believer* August 2007. 12 April 2008. <www.believermag.com/issues/200708/?read=interview_simon>.

Inner Harbor Project I Renewal Plan. Urban renewal and Housing Agency. Baltimore, 1967.

Jenkins, Steven. "Copying No One: Agniezska Holland Challenges the Maestro." *GreenCine* 10 November 2006. <http://www.greencine.com/article?action=view& articleID=360>.

Jensen, Brennen. "Lives Lost: One." *Baltimore City Paper* 3 September 2003. <http://www.citypaper.com/news/story.asp?id=2321>.

Johnson, James H., Grover C. Burthey III, and Kevin Ghorm. "Economic Globalization and the Future of Black America." *Journal of Black Studies* 38.6 (2008): 883–899.

Johnson, Steven. "Watching TV Makes You Smarter." *The New York Times* 24 April 2005. <http://www.nytimes.com/2005/04/24/magazine/24TV.html>.

Kennedy, Liam. *Race and Urban Space in Contemporary Culture*. Edinburgh: Edinburgh University Press, 2000.

King, Stephen. "Setting off a 'Wire' Alarm." *EW.com* 25 August 2006. <http://www.ew. com/ew/article/0,,1333799,00.html>.

Klein, Amanda Ann. "The Truth You Say? The End of *The Wire*." *PopMatters* 14 March 2008. <http://www.popmatters.com/pm/features/article/56051/the-truth-you-say/>.

Kois, Dan. "Everything you Were Afraid to Ask about '*The Wire*.'" *Salon.com* 1 October 2004. 12 April 2008. <dir.salon.com/story/ent/feature/2004/10/01/the_wire/index. html?pn=4>.

Kozloff, Sarah. "Narrative Theory and Television." *Channels of Discourse, Reassembled: Television and Contemporary Criticism.* Ed. Robert C. Allen. London: Routledge, 1992. 67–100.

Kronman, Anthony T. *The Lost Lawyer: Failing Ideals of the Legal Profession.* Cambridge: Belknap Harvard, 1993.

Kübler-Ross, Elisabeth, and David Kessler. *On Grief and Grieving.* New York: Scribner, 2005.

Lanahan, Lawrence. "Secrets of the City: What *The Wire* Reveals about Urban Journalism." *Columbia Journalism Review* (January/February 2008): 23–31.

Landy, Marcia. *Genres: Cinema and Society, 1930–1960.* Princeton: Princeton University Press, 1991.

Lane, Alycee J. "Black Bodies/Gay Bodies: The Politics of Race in the Gay/Military Battle." *Black Studies Reader.* Ed. Jacqueline Bobo, Cynthia Hudley and Claudine Michel. New York: Routledge, 2004. 315–328.

Lefkowitz, Monroe M., Leonard D. Eron, Leopold O. Walder and L. Rowell Huesmann. *Growing Up To Be Violent: A Longitudinal Study of the Development of Aggression.* New York: Pergamon, 1977.

———. "Television Violence and Child Aggression: A Follow-up Study." *Television and Social Behavior: Reports and Papers, Volume III: Television and Adolescent Aggressiveness.* Ed. George A. Comstock and Eli A. Rubinstein. Baltimore: National Institute of Mental Health, 1972. 35–135.

Levine, Stuart. "Voters Explain Why They're Not High on 'The Wire.'" *Variety.com* 21 August 2005. <http://www.variety.com/article/VR1117927818.html>.

Macek, Steve. *Urban Nightmares: The Media, the Right, and the Moral Panic over the City.* Minneapolis: University of Minnesota Press, 2006.

Marc, David. *Demographic Vistas: Television in American Culture.* Philadelphia: University of Pennsylvania Press, 1984.

Marshall, C.W. and Tiffany Potter. "The Life and Times of Fuzzy Dunlop: Herc Hauk and the Modern Urban Crime Environment." *Darkmatter* 4 (2009). <http://www.darkmatter101.org/site/2009/05/29/the-life-and-times-of-fuzzy-dunlop-herc-and-the-modern-urban-crime-environment/>.

Marx, Gary T. *Undercover: Police Surveillance in America.* Berkeley: University of California Press, 1988.

Marx, Karl. *Capital: A Critique of Political Economy, Volume I.* Trans. Ben Fowkes. New York: Penguin, 1977.

———. *The Economic and Philosophic Manuscripts of 1844.* Trans. Dirk Struik. New York: International, 1964.

Maryland Lawyer's Rules of Professional Conduct. American Legal Ethics Library. <http://www.law.cornell.edu/ethics/md/code/>.

McLane, Robert. "The Fire." *People and Problems.* Ed. Fabian Franklin. New York: Henry Holt and Company, 1908.

McMillan, Ali [Alasdair]. "Dramatizing Individuation: Institutions, Assemblages, and *The Wire*." *Cinephile* 4.1 (Summer 2008): 42–50.

Miller, Arthur. "Tragedy and the Common Man." *The Theatre Essays of Arthur Miller*. 2nd edn. Ed. Robert A. Martin and Steven R. Centola. New York: Da Capo Press, 1996. 3–7.

Miller, D. A. *The Novel and the Police*. Berkeley: University of California Press, 1988.

Miller, Jody. *Getting Played: African American Girls, Urban Inequality, and Gendered Violence*. New York: NYU Press, 2008.

Mittell, Jason. "Narrative Complexity in Contemporary American Television." *The Velvet Light Trap* 58 (Fall 2006): 29–40.

Model Code of Judicial Conduct, 2007. Ed. Center for Professional Responsibility. Chicago: American Bar Association, 2007.

Murphy, Joel. *One on One with Michael Ostroff*. 14 February 2008. <http://www. hobotrashcan.com/2008/02/14/one-on-one-with-michael-kostroff/>.

Murrell, Jr., Peter C. "Digging Again the Family Wells: A Freirian Literacy Framework as Emancipatory Pedagogy for African American Children." *Mentoring the Mentor: A Critical Dialogue with Paulo Freire*. Ed. Paulo Freire. New York: Peter Lang, 1997. 19–58.

Ndalianis, Angela. "Television and the Neo-Baroque." *The Contemporary Television Series*. Ed. Michael Hammond and Lucy Mazdon. Edinburgh: Edinburgh University Press, 2005. 83–101.

Neal, Mark Anthony. *New Black Man*. New York: Routledge, 2006.

Neale, Steve. "Melodrama and Tears." *Screen* 27 (1986): 6–22.

Newman, Michael Z. "From Beats to Arcs: Toward a Poetics of Television Narrative." *The Velvet Light Trap* 58 (Fall 2006): 16–28.

Nietzsche, Friedrich. *Beyond Good and Evil: Prelude to a Philosophy of the Future*. Trans. Helen Zimmern. New York: Russell and Russell, 1964.

Noble, Nina Kostroff. Commentary. *The Wire*, 3.01. "Time After Time." DVD. HBO Home Video, 2007.

Nochimson, Martha. "Tony's Options: *The Sopranos* and the Televisuality of the Gangster Genre." *Senses of Cinema* 29 (November–December 2003). <http://www. sensesofcinema.com/contents/03/29/sopranos_televisuality.html>.

Nora, Pierre. "Between History and Memory: Les Lieux de Mémoire." *Memory and Counter-Memory*. Special issue of *Representations* 26 (Spring 1989): 7–24.

Okazawa-Rey, Margo. "Economic, Social, and Racial Justice: The Survival of the African-American Family." *Journal of Health & Social Policy* 9.1 (1997): 15–21.

Olson, Sherry H. *Baltimore: The Building of an American City*. Baltimore: The Johns Hopkins University Press, 1997.

O'Mara, Richard. "Backstory: Baltimore—'Home of 1,000 Slogans.'" *Christian Science Monitor* 5 January 2006. <http://www.csmonitor.com/2006/0105/p20s01-lihc.html>.

O'Rourke, Meghan. "Behind *The Wire*: David Simon on Where the Show Goes Next." *Slate* 1 December 2006. <http://www.slate.com/id/2154694/>.

Owens, Hamilton. *Baltimore on the Chesapeake*. Garden City, NY: Doubleday, Doran & Company, Inc., 1941.

Pearson, Felicia and David Ritz. *Grace after Midnight: A Memoir*. New York: Warner Books, 2007.

Persuad, Randolph B., and Clarence Lusane. "The New Economy, Globalisation, and the Impact on African Americans." *Race & Class* 42.1 (2000): 21–34.

Plato. *The Republic.* Trans. G. M. A. Grube. Indianapolis: Hackett, 1974.

Raney, Arthur A. "Punishing *Media Criminals* and Moral Judgment: The Impact on Enjoyment." *Media Psychology* 7.2 (2005): 145–163.

Reddy, Maureen T. *Traces, Codes, and Clues: Reading Race in Crime Fiction.* New Brunswick, NJ: Rutgers University Press, 2003.

Rose, Brian G. "*The Wire.*" *The Essential HBO Reader.* Ed. Gary R. Edgerton and Jeffrey P. Jones. Lexington: University Press of Kentucky, 2008. 82–91.

Rosenblatt, Paul C., and Beverly R. Wallace. *African American Grief.* New York and Hove: Routledge, 2005.

Rozhon, Tracie. "Old Baltimore Row Houses Fall Before Wrecking Ball." *New York Times* 13 June 1999. <http://www.nytimes.com/1999/06/13/us/old-baltimore-row-houses-fall-before-wrecking-ball.html>.

Russell, Margaret. "Law and Racial Reelism: Black Women as Celluloid 'Legal' Heroines." *Feminism, Media, and the Law.* Ed. Martha Fineman and Martha T. McCluskey. New York: Oxford University Press, 1997. 136–145.

Ryan, Maureen. "'The Wire' Comes Full Circle in its Gripping Finale." *The Chicago Tribune.com* 9 March 2008. <http://featuresblogs.chicagotribune.com/entertainment_tv/2008/03/the-wire-comes.html>.

———. "'Wire' Man Wants You To Care." *Chicago Tribune* 13 January 2008. <http://archives.chicagotribune.com/2008/jan/13/entertainment/chi-0113_wirejan13>.

"Scene of the Crime." *Homicide: Life on the Street.* Dir. Kathy Bates. NBC. 12 April 1996.

Scharf, Thomas J. *The Chronicles of Baltimore.* Port Washington, NY: Kennikat Press, 1972.

———. *History of Baltimore City and Baltimore County.* Baltimore: Regional Publishing Company, 1971.

Schiappa, Edward. *Beyond Representational Correctness: Rethinking Criticism of Popular Media.* Albany: State University of New York Press, 2008.

Sheehan, Helena and Seamus Sweeney. "*The Wire* and the World: Narrative and Metanarrative." *Jump Cut* 51 (forthcoming 2009).

Shelden, Randall G., Shannon K. Tracy, and William B. Brown, eds. *Youth Gangs in American Society.* 2nd edn. Belmont, CA: Wadsworth/Thomson Learning, 2001.

"Silo Point Luxury Condominiums." 2007. <http://www.silopoint.com>.

Simon, David. *Homicide: A Year on the Killing Streets.* New York: Ivy Books, 1991.

———. "Introduction." *The Wire: Truth Be Told.* Rafael Alvarez. New York: Pocket Books, 2004. 2–34.

———. Commentary. *The Wire,* 1.01. "The Target." DVD. HBO Home Video, 2004.

———. Commentary. *The Wire,* 3.01. "Time After Time." DVD. HBO Home Video, 2007.

Simon, David and Edward Burns. *The Corner: A Year in the Life of an Inner-City Neighborhood.* New York: Broadway, 1997.

Smith, Evan. "Thread Structure: Rewriting the Hollywood Formula." *Journal of Film and Video* 51, 3–4 (1999): 88–96.

Smith, Van. "Redemption Song and Dance." *Baltimore City Paper* 19 March 2008.

Stalnaker, Maria. "Agnieszka Holland Reads Hollywood." *Living in Translation: Polish Writers in America.* Ed. Halina Stephan. New York: Rodopi, 2003. 313–330.

Stanley, Alessandra. "So Many Characters, Yet So Little Resolution." *New York Times. com* 10 March 2008. <http://www.nytimes.com/2008/03/10/arts/television/10stan. html?hp=&pagewanted=all>.

Stark, Steven D. "Perry Mason Meets Sonny Crockett: The History of Lawyers and Police as Television Heroes." *University of Miami Law Review* 42 (1987–88): 229–284.

Sternbergh, Adam. "Sternbergh on 'The Wire' Finale: The Anti-'Sopranos.'" *New York Magazine.com* 10 March 2008. <http://nymag.com/daily/entertainment/ 2008/03/ sternbergh_on_the_wire_finale.html>.

Suderman, Peter. "Tension City." *National Review* 60.7 (21 April 2008): 59–60.

Surette, Ray. *Media, Crime and Criminal Justice: Images, Realities and Policies.* 3rd edn. Belmont, CA: Wadsworth, 2007.

Szanton, Peter. *Baltimore 2000: A Choice of Futures: A Report to the Morris Goldseker Foundation.* Baltimore: The Foundation, 1986.

Talbot, Margaret. "Stealing Life: The Crusader Behind 'The Wire.'" *The New Yorker* 22 October 2007. <http://www.newyorker.com/reporting/2007/10/22/071022fa_fact_talbot>.

Thompson, Kristin. *Storytelling in Film and Television.* Cambridge, MA: Harvard University Press, 2003.

"To Build a New and Greater Baltimore." *Baltimore Sun* 10 February 1904: 1.

"Twenty-Four Blocks Burned in Heart of Baltimore." *Baltimore Sun* 8 February 1904: 1.

Tyree, J. M. Rev. of *The Wire*: The Complete Fourth Season [DVD]. *Film Quarterly* 61.3 (Spring 2008): 32–38.

Urbina, Ian. "From Two Broken Lives to One Beginning." *New York Times* 9 August 2007. <http://www.nytimes.com/2007/08/09/us/09baltimore.html>.

Vidler, Anthony. *The Architectural Uncanny: Essays in the Modern Unhomely.* Cambridge, MA: MIT Press, 1992.

Ward, Stephen V. "'Cities are Fun!': Inventing and Spreading the Baltimore Model of Cultural Urbanism." *Culture, Urbanism and Planning.* Ed. Javier Monclús and Manuel Guàrdia. Aldershot: Ashgate, 2006. 271–285.

Watkins, S. Craig. *Representing: Hip Hop Culture and the Production of Black Cinema.* Chicago: University of Chicago Press, 1999.

Weisberg, Jacob. "*The Wire* on Fire: Analyzing the Best Show on Television. *Slate.com.* 13 September 2006. <http://www.slate.com/id/2149566/>.

Williams, Linda. "Melodrama Revised." *Refiguring American Film Genres: Theory and History.* Ed. Nick Browne. Berkeley: University of California Press, 1998. 42–88.

———. *Playing the Race Card: Melodramas of Black and White from Uncle Tom to O. J. Simpson.* Princeton: Princeton University Press, 2001.

Wilson, Christopher P. *Cop Knowledge: Police Power and Cultural Narrative in Twentieth-Century America.* Chicago: University of Chicago Press, 2000.

Wilson, David. *Cities and Race: America's New Black Ghetto*. London and New York: Routledge, 2007.

———. "City Transformation and the Global Trope: Indianapolis and Cleveland." *Globalizations* 4.1 (2007): 29–44.

Wiltz, Teresa. "Down to 'The Wire': It's a Wrap for Gritty TV Series." *The Washington Post* 3 September 2007. <http://www.washingtonpost.com/wp-dyn/content/article/2007/09/02/AR2007090201454.html>.

Wink, Joan. *Critical Pedagogy: Notes from the Real World*. 2nd edn. New York: Longman, 2000.

Zavattini, Cesare. "Some Ideas on the Cinema." *Vittorio De Sica: Contemporary Perspectives*. Eds. Howard Curle and Stephen Snyder. Toronto: University of Toronto Press, 2000. 50–61.

Ziehl, Susan C. "Forging the Links: Globalisation and Family Patterns." *Society in Transition* 34.2 (2003): 320–337.

Zitrin, Richard and Carol M. Langford. *The Moral Compass of the American Lawyer*. New York: Ballantine, 1999.

Episode List

Episode	Sequential Numbering	Title	First Aired
Season One			
1.01	01	The Target	2 Jun 2002
1.02	02	The Detail	9 Jun 2002
1.03	03	The Buys	16 Jun 2002
1.04	04	Old Cases	23 Jun 2002
1.05	05	The Pager	30 Jun 2002
1.06	06	The Wire	7 Jul 2002
1.07	07	One Arrest	21 Jul 2002
1.08	08	Lessons	28 Jul 2002
1.09	09	Game Day	4 Aug 2002
1.10	10	The Cost	11 Aug 2002
1.11	11	The Hunt	18 Aug 2002
1.12	12	Cleaning Up	1 Sep 2002
1.13	13	Sentencing	8 Sep 2002
Season Two			
2.01	14	Ebb Tide	1 Jun 2003
2.02	15	Collateral Damage	8 Jun 2003
2.03	16	Hot Shots	15 Jun 2003
2.04	17	Hard Cases	22 Jun 2003
2.05	18	Undertow	29 Jun 2003
2.06	19	All Prologue	6 Jul 2003
2.07	20	Backwash	13 Jul 2003
2.08	21	Duck and Cover	27 Jul 2003
2.09	22	Stray Rounds	3 Aug 2003
2.10	23	Storm Warnings	10 Aug 2003
2.11	24	Bad Dreams	17 Aug 2003
2.12	25	Port in a Storm	23 Aug 2003

Episode	Sequential Numbering	Title	First Aired
Season Three			
3.01	26	Time After Time	19 Sep 2004
3.02	27	All Due Respect	26 Sep 2004
3.03	28	Dead Soldiers	3 Oct 2004
3.04	29	Hamsterdam	10 Oct 2004
3.05	30	Straight and True	17 Oct 2004
3.06	31	Homecoming	31 Oct 2004
3.07	32	Back Burners	7 Nov 2004
3.08	33	Moral Midgetry	14 Nov 2004
3.09	34	Slapstick	21 Nov 2004
3.10	35	Reformation	28 Nov 2004
3.11	36	Middle Ground	12 Dec 2004
3.12	37	Mission Accomplished	19 Dec 2004
Season Four			
4.01	38	Boys of Summer	10 Sep 2006
4.02	39	Soft Eyes	17 Sep 2006
4.03	40	Home Rooms	24 Sep 2006
4.04	41	Refugees	1 Oct 2006
4.05	42	Alliances	8 Oct 2006
4.06	43	Margin of Error	15 Oct 2006
4.07	44	Unto Others	29 Oct 2006
4.08	45	Corner Boys	5 Nov 2006
4.09	46	Know Your Place	12 Nov 2006
4.10	47	Misgivings	19 Nov 2006
4.11	48	A New Day	26 Nov 2006
4.12	49	That's Got His Own	3 Dec 2006
4.13	50	Final Grades	10 Dec 2006
Season Five			
5.01	51	More With Less	6 Jan 2008
5.02	52	Unconfirmed Reports	13 Jan 2008
5.03	53	Not for Attribution	20 Jan 2008
5.04	54	Transitions	27 Jan 2008
5.05	55	React Quotes	3 Feb 2008
5.06	56	The Dickensian Aspect	10 Feb 2008
5.07	57	Took	17 Feb 2008
5.08	58	Clarifications	24 Feb 2008
5.09	59	Late Editions	2 Mar 2008
5.10	60	—30—	9 Mar 2008

Notes on Contributors

David M. Alff is a doctoral student in the English Department at the University of Pennsylvania. He is immensely thankful to those who helped in formulating and revising this essay, including Katrin Rowan, Elizabeth Blum, Phillip Maciak, and Katie Price.

Ralph Beliveau is on the faculty in the Gaylord College of Journalism and Mass Communication at the University of Oklahoma. He studies critical media pedagogy, rhetorical theory, and media criticism.

Laura Bolf-Beliveau is an assistant professor in the English Department at the University of Central Oklahoma. As English Education Program Coordinator, she prepares future teachers. Her research studies how new teachers engage in social justice pedagogy.

Elizabeth Bonjean is currently a Visiting Assistant Professor of Theatre at the University of Texas at Austin. She teaches courses in dramatic literature, theatre history, critical theory, and play analysis. Elizabeth received her Ph.D. from the University of Washington, Seattle.

Ryan Brooks is a senior Ph.D. student in English Studies at the University of Illinois, Chicago. He has presented conference papers on Charles W. Chesnutt, Ralph Ellison, Hardt and Negri, and William S. Burroughs. His fields of interest include Transatlantic Modernism, Postmodern and Contemporary Fiction, and Political Theory.

Peter Clandfield teaches in the Department of English Studies at Nipissing University in North Bay, Ontario. He is author or co-author of several articles and book chapters about fictional representations of urban development, and he plans a book-length project on the same subject.

Amanda Ann Klein is an Assistant Professor of Film Studies at East Carolina University. She has published on topics ranging from the films of Jean-Luc Godard to fan magazines and reality television. She is currently completing a manuscript about film cycles and popular culture.

Kathleen LeBesco is Professor of Communication Arts at Marymount Manhattan College, where she teaches about communication theory, cultural studies, and popular culture. She is author of *Revolting Bodies? The Struggle to Redefine Fat Identity* (University of Massachusetts) and has published extensively about the politics of representation.

Stephen Lucasi is a Ph.D. Candidate in English at the University of Connecticut. His dissertation, 'False to the Past: Slavery and the Historical Fictions of National Identity,' explores theories of post-national identification through contemporary American historical literature of slavery.

C. W. Marshall is Associate Professor of Classics at the University of British Columbia. He is the author of *The Stagecraft and Performance of Roman Comedy* (Cambridge, 2006). With Tiffany Potter, he edited *Cylons in America: Critical Studies in Battlestar Galactica* (Continuum, 2008).

Courtney D. Marshall is completing her Ph.D. in English at the University of California, Los Angeles. She works in critical race theory and black feminist criticism. Her current project is on the black female body in narratives of lynching and capital punishment.

Alasdair McMillan is an M.A. candidate at the University of Western Ontario's Centre for the Study of Theory and Criticism. Alongside ongoing research in continental philosophy and media theory, he has previously written on *The Wire*, Foucault, and Deleuze.

Kevin McNeilly is Associate Professor in the Department of English at the University of British Columbia. He teaches Cultural Studies and Contemporary Literatures.

Ted Nannicelli is a Ph.D. candidate in the Film Studies Department at the University of Kent, Canterbury, where he is researching the ontology of the screenplay.

James Braxton Peterson is Assistant Professor of English at Bucknell University, and was the founding Media Coordinator for the Harvard University Hip Hop Archive. His forthcoming book explores in detail the lyrics and life of Tupac Shakur (Praeger/Greenwood Press).

Tiffany Potter teaches English at the University of British Columbia, specializing in eighteenth-century theatre and fiction, and ideas of gender, sexuality, and North American indigeneity. With C. W. Marshall she edited *Cylons in America: Critical Studies in* Battlestar Galactica (Continuum, 2008).

Jason Read is Assistant Professor of Philosophy at the University of Southern Maine. He is the author of *The Micro-Politics of Capital: Marx and the Prehistory of the Present* (SUNY, 2003). His current research is on the ontology of social relations and a critique of neoliberalism.

Lynne Viti, a native of Baltimore, is a senior lecturer in the Writing Program at Wellesley College, where her courses focus on legal studies. A member of the Massachusetts Bar and a practicing attorney, she previously served as a law clerk and later Chief Law Clerk to justices of the Massachusetts Superior Court.

Afaa M. Weaver holds the endowed chair as Alumnae Professor of English at Simmons College. His latest collection of poetry is *The Plum Flower Dance: Poems 1985 to 2005* (University of Pittsburgh, 2007). His official website is www.afaamweaver.com.

Index